# Urban Policy and Politics in Britain

## DATE DUE

# Contemporary Political Studies

Series Editor: John Benyon, *University of Leicester*

# Urban Policy and Politics in Britain

Dilys M. Hill

First published in Great Britain 2000 by
**MACMILLAN PRESS LTD**
Houndmills, Basingstoke, Hampshire RG21 6XS and London
Companies and representatives throughout the world

A catalogue record for this book is available from the British Library.

ISBN 0–333–73921–3 hardcover
ISBN 0–333–73922–1 paperback

First published in the United States of America 2000 by
**ST. MARTIN'S PRESS, INC.,**
Scholarly and Reference Division,
175 Fifth Avenue, New York, N.Y. 10010

ISBN 0–312–22745–0

Library of Congress Cataloging-in-Publication Data
Hill, Dilys M.
Urban policy and politics in Britain / Dilys M. Hill.
p.   cm. — (Contemporary political studies)
Includes bibliographical references (p.   ) and index.
ISBN 0–312–22745–0 (cloth)
1. Urban policy—Great Britain.   2. Urban renewal—Great Britain.
3. Cities and towns—Great Britain.   I. Title.   II. Series:
Contemporary political studies (St. Martin's Press)
HT133.H555   1999
307.76'0941—dc21                                          99–33861
                                                                        CIP

This book is printed on paper suitable for recycling and made from fully managed and
sustained forest sources.

10   9   8   7   6   5   4   3   2   1
09   08   07   06   05   04   03   02   01   00

Printed in Hong Kong

# Contents

# Acknowledgement

Crown copyright is reproduced with the permission of the Controller of Her Majesty's Stationery Office.

# List of Figures, Boxes and Tables

ix

## Tables

# Abbreviations

| | |
|---|---|
| ACORN | 'A Classification of Residential Neighbourhood' |
| CBI | Confederation of British Industry |
| CDP | Community Development Project |
| CORA | 'community, opportunity, responsibility, accountability' |
| CLD | Commission for Local Democracy |
| CRCs | Community Relations Councils |
| CCT | compulsory competitive tendering |
| DATs | Drug-Action Teams |
| DBFO | 'design, build, finance and operate' |
| DEA | Department of Economic Affairs |
| DETR | Department of the Environment, Transport and the Regions |
| DfEE | Department for Education and Employment |
| DOE | Department of the Environment |
| DTI | Department of Trade and Industry |
| EAGGF | European Agricultural Guidance and Guarantee Fund |
| EAZs | Education Action Zones |
| EMAG | Ethnic Minorities Achievement Grant |
| ERDF | European Regional Development Fund |
| ESDP | European Spatial Development Perspective |
| ESF | European Social Fund |
| EZs | Enterprise Zones |
| FAS | Funding Agency for Schools |
| GLC | Greater London Council |
| GMS | grant-maintained status |
| GORs | Government Offices of the Regions |
| HAZ | Health Action Zones |
| HIE | Highland and Islands Enterprise |
| HIP | Housing Investment Programme |
| IDA | Improvement and Development Agency |
| ILEA | Inner London Education Authority |
| ILRs | independent local radio stations |
| IT | information technology |

| | |
|---|---|
| LDA | London Developement Agency |
| LEAs | local education authorities |
| LECs | local enterprise companies |
| LETS | local exchange trading systems |
| LGA | Local Government Association |
| LGWCS | local government women's committees |
| LPP | Local Policing Plan |
| LSVT | Large Scale Voluntary Transfer |
| OFSTED | Office of Standards in Education |
| OHMI | Office of Her Majesty's Chief Inspector of Schools in Wales |
| PFI | private finance initiative |
| PPGs | Planning Policy Guidance notes |
| Quangos | Quasi-nongovernmental organisations |
| RDAs | Regional Development Agencies |
| RDC | Rural Development Commission |
| RPG | Regional Planning Guidance |
| SE | Scottish Enterprise |
| SEN | special educational needs |
| SMEs | small and medium-sized enterprises |
| SOC | School Organisation Committee |
| SRB | Single Regeneration Budget |
| SSAs | Standard Spending Assessments |
| TECs | Training and Enterprise Councils |
| TPP | Transport Policies and Programmes |
| UDCs | Urban Development Corporations |
| UNCED | United Nations Conference on Environment and Development (Rio de Janeiro) |
| UP | Urban Programme |
| UPAs | Urban Programme Authorities |

# 1

# Introduction: the Urban Experience

In Britain, where a large proportion of the population lives in towns and cities, virtually all aspects of policy and politics could be said to be urban. This book, however, is specifically focused on the major urban problems of physical dereliction, economic decline and social exclusion, and the accompanying issues of community safety, environmental quality and racial harmony. These are sometimes called the 'wicked issues' because of their multifaceted nature, the way they cross service and agency boundaries, and because they have no immediately 'obvious' solutions.

Tackling these issues and trying to raise standards in education, health and housing dominate the political agenda. Governments at both central and local level have long been criticised for the fragmented, ad hoc and uncoordinated attempts to solve poverty and dereliction in our cities. At the beginning of the twenty-first century these issues have a new urgency: the inadequacies of previous solutions have produced cities with segregated populations, with extremes of wealth and poverty. To create more prosperous and inclusive cities more integrated strategies are under way, with new regional structures and, in towns and cities, new possibilities for political leadership through elected mayors. The present scene is thus one of energy and promise, with new ways of working together between public, private and voluntary bodies. New developments to improve city life are gathering momentum and there is a new dynamism to urban politics.

A reinvigorated approach to urban life is urgently needed because the magnitude of the problems is grave, with real concern that Britain could go the way of some North American cities with their bleak neighbourhoods and alienated residents suffering high unemployment, discrimination and crime. As the Social Exclusion report of September 1998 put it, over the last generation Britain has become a more divided society. The worst neighbourhoods have become no-go areas for some and no-exit zones for others (Cm 4045:9). Unless communities can be brought back into an active role in the regeneration process at grass-roots level then social polarisation could widen. It is not just deprived neighbourhoods that call out for help. The quality of life – curbing traffic and pollution, getting access to good housing and schools, and improving safety – concerns everyone.

These are not new concerns. As this book shows, since the late 1960s there have been numerous attempts to solve poverty, discrimination and decay in Britain's towns and cities. These problems have come about for a variety of reasons. Declining traditional industries and the fall in unskilled jobs have been accompanied by high male and youth unemployment. Other problems have come from changing family structures and poor schools. But governments too have contributed to the malaise, with poor housing design and allocation policies that concentrate poor people in neighbourhoods where few have jobs. In the last half-century, government policy has moved from planning to markets, from public sector dominated to mixed public–private systems of service delivery and from bureaucratic pluralism to consumer choice and quality standards. Understanding how and why these momentous changes have come about requires insights into the ideas which underpin the search for solutions. This book demonstrates the theoretical bases of contemporary urban policy and the ways in which it is evolving under the Labour administration elected in 1997 after 18 years of Conservative government. In particular, it considers the extent to which Tony Blair's 'Third Way' approach can provide the foundation of a revitalised urban democracy for the twenty-first century.

A distinctive feature is the attention given to issues of social exclusion and local democracy. Urban policy is not just about physical development: it is about how people can take an active part in social and political decisions that affect them all. Debates on policy are thus wide-ranging, covering not only the practicalities of tackling urban regeneration, civil order and raising service standards, but also the wider questions of political leadership and the ultimate goals of justice and fairness.

The purpose of this chapter is to set the scene for what follows by considering how we have come to understand urban policy and the key issues which are at its core.

## Exploring the urban world

*Box 1.1*   The traditional concerns of urban policy

- Land-use and strategic planning, including questions of development control; journey-to-work and retail patterns; capital and labour mobility; residential, industrial and commercial location.
- Physical and economic regeneration of the 'inner-city' through specific programmes to foster entrepreneurship and partnerships between public, private and voluntary bodies.
- Improving the quality of life for all city dwellers by tackling crime, environmental pollution, traffic and improving standards in housing and education; balancing social need and economic opportunity.
- Targeting the most deprived areas with increased resources and innovative solutions, such as the Action Zones for Education, Employment and Health.
- Working for the just and fair city: empowering communities; increasing citizens' voices and involvement; encouraging harmonious social relations between groups; countering discrimination and exclusion.

Box 1.1 summarises the key issues and problems which have dominated urban policy in post-war Britain. Although these appear diverse, they are all concerned with improving the quality of life in cities. Both central and local governments are involved in trying to solve these problems and do so through a mix of public and private provision of services. Urban problems have intensified as economic restructuring and social and demographic changes have created a growing polarisation between groups and between neighbourhoods. What is more British urban policy has traditionally provided town planning, education, mass transit and public housing well beyond inner-city neighbourhoods (Mossberger and Stoker, 1997). The result is that local provisions vary between cities and as circumstances change, though economic renewal and individual and social wellbeing remain the major goals of the urban political agenda.

Talking about 'urban policy' raises questions of what we mean by 'the urban' in a society such as Britain where life is essentially urbanised in the sense that everyone shares in common patterns of consumption, service standardisation and delivery, the market society and mass culture. 'The urban' is used in a variety of ways, among different academic disciplines and practitioners. For example, while geographers are concerned with how problems are situated in territory (patterns of settlement, journey-to-work and retailing for example), sociologists study the urban as the setting for social relations and political scientists examine decision-making and the exercise of power within governmental units (for examples of these approaches, see Agnew, 1993; Giddens, 1985; Urry, 1985; 1990). Other commentators claim there is no clear 'urban' referent as such (Dowding, 1996). This is so, it is argued, because the social and economic problems of cities are structural and require national solutions, not ones based on targeted areas or focused on the behaviour and attitudes of individuals and families. Solutions to the urban crisis and the promotion of economic growth and wellbeing, must be generic rather than locality-specific. Thus there are no 'urban' issues as such, just simply issues that face everybody (Kirby, 1995).

To ordinary people such concerns may seem of little relevance. Common sense dictates that the urban is recognisable as such, consisting of built-up areas with their concentrated populations, employment, retail and leisure facilities and with particular problems that call for solution, perhaps most obviously traffic, crime and dereliction. A pragmatic approach to people's appreciation of these issues is to begin with the local scale. People are most familiar with their immediate environment, which expands from the neighbourhood to the total built-up area and its wider setting. From this it can be concluded that it is the city region which more accurately reflects how urban centres influence their suburban and rural hinterlands. The result is that it is impossible to agree on an exact, bounded area for analysis, because the legal/administrative definition of urban units is too restricted. Other critics have been more trenchant. For some on the left urban was a redundant category in the operation of modern capitalism which had to be seen as a ubiquitous pattern of economic relations. For those on the right, government intervention itself was suspect. There was no need for a specific 'urban' policy and state direction: government's role was to support market solutions and promote enterprise and individual, not collective, responsibility.

In this book, however, the argument is that while urban phenomena can never be independent of the wider society, the local arena is vital in people's lives. This is the scale at which we interact with our environment, at which firms make investment decisions, where governmental, private and voluntary bodies operate, where we work and mix with other people, where we have a direct link with politicians and groups to defend our interests and meet our demands (Cooke, 1989). Thus the urban is a legitimate and crucial area of action and analysis. Modern mass society has not made the local arena redundant. Despite economic globalisation and the powerful effects of telecommunications and of work and leisure mobility, locality matters. The argument that the globalisation of economic life makes all local politics global politics, where cities must play the growth game to compete with others within the international division of labour, must be seen alongside the search for solutions within cities. Similarly, the explosion of communication through the Internet and the World Wide Web does not mean homogeneity and standardisation. Many disparate voices claim a hearing: minorities, and interests of all kinds, gain access to the network of information. The importance of the local thus has two dimensions: the variation between different towns and cities and the role of civic life within cities. The variation between cities which arises from different political and economic profiles must, this book argues, be recognised if local democracy is really to flourish. Of equal importance is the fact that cities are the fora of civil society, offering the potential for involvement in decision-making, understanding and working with others, allocating resources and resolving conflict. Urban life is political life, the stage for important issues and their resolution. Thus the study of the urban is a study of these relations.

To say this is to recognise that local areas are profoundly shaped by their role in modern capitalist society where businesses divide their operations into particular labour markets and local authorities compete for investment (Massey, 1984; Day and Murdoch, 1993). But at the same time the local area is important because the people who live there invest meaning in it; that is, they feel a sense of belonging and recognition. This investment of meaning turns locality into community: towns and cities are more than impersonal and anonymous physical surroundings, they are communities. Community, however, remains a contested concept (Hill, 1994); communities are not necessarily homogeneous and may be divided by conflict rather than united in harmony.

Urban politics and policy are thus shaped by the global and the local, by the different interests that are located in the city and by the attachments that people have to their communities. These policies and politics are marked by struggle as well as consensus. Political struggles have arisen over the policies for the disadvantaged, particularly in relation to ethnic minorities and, to a lesser extent, over the position of women as a marginalised group. Ethnic minorities and their concentration in deprived areas raise questions of whether policy should be targeted on particular groups of people or on specific neighbourhoods. Other groups have similar concerns. For feminists, local space is seen as the site of struggle and of women's position as disadvantaged and marginalised (Little, 1994). This has had an impact on urban politics, where women have sought to improve their representation on local councils, to gain access to decision-making through group recognition and to influence the outcomes of physical planning. Allied to this are questions of the accessibility and safety of public space, problems of transport and the design of estates (Higgins and Davies, 1996).

From these different approaches it is clear that 'place matters' and that place is not an abstract space but the location where problems arise and people try to work out their relations with each other. Conflicts between interests express themselves in place and are reflected in local politics. An important part of this political dialogue is the problem of those excluded from social and political society: those who are not mobile, who are without work and find themselves trapped in inner cities or peripheral housing estates in a ghettoised life style. The focus on economic and social polarisation and on 'social exclusion' will drive the urban policy agenda for a considerable period: the 1998 report of the government's Social Exclusion Unit emphasised that solving the problems would take 10–20 years. The distinctive contribution of this book is to highlight how past and present policies are meeting these challenges.

Urban politics, then, is grounded in local space and the relations between people lived out in localities:

> localities are theoretical and practical necessities in modern democracies. They are the point at which subjects with electoral rights vote, where most of the services provided by the state's welfare agencies are consumed, and where the day-to-day organisation of formal and informal political resistance or proactivity towards central institutions is carried out.
>
> (Cooke, 1990a: 133)

If, as this book claims, 'locality matters' to the conduct of urban affairs, then we must expect and endorse diversity and variation in urban politics and policy. Variations occur as the result of: voting patterns and party allegiances; residential patterns of urban cities with a high-density core, suburbs and 'rurban' hinterland; the nature of economic activity and its manufacturing/service mix. These variations remain influential in spite of the supposed 'nationalisation' of politics whereby people's local election choices are influenced by national events. In fact, urban politics will become increasingly important as the democratic arena reflects more pluralistic ways of working between local councils, business and voluntary groups.

## The challenges ahead

A key element of this book is to show how urban policy has evolved over the past three decades, as a key to understanding the changes that are in the making. From its welfarist beginnings in the late 1960s, urban policy changed dramatically under the radical agenda of Conservative governments in the 1980s and early 1990s. Labour's election victory in 1997 promised important new directions, but there has also been a continuing emphasis on value-for-money services and partnerships with the private and voluntary sector: that mixed economy of provision and its emphasis on quality and consumer satisfaction which has become a major feature of urban policy. The question to be addressed is whether we are entering a new era of a 'third way' between state collectivist solutions and *laissez faire* capitalism, as Labour claims, or just seeing the stabilisation of a public–private provision of services that have emerged from the previous Conservative revolution?

The challenge centres on those economic and social problems that appear so entrenched and intractable in Britain's towns and cities. Three areas stand out: physical deterioration, economic decline and poverty – the last an unfashionable term for which social deprivation has become a synonym. Concerns for these issues have their roots in programmes to address 'inner-city' decline in the 1960s, but the the first formal expression of urban policy was the Labour government's 1977 White Paper *Policy for the Inner Cities* which pressed for a more coherent strategy across departmental boundaries at both central and local levels (Cmnd 6845, 1977). The causes of urban malaise became the subject of much more controversy and debate in the 1980s. As this book shows, arguments taken from new right thinking and public choice theory challenged the power of local bodies and their bureaucracies. Instead, these critics argued, public sector provision should be replaced by entrepreneurial, market remedies and individual choice and responsibility. These criticisms were reflected in important theoretical developments, both in the 1980s and again at the turn of the century. In the 1980s there was increased theoretical interest in the influence of the new right on modern conservatism, on explanations taken from political economy and on neopluralist and neo-elitist approaches. Now, the stress by Prime Minister Blair on a 'third way' that draws on evidence-based research ('what works' is what matters) echoes ideas on both sides of the Atlantic. At the same time, European influences have had an important influence on policy direction, with localities seeking funding from the European Union. Policies have not become 'Americanised' or 'Europeanised' but they do operate within an international intellectual and structural framework.

The international dimension has not made cities redundant as a site of action. On the contrary, they claim renewed attention as the state becomes 'hollowed-out', with decisions passing upwards to supraregional bodies such as the European Union and down to the regions and localities within countries. The Labour government's devolution to Scotland and Wales, decentralisation to the new Regional Development Agencies and promise of further empowerment of communities and individuals is in the mainstream of these developments.

These theoretical and practical issues drive what central and local governments do. While central government lays down the legal framework, sets standards and directs major resources, local authorities devise strategies and programmes, in cooperation with other public and private agencies, to meet local needs and demands. Tension can arise between central and local governments over both priorities and strategies; one of the conclusions of this book is that truly revitalised local action must recognise and facilitate variation and local choice. Nor are cities homogeneous internally: areas are distinguished by ethnic, racial and economic diversity. These spatial and demographic differences are a vital element in urban politics, with resources and projects being increasingly targeted on the most deprived areas.

What has been remarkable in this changing scene has been the robustness of local institutions. Though local councils cannot override external economic factors they can be key actors in revitalising communities. This is so, even though policy over the past three decades has been criticised as short-term and fragmented. Now, not only must local authorities re-establish a lead role in urban affairs, albeit in partnership with other interests, local people must also become more actively involved in the renewal of their communities. New methods of consultation and involvement are essential if local democracy is to be modernised to be 'In Touch with the People' as the government White Paper of July 1998 puts it (Cm 4014, 1998).

These developments are themselves the subject of critical analysis. As this book shows, questions of democratic politics, their accessibility and accountability, are at the heart of action. But no one theoretical approach dominates debate and it is difficult to derive a set of long-term solutions from the analysis. If there has been a consensus, it is one of a mixed economy of provision involving public, private and voluntary sectors. Economic growth and social inclusion are the main goals of policy. This in turn means increased targeting of groups and areas, empowering people and communities and addressing the problems of ethnicity and race. Building partnerships, a key aim of Labour's modernising project, is highlighted in the examples of cooperation between local authorities and self-managing schools and in strategic working between the police and local councils. Similar partnership working will drive the 'New Deal for Communities' approach to run-down areas, tackling the causes of poor health in Health Action Zones and bringing together local councils and Regional Development Agencies to reverse economic decline. Legislation in the near future will also place a new duty on local councils to promote the economic, social and environmental wellbeing of their areas and put sustainable development more firmly into urban decision-making.

## The scope of this book

Five themes are developed in this book to investigate the challenges facing the urban agenda. The first theme sets the key issues of urban policy in their historical setting and examines the principles that underpin decisions. The second examines the framework of policy set by central and local government and by the European Union. The third theme looks at contemporary urban politics and how citizens take part as councillors, voters and members of different groups and interests. The fourth theme addresses the pressing problems of urban life: social exclusion, economic and physical change, community safety and implementing new initiatives to raise standards in education, community care, housing and the environment. The fifth and final theme looks at Labour's modernisation project, with its focus on elected mayors and local cabinets, to foster an expanded local democracy with better services and empowered communities.

Chapter 2 begins the exploration of these themes by demonstrating how policy has developed over the past half-century. Urban policy has its modern beginnings in the post-1945 establishment of the welfare state, with its twin influences of a new land-use planning system and universal services delivered locally to national standards. This position began to erode in the 1960s with the 'rediscovery of poverty', that is the evidence that the welfare state had not eliminated the problems faced by the most vulnerable in society. Governments responded by introducing specific programmes for particular areas, in distinction from former policy which set common solutions to common problems. A succession of projects followed. Conservative governments after 1979 introduced more market-orientated and entrepreneurial solutions. Planning regulations were eased for targeted projects and business encouraged to take a greater part in local affairs. New bodies outside the control of local authorities were set up to meet these aims. The judgement of the success of the many initiatives is that outcomes have been mixed. A major criticism has been of the extent to which projects have been property rather than people-orientated. The coming of a Labour government in 1997 continued and increased the targeting of resources and projects, while placing a new emphasis on tackling the worst neighbourhoods and fostering greater community involvement.

Chapter 3 explores the theories that have underpinned these developments. State–economy relations are at the heart of those ideas of neoconservative and neoliberal conservatism known as the New Right. The analysis then broadens out to look at the globalisation thesis. These debates range over a number of political economy approaches, but also take account of the role that social theory – in particular that on community and communitarianism – has played. A further element of the theoretical debate has been neopluralist and neo-elitist analyses which centre around the role of business and other interests in urban politics and the part that the plurality of ethnic, gender, environmental and other groups play in the exercise of political power.

Chapter 4 looks at the context of policy, at the structure of local government, the move to a regional dimension, the power of central government and the growing influence of the European Union on local decisions. These forces provide a complex framework within which decisions are taken. Over the past two decades not only has the system of local government changed, local councils have moved significantly from providing most local services to an enabling role overseeing services provided by public, private and voluntary bodies. Councils have lost powers upwards, as central government imposed tighter financial and other controls and downwards to the private sector, schools and other bodies. Relations between the centre and the localities became strained as local authorities were displaced from their traditional role as multipurpose providers of services. Chapter 4 explores the attempts being made under a Labour government to rebuild trust between central and local government in order to work together to tackle urgent urban problems. Tackling these issues now goes beyond the nation-state, with the European Union having a growing influence in providing funds and exploring new solutions. Urban issues are thus addressed through an interconnected network of local, national and European bodies.

Chapter 5 explores urban politics and the new emphasis on decentralisation and inclusion that are part of the Labour government's strategy. This in turn raises issues of accountability and the complexity of urban governance brought about by the introduction of non-elected bodies. Urban politics is the prime setting for the exercise of citizenship and participation, but a paradox remains over the realities of low voter turnout and the dominance of middle-class, middle-aged patterns of involvement.

Chapter 6 examines the ways in which councils are tackling economic decline and physical decay through Single Regeneration Budget projects and anti-poverty strategies. It shows that urban deprivation is multifaceted and that effective responses must address problems of crime, poor housing, ill-health, sustainable development and raise standards in education and other services. The Labour government is trying to remedy these defects by bringing social and community issues back into regeneration projects, giving local people more say in how decisions are made and implemented. The chapter also shows the innovations that are being introduced to improve community safety, tackle failing schools, develop a 'New Deal' for the worst council estates, impose new ways of working into health and community care and make cities better environments in which to live. It is the quality of city life for all its residents which is important, ensuring safe streets, a clean environment, good schools and health.

These are the concerns of Chapter 7, which looks at the wide range of proposals that the Labour government is putting in place. The emphasis remains on the strategic, 'enabling' authority, working in partnership with other bodies. Labour's objective is to give greater power to local people and make local leaders more responsive. Elected mayors and greater consultation will, it is argued, bring fundamental changes to urban politics. This is the 'third way' of Prime Minister Blair's philosophy; Chapter 7 explores the meaning and persuasiveness of this approach as the foundation of urban action. Labour's agenda is moving ahead rapidly; devolution to Scotland and Wales has already taken place and an elected Mayor and Assembly will soon be at work in London. These changes raise important issues of when, and if, elected bodies will be introduced in the English regions, what the powers of city mayors versus regional assembly leaders might be and what powers local councils can expect in the future.

Chapter 8 draws together the findings of the previous chapters. Though services must be provided for all local citizens, it is the pressure of economic decline and social deprivation that has dominated urban policy. The aim must be the just and fair city, goals that are thrown into sharp relief by the claims of the Labour government.

**Conclusion**

The distinctiveness of this book is to show the present and future prospects for achieving an urban policy that is coherent, long-term and strategic. This is essential if it is to overcome the 'initiative-itis' of approaches of the past 20 years. The book shows that developing a coherent strategy is difficult and controversial, taking place within an economy that has seen major changes and local authorities that have lost their monopoly of service provision. The days of the multipurpose local authority have gone. In its place the enabling authority must guide strategy while facilitating a system of urban politics which is based in partnership with other bodies. At the same time, action must remain responsible and responsive to citizens as both voters and consumers.

The atmosphere of change is palpable. But modernisation must have a purpose. The four values set out at the beginning of Prime Minister Blair's Fabian pamphlet suggest that purpose: equal worth, opportunity for all, responsibility and community (Blair, 1998b). To achieve these purposes, governments will have to devise programmes to meet formidable challenges: rich and poor areas existing side-by-side, crime and decay, and continued migration of families to satellite towns and rural areas. Within cities, populations are segregated and the poorest neighbourhoods suffer physical degradation and social and economic malaise. The Social Exclusion Unit is taking steps to combat poverty but there is no great crusade against poverty and injustice; in that sense the 'third way' has yet to produce the big idea (but see: Giddens, 1998b). Nevertheless the government argues that it is delivering improvements to everyone's quality of life. In 1999 its three-year targets were set out in a Department of the Environment, Transport and the Regions Public Service Agreement. The targets were: to reduce the number of people sleeping rough by two-thirds; cut the backlog of council house repairs by at least a quarter of a million; improve 1.5 million council houses; deliver 50 regeneration projects in the worst neighbourhoods; ensure 60 per cent of new homes are built on 'brown-field' sites. These targets show the government's determination to make real differences to city life.

The need for action, as this book shows, is urgent. Preventing that 'death of the city' of American fears, where residents and business flee to the suburbs and beyond to leave dereliction at the city's heart, is a demanding and rewarding challenge for practitioners and policymakers alike. This book pursues these challenges with optimism, seeing not despair but positive hopes of an urban renaissance and fresh commitment to achieving the good city.

# 2

# Seeking Solutions:
# Urban Policy since 1945

The present chapter shows how successive governments since 1945 have struggled with the problems of rebuilding and revitalising cities and their economies. Such a review is essential to understanding the key issues, how policy has evolved and the strengths and weaknesses of different approaches. Britain, like other advanced societies, must be concerned with the state of its cities, not only because local economic growth and decline affects national prosperity, but also because states must assert their own legitimacy and maintain civil order (Gurr and King, 1987). Since late Victorian times British governments have tried to address physical decay, public health, housing need, crime and poverty through urban policies that relied on a comprehensive structure of local government and effective local implementation. In the twentieth century, under the pressure of technological, communication and economic changes and the upheavals of two World Wars, urban and regional policy has become an important part of the national political agenda.

After 1945, urban policy developed in two directions. The first was that governments had to redress the economic consequences of uneven development between cities and regions, in particular the legacy of the physical and economic decline of the major industrial areas – the 'Depressed Areas' of the 1930s. Regional economic policy promoted development in these declining areas through aid for infrastructure and through selective financial incentives. At the same time the programme for 21 New Towns around the major conurbations (particularly London) was meant to disperse population away from densely populated centres. In the cities and towns, 'urban policy' focused on physical infrastructure, primarily slum clearance and on the dispersal of people to new housing on peripheral estates. These objectives were met largely through the land-use planning system set up after 1947 and regional economic measures. The second policy development arose out of the establishment of the welfare state, with governments determining universal services to be locally delivered to nationally determined standards and funding.

From the late 1940s onwards legislation to meet these goals covered education, public health, personal social services and unemployment and pension benefits, together with the establishment of the National Health Service. Central control over services increased as government funding grew and as ministerial circulars and regulations set out guidelines. But the centre was not completely dominant: local councils, the associations of local authorities and the professional groups of local officers made substantial contributions to policy. In this way localities and central governments were cemented into a pattern of policy communities (Rhodes, 1988; Gray, 1994). These patterns of influence widened in the 1970s as national and local policy for cities and regions was affected by European Union initiatives. As British spending on regional incentives declined in the 1980s, so that provided by European Union Structural Funds grew. In overall amounts, the grant aid is small but makes important contributions to action in particular towns and cities.

The chapter sets out the structure of these foundations of urban policy. It begins by considering how, after 1945, urban needs were addressed through the planning system. The British tradition has given a prime place to land-use planning as a major policy tool with which to confront problems arising from industrialisation and urbanisation. After World War II governments faced pressing tasks of reconstructing war-damaged cities, meeting pent-up housing demand and rebuilding the economy. Although there was already a long history of intervention in public health, law and order and other urban problems, the changes of the late 1940s brought legislation to address these issues systematically nationwide. The system laid down in the 1947 Town and Country Planning Act has proved remarkably robust; it has survived modification and consolidation to remain the basis of strategic and local physical planning and development for over 50 years. Parallel to the control of land-use and development, governments also tried to redress the imbalance between rich and poor regions through additional investment and regional planning structures.

At the same time that the formal system of planning was laid down, the foundations of the welfare state were established with the aim of providing universal services to national standards and delivered to a substantial degree by local authorities. By the 1960s, however, both the planning system and the coverage of the welfare services were being called into question. This chapter shows how the rediscovery of poverty on both sides of the Atlantic drove the search for new solutions. Not only had poverty not been eliminated by the welfare state, tensions over immigration and race relations appeared to be growing. The solution was to concentrate resources more specifically on deprived areas, though controversy arose over the programmes and their outcomes. In the mid-1970s there were determined attempts to meet these criticisms by establishing coherent policies for the inner cities. This chapter highlights the difficulties that were experienced as the focus on the 'inner-city' raised issues as to whether policy should be directed primarily at physical regeneration of particular areas or aimed at poor individuals and families wherever they lived.

After 1979 Conservative governments challenged the post-war assumptions that state planning and intervention were the best solutions. The chapter examines the Conservatives' radical agenda to show how the structures and processes of urban policy were changed substantially to meet Conservative objectives. The emphasis on deregulation, private rather than public solutions and new agencies to deliver services, reduced the role of local authorities and gave business an important place in urban politics. And towns and cities had to compete for government funding: it was no longer sufficient to demonstrate that social needs existed and should be met. Needs had to be prioritised, efficiency demonstrated and projects evaluated by civil servants against a limited regeneration budget. Competing for funds, the chapter shows, became the key feature of urban policy from the late 1980s into the 1990s. It is clear that policy in the the last decade-and-a-half has been, for all its efforts to provide coherent solutions, essentially a series of ad hoc responses to crises and competing priorities. How then should policy be judged? The chapter shows that while gains have been made, they have been modest and distributed unevenly as between the most deprived and other needy areas.

If the era from 1979 to the mid-1990s was a mixture of ideology and pragmatism, fragmentation within a search for coherence, what is the next decade likely to bring? In the year 2000 what is happening is that the traditional physical determinism of the planning system on the one hand and the supply-side 'trickle-down' economic solutions of the Conservative years on the other, are being reordered – if not wholly replaced – to foster a more just and inclusive society. There is a new urgency to find solutions to multifaceted urban stress: unemployment and low skills, concentrated in areas of deprivation, apathy and social exclusion. Here the chapter considers whether we are moving to a new consensus based on a mix of public and private sectors and drawing on partnerships between them. 'What works' is almost claiming the status of an ideology or motivating principle. The chapter concludes by drawing the themes of this historical overview together to form the framework against which current policy developments must be seen.

## Meeting needs through the planning framework

Governments have a prime interest in making cities safe and vibrant places to live. After 1945 it was physical planning that drove this urban policy, in order to meet the urgent demand for housing and reconstruction. The planning system at this time was rooted in those nineteenth-century reforms which tackled the pressing needs of public health, housing and crime. Starting with model bye-laws to build housing, by the early twentieth century local councils were accumulating powers to address the worst problems of slums and insanitary conditions in more comprehensive and coordinated ways: that is, to plan. The powers conferred by the 1909 Housing, Town Planning, Etc. Act and subsequent legislation, though limited, provided the basis for the future land-use planning system. In the inter-war years planning acquired another dimension, based on economic issues and covering wider regional, as opposed to city, areas. Thus planning came to have a dual meaning – the physical and the economic – and to involve national governments as well as local councils.

These developments came to fruition in the years following World War II. Under the Labour governments of 1945–51, policy to address urban issues had a clear remit: to rebuild cities after wartime destruction, meet the pent-up housing demand and establish national standards. This period was, as Chapter 3 shows, a 'Fordist' era of mass production and mass consumption in which local authorities delivered the major services of the welfare state. As well as the planning and reconstruction of cities, there was a wider problem of uneven development between regions. This was met through the Distribution of Industry Act 1945 and other legislation that directed investment and incentives to the worst affected industrial areas. Subsequently, the Labour government of 1964 set up the Department of Economic Affairs (DEA) to meet these needs through a National Plan and

Economic Planning Councils (representing a cross-section of public and private interests) and Economic Planning Boards (of civil servants) in the eight English regions, together with the separate regions of Scotland and Wales. The DEA's achievements were limited. It was disbanded in 1969 with its economic planning functions passing to the Treasury and its regional responsibilities to the then Ministry of Housing and Local Government.

As the 1970s wore on, economic restructuring through national planning policies was increasingly questioned. The Conservative government of 1979 wound up the Regional Economic Planning Boards and Councils and introduced different and more market-orientated perspectives. In the 1980s the broad objectives of Conservative regional policy were to reduce employment imbalances and encourage growth potential from within the regions, not from special government measures. This emphasis on indigenous potential replaced the aim of shifting activity from one area to another which had marked previous policy. A degree of selective regional assistance was retained and applied throughout Britain. In organisational terms, however, Scotland and Wales were treated differently. In Scotland, there were three separate bodies: the Scottish Development Agency, the Highlands and Islands Development Board and the Training Agency. In 1991 these were consolidated into Scottish Enterprise (SE) and Highlands and Islands Enterprise (HIE), with the Scottish Office responsible for regional policy. The majority of SE and HIE activity is carried out by 22 Local Enterprise Companies (LECs), private companies operating under contract whose directors are drawn primarily from the private sector. In Wales the Welsh Office is responsible for regional policy and executive powers are held by the Welsh Development Agency and the Development Board for Rural Wales. In both Scotland and Wales these structures will be affected by the new devolution arrangements (see Chapter 7).

By contrast to the disagreements and changes surrounding regional policy, the period between 1947 and 1979 in land-use planning was largely one of evolution around a common core structure. The landmark was the Town and Country Planning Act of 1947 which required local authorities to produce plans for their areas and gave them powers over the control of development. This Act and subsequent legislation offered certainty to meet problems through negotiated and consensual solutions. Urban dereliction, the shortage of housing, the mismatch between people, jobs and homes, could all be met by rational planning strategies. This does not mean that there were no conflicts or contradictions. Disputes existed between conurbations and surrounding counties and districts, largely over the erosion of the green belt and the siting of new towns. Solving such disputes by moving to a wider city–regional planning base was constrained by existing local government boundaries. These strains led to changes to the planning system in the 1960s and a greater emphasis on strategic planning at the county level to integrate town and countryside developments.

Beginning with the 1947 legislation, then, a nationwide system of development plans and development control was introduced into England and Wales (the system differed in Scotland and was subsequently amended by the 1973 Local Government (Scotland) Act when the local government system there was reformed). The 1968 Town and Country Planning Act, as amended in 1971, continued the tradition of the 1947 legislation, but introduced new forms of development plans within a two-tier county and district system. Under this new system County Councils prepared structure plans dealing with wider strategies, while District Councils were responsible for local plans. The two-tier system required cooperation and collaboration between counties and districts and there were considerable strains in the relationship as districts sought greater powers to control developments in their own areas more closely.

The two-tier system of county structure plans and district plans, however, remained the basis of planning. A major modification in the 1980s came with the changes to the way local government was organised in the major conurbations and London. In 1986 the Greater London Council (GLC) and the six metropolitan counties of the West Midlands (based on Birmingham), Merseyside (Liverpool), Manchester, South Yorkshire (Sheffield), Tyne and Wear (Newcastle) and West Yorkshire (Leeds) were abolished. Their powers, including planning powers, were transferred to the lower tier authorities, the metropolitan districts and the London boroughs. Within these lower-tier authorities unitary plans, covering both the strategic and local elements, were combined for each district, leaving the wider conurbation with no formal, overall strategic approach to matters such as transport and development. This criticism was particularly sharp in London, where it was claimed that the abolition of the GLC had left a massive deficit of strategic planning for the London region. The Labour government believes that the new system of an elected mayor and assembly in London will address these problems (see Chapter 7).

In 1990, planning legislation was consolidated by four Acts: the Town and Country Planning Act, the Planning (Listed Buildings and Conservation Areas) Act, the Planning (Hazardous Substances) Act and the Planning (Consequential Provisions) Act. The 1990 Town and Country Planning Act provided for a new system by which development plans consist of structure plans and local plans. In addition, following the reform of the local government structure after 1992, those districts which became Unitary Authorities assumed both the structure and local planning powers formerly shared with the county councils (for the particular changes in Wales and in Scotland, see Jarvis, 1996; Hayton, 1996b). These changes, and the introduction of the Planning Policy Guidance notes (PPGs) by the Department of the Environment, both increased central oversight and put formal plan-making and environmental issues at the centre of the system. It is notable, however, that of the 25 or so PPGs published by the mid-1990s, none dealt with women and planning, nor with ethnic minority, disability, or access issues (Greed, 1996). What emerged was a more centralised urban planning framework with a higher degree of uniformity in planning practice (Allmendinger and Tewdwr-Jones, 1997). At the regional level, the rationale for the Regional Planning Guidance (RPG) system was that it provided a wider geographical framework, with a longer time-span, within which local authorities' own development plans could operate.

The Labour government of 1997 merged transport and the environment into a single Whitehall department, the Department of the Environment, Transport and the Regions (DETR) and gave it responsibility for coordinating planning, environmental and regional issues and bringing transport to the heart of these endeavours – a massive governmental brief. The objectives were ambitious and wide-ranging. They were: to modernise the planning system to improve the input of regional stakeholders; promote sustainable development; incorporate a European dimension and speed up the preparation and adoption of development plans. Planning will remain under local democratic control by local councils, but the new Regional Development Agencies (RDAs) will have a key role in contributing a regional perspective. This will place a premium on good relations between the RDAs, the government's regional administrative structure (the Government Offices of the Regions (GORs) ) and local authorities. It remains too soon to judge whether this will mean a real move to a more collaborative planning system involving multiple stakeholders, rather than the emphasis on regulation that has been the traditional basis of land planning and resource management (for an analysis of collaborative planning, see: Healey, 1998).

Changes will certainly result from the coming into operation of the Regional Development Agencies in April 1999. Though the RDAs will not be able to overrule local planning authorities, both parties will have to work together on planning issues and this is likely to prove a very demanding task, given the disputes over the siting of major developments, particularly large-scale housing projects, roads and new retail centres. Uncertainties also arise from the increasing European Union interest in planning matters. In 1991, the European Commission published *Europe 2000* on territorial developments, including regional and environmental issues. This was followed in 1994 by *Europe 2000+* which prefigured a 'European spatial development perspective' and a 'Compendium on planning systems and policies in Member States' (Commission of the European Communities, 1994). The EU is continuing to work on a European Spatial Development Perspective (ESDP) and although there have been statements denying that this would preempt national or regional responsibilities, uncertainties remain as to what harmonisation across member states will entail.

## Rediscovering poverty

The planning system established in 1947, although it has undergone considerable modification, remains the framework for the land-use and development elements of urban policy. In the 1960s, however, the 'rediscovery of poverty' on both sides of the Atlantic changed the focus of urban policy from land-use planning and regional economic measures to programmes to meet social needs. These developments energised the search for new solutions.

'Urban policy' for the three decades after 1945 operated through a national legislative framework and local action. It came increasingly to be equated with the problems of the 'inner-city', a place and a term notoriously difficult to define (Hill, 1994). In some sense, the inner-city is a place, a geographical locality marked by physical and economic decline. But major areas of deprivation are not confined to the city core (or, more correctly, to the manufacturing and residential areas around the commercial centre). Some of the worst features of poverty are to be found in the 1960s council housing estates on the city periphery. The general consensus has been that 'inner-city' problems were multiple and interwoven, centred on unemployment, low investment, low educational achievement, poverty and poor health, high crime rates and large numbers of one-parent families. But urban policy defined as inner-city deprivation in practice raised issues as to whether it was directed primarily at places or at people. That is, are resources best directed to infrastructure and physical regeneration of particular areas, or to programmes aimed at deprived individuals and families? Though policymakers argued that this was a false distinction, since projects were targeted at areas where there were large concentrations of those in need, the difficulties remained.

In the major cities in particular there were pressures to widen the purposes of planning to meet the needs for economic and social improvements as well as physical development. The transatlantic policy remedy for deprivation was to introduce very localised projects mixing redevelopment and social services. In place of universal services for all needy people who qualified for aid, wherever they lived, programmes would be targeted selectively on areas which were perceived as having high concentrations of populations in acute poverty. In Britain, from the 1960s onwards these new objectives were met through a variety of anti-poverty programmes which, unlike the universality of land-use planning or unemployment or social security benefits, were specific and targeted by area, concerned with the run-down city neighbourhoods and with particular social and racial issues (Edwards and Batley, 1978; Higgins, Deakin, Edwards and Wicks, 1983). The successes of the planning system were recognised, particularly in controlling development, building new towns and improving housing and other conditions. But this process was seen as essentially a reaction to the Victorian urban legacy of slums and congestion, ill-suited to the late twentieth century problems of social exclusion and unemployment. Indeed, it arguably made problems worse, with tower blocks and 'sink' estates of deprivation (Shaw and Robinson, 1998).

The contention was that the welfare state had residualised but not eliminated poverty, and racial tensions in Britain raised fears that the rioting and alienation of United States' experience threatened similar prospects in this country. Indeed, the response of the Wilson government was in part a reaction to the assertion by Enoch Powell MP, at the time of the 1968 Race Relations Bill, that urban unrest would follow rising numbers of immigrants. Immigration and discrimination in employment and housing revealed settlement patterns in which minorities were concentrated in inner areas with high levels of poverty. These patterns of economic and residential polarisation had accelerated. Populations were moving from city cores to the periphery, creating city regions marked by central business, commercial and retail districts surrounded by run-down 'inner-city' neighbourhoods and with expanding suburban residential areas.

From the 1960s, in the face of these changes, 'urban policy' became coterminous with 'inner-city' policy, targeting projects on areas marked by poverty and in many cases, immigration. In this context it is notable that the first specifically inner-city policy was devised by the Labour government's 1968 Urban Programme. This was closely tied to issues of 'race' and racism and had followed the introduction of special grants, for up to 75 per cent of approved expenditure, under Section 11 of the 1966 Local Government Act to support additional services in areas with large ethnic minority populations. The Urban Programme was developed by the Home Office in 1968 and formalised by the 1969 Local Government Grants (Special Needs) Act. At the same time the policy of specific targeting on areas gained momentum, with the setting up of Housing Action Areas, General Improvement Areas and Education Priority Areas. In addition the Community Development Projects, modelled on American programmes and emphasising local participation, were set up both as an anti-poverty strategy and as a means of researching into the effects of policy (for a history of the measures of the 1960s and 1970s, see Edwards and Batley, 1978).

Not everyone agreed with the emphasis on targeting. In particular the Community Development Projects, another Home Office initiative set up in 1969, ended in 1976 after clashes between area teams and local and central government over the purpose of such efforts. The Community Development Project (CDP) report rejected the area-based, social pathology explanation of urban poverty (Community Development Project, 1977). Taken largely from the American War on Poverty programme of the 1960s, the social pathology argument had been that there was a 'culture of poverty' by which individuals and families were trapped in a 'cycle of poverty', perpetuated from one generation to the next. The CDP report rejected this analysis. Poverty, it argued, arose from defects in the economic and social structure of society rather than from individual shortcomings. It could only be remedied by national policies on employment and income, not by localised solutions. Controversial at the time, this emphasis on the socioeconomic, rather than the behavioural, foundations of inner-city poverty became part of policy orthodoxy. And targeting itself became a key feature of all subsequent urban policies.

Policy is not driven solely by expert opinion or by judgements on past efforts. Since the late 1960s the place of urban policy on the political agenda has waxed and waned as much in relation to political pressure – the concern over social unrest, the search for electoral support, the wish to make moral statements – as to questions of distributive policies and welfare needs. Policies also gave rise to controversy over the differing perspectives and priorities of central and local government, as the CDP itself showed. The Urban Programme and the Community Development Projects of the 1960s and 1970s called for cooperation between central and local governments. The policies were set nationally and involved local authorities as partners in targeted neighbourhood work. Much of the central government funding was time-limited, though many of the projects were eventually taken into mainstream provision by local authorities. But although racial issues were a catalyst of policy, racial disadvantage and exclusion were rarely addressed directly.

Critics have also argued that urban policy was intractable: competitive and fragmented and property- rather than people-driven. Outcomes have been equally uneven, yielding no permanent solutions. The unevenness of outcomes has mirrored the eclecticism of influences on policy. Different solutions have been tried and rejected over time and taken from a wide range of sources within different academic disciplines and from different countries, particularly from the United States.

Despite these criticisms, from the mid-1970s onwards there were determined efforts to address urban problems directly and more comprehensively. These efforts took a new turn with the Labour government's 1977 White Paper, *Policy for the Inner Cities* (Cmnd 6845). The 1977 White Paper and the Inner Urban Areas Act of 1978 changed the focus from social action to a new policy of inner-city economic regeneration. At the same time help for those left outside the economic mainstream, as developed through the Urban Programme, would remain a continued welfare commitment. Labour's 1977 White Paper has been seen as a definitive stage in the development of a strategic urban policy, giving it a permanent place on the political agenda (Lawless, 1996). Often judged as the best statement of urban policy ever made, the White Paper promoted the reversal of economic decline as the key to urban renewal. But it was not, as some argued, rigidly economistic; it highlighted the importance of race relations, the need for population balance and the significance of public involvement. Peter Shore, the Secretary of State for the Environment, claimed that the White Paper was the first comprehensive policy for the inner cities. The government promised better coordination between departments at central and local level to integrate all relevant agencies into a concerted approach to the many sources of urban distress. The physical, economic and social decline of inner cities had to be halted through what was a radically new objective, that of turning away from the focus on individual pathology (people's attitudes, behaviours and lifestyles) to basic economic causes. The difficulty remained, however, that coordination and comprehensiveness were elusive. Governments continued to use successive programmes to meet problems as they arose; a range of initiatives that were marked more by their fragmentation than by their coherence.

**From planning to markets**

After 1979 urban policy was driven by the ideological stance of successive Conservative governments, shaped by increasing central control and direction and characterised by an emphasis on business investment. The Conservatives' radical agenda was to promote deregulation and entrepreneurship. Conservative governments saw the purpose of planning as being to aid the market rather than to manage or control it. To this end, governments set limits to local authority spending, introduced a large body of legislation which controlled how councils operated and set up new bodies with specific tasks to act alongside local councils.

The government's deregulation agenda had two major impacts on urban policy. The first and most radical change was to remove physical and economic regeneration powers from local authorities and give them to separate appointed bodies, the so-called quasi-nongovernmental organisations (Quangos). The 1980 Local Government, Planning and Land Act established the Urban Development Corporations as Quangos outside local authority control and extended planning deregulation to newly defined areas of inner cities designated as Enterprise Zones and Simplified Planning Zones. The aim in all three situations was to target particular areas of towns and cities, using private finance and involving business leaders and other important local interests, to bypass what were seen as slow and restrictive local councils. When the Enterprise Zones and the Urban Development Corporations came to the end of their time-limited operation in the late 1990s, the Labour government's introduction of Regional Development Agencies again called into question the precise operations of local authority planning regimes. As was shown above, the RDAs will not override local authority planning but the two levels will be required to work together and how this will operate in practice remains to be established.

The second and related effect of the 1979 Conservative government's move from planning to a market approach was the shift to greater deregulation of development controls in order to encourage employment creation. But the government was under pressure from a different direction to maintain and expand certain aspects of planning intervention: that relating to the environment. These pressures came from both the public's increasing concern over environmental issues and from the wider influence of international bodies and the European Community. The result was that the government was eventually to introduce, in 1990, an Environmental Protection Act (see Chapter 6 for the impact of environmental issues). This and subsequent action marked the growing importance of environmental controls in urban policy even for governments wishing to shift from regulation to markets.

Conservative governments, influenced by the new right emphasis on the market and a reduced role for the state both in economic and welfare provision, followed a supply-side approach. This gave primacy to the private sector, which was encouraged through deregulation and financial aid and by the incorporation of business into public–private partnerships. The use of 'partnership' changed. Whereas this had previously meant cooperation between central and local governments, it now meant cooperation with the private sector, encouraged through measures to draw in private investment and the direct involvement of business in taking decisions and running projects.

It has to be recognised, however, that there was another element to these developments. On entering office, the government appeared to have little particular interest in the urban social programmes of its predecessors. While it did continue the funding of the Urban Programme operating in the Urban Priority Areas and elsewhere, it down-graded its importance. What drew attention back to social conditions were the urban riots of the early 1980s, initially in London and Liverpool in 1981 and subsequently in other towns and cities. Building on the provisions available in the 1980 Act, Michael Heseltine, the Secretary of State for the Environment, made determined efforts to set up consultative groups of business interests and galvanise private investment in cities. At the same time the law and order implications of the urban unrest gave rise to investigations into the causes of disorder (for example the Scarman Report on the 1981 riots in Brixton: see Chapter 6) and to a re-evaluation of the role of civil order and community safety in city regeneration. The strong emphasis on the private sector was also boosted by partnerships between central government and a variety of bodies at the local level (in the City Action Teams and Task Forces for example). City Action Teams were set up in 1985 to bring different agencies together (their work continued for a decade and was eventually subsumed into the Government Offices of the Regions in 1994). The Task Forces were established in 1986 and were made up of civil servants from Whitehall and secondees from business and the local authority. The aim of both initiatives was to ensure that government policy objectives were being actively pursued in the localities and to improve coordination between agencies at the local level.

The central emphasis of Conservative policy, on private investment and business involvement, was established early in the Conservative government's first term, with the 1980 Local Government, Planning and Land Act setting up the Enterprise Zones (EZs) and Urban Development Corporations (UDCs). Judgements of the effectiveness of these flagship policies have been mixed. Between 1981 and 1984 25 EZs were designated for 10-year periods. By the end of that time, some 68 000 jobs were located in the EZs and almost 80 per cent of the land area had been developed. The legacy of dereliction had been effectively tackled and there was considerable environmental improvement. But doubts remained over the extent to which employment and development were additional or merely transferred from other areas in response to the financial incentives (Department of the Environment, 1995a). There were similar mixed outcomes from the Urban Development Corporations. Seen as the flagship of Conservative urban policy, the first two were set up in London Docklands and on Merseyside in 1981, with the remaining ten in other conurbations in four tranches up to the mid-1980s. Though the 1980 Act had no clear definition of 'regeneration', the emphasis was on property-led development.

UDCs are now seen as the classic 1980s regeneration initiative, exhibiting the key features of government-imposed, property-orientated and private sector-dominated policies (Parkinson, 1996). The UDCs had parallels with the United States' Urban Development Action Grants, with their aim of 'leveraging' (in Britain, levering) private investment into projects by priming them with public subsidies, cleared sites, reduced regulation of land-use and a favourable financial regime. In this way, it was hoped, long-term growth would become self-sustaining. Time-limited bodies that came to an end between 1995 and 1998, the UDCs were considered by Conservative governments as successes in achieving their objectives, with over £11 billion of private investment attracted against a total grant in aid of just over £3 billion (Cm 3207, 1996). On the other side were commentators who criticised the business domination of the UDCs, their limited social objectives and their isolation from local community involvement. The largest of the projects, the London Docklands Development Corporation, was a particular focus of criticism on these grounds. It remains the case, however, that the UDCs reflected an important change of direction from a needs-based policy to a supply-side approach that aimed to attract private enterprise into specifically defined areas. These objectives, moreover, were deliberately set outside normal local authority provision, even though there were local representatives on the boards of the UDCs. The use of the Quango UDCs introduced a new organisational form into urban affairs – and one which has outlasted the operation of the UDCs themselves.

These new organisational, public–private forms of urban action have not disappeared and, as Chapter 7 shows, are growing in diversity under Labour. Though the UDCs themselves were given limited time to achieve their objectives, Conservative governments continued to use this organisational form as part of its policies. One of the major Quangos that persists, and which the Conservatives saw as a leading initiative in providing the enterprise and skills training that were so vital to regeneration, are the Training and Enterprise Councils. In 1990, as part of its continued determination to stimulate business involvement, a programme of Training and Enterprise Councils (TECs; in Scotland, Local Enterprise Companies, LECs) was announced. By 1991 England and Wales were covered by 81 TECs with 22 LECs in Scotland. The TECs have appointed boards on which at least two-thirds of the 8–15 members have to be business leaders (including the chairman). As hybrid bodies, they are private companies with public roles. Outside the metropolitan areas the TECs cover areas larger than individual cities, normally the county. TECs have made a modest contribution to improving training and promoting economic regeneration, but their impact has not been as dramatic as had been hoped (Employment Committee, 1996).

Local authorities have sought to establish close relationships with the TECs. After 1993 the TECs were drawn into the Single Regeneration Budget process, when they were encouraged to collaborate with local authorities and other local interests in bidding for, and taking a lead in, Single Regeneration Budget funds. TECs also have a leading role in the network of local business-support partnerships known as Business Links. The importance of TECs goes beyond the question of their unelected Quango status. They represent an important element in the framework of policy implementation. As John points out, TECs represent a new intervention system: 'a nationwide multi-functional decentralised central administration, introduced very slowly, like a prefecture in embryo' (John, 1994a: 425). By contrast, evaluation of their role as leading delivery agents of education and training to young school-leavers and the adult unemployed has been mixed. While recognising the numbers of young people that have gone through the system, there is criticism of TEC provision, particularly in relation to the more disadvantaged school-leavers. As a result, the role of TECs in the policy framework may change again. Their role was reviewed by the Labour government in the autumn of 1998; while business leadership is likely to remain in place, the TECs may become more subservient to the new Regional Development Agencies.

Because the Conservative party was in office for such a long period, it enjoyed considerable opportunity to make substantial changes to the policy framework of urban regeneration. At the centre of these changes was the objective of curtailing local authority spending, in order to promote economic growth while defeating inflation. These actions, together with the curtailment of the planning regime described above, would bring benefits not only in increased business investment in cities but in giving greater choice to individuals.

A notable feature of this change of direction and of the rationale for policy was that for the first eight years of this long period of Conservative rule, there was no formal publication of aims and objectives. It was not until 1987 that a comprehensive statement appeared. This came out of the 1987 election victory when Prime Minister Thatcher announced in her election night speech: 'We have a big job to do in those inner cities... because we want them too next time'. The result was not, however, new legislation but the publication, in March

1988, of a glossy brochure, *Action for Cities* (Department of the Environment, 1988) and, in Scotland, *New Life for Urban Scotland* (Scottish Office, 1988). The documents are important because they were the first formal statements of the aims of urban policy since the Conservatives had entered office in 1979. They emphasised the need to consolidate programmes and grants, achieve greater coordination between Whitehall Departments, a reaffirmation that the state's role was to facilitate private entrepreneurship and to stress that economic development had priority over social needs. These objectives were reinforced by actions taken over how local council services should be delivered. Where services could not be provided through the market by privatisation, then market surrogates would be applied. Local councils were required, through the Compulsory Competitive Tendering (CCT) introduced in 1988, to put their services out to tender to the private sector and, in services retained in-house, to operate internal tendering systems through the use of trading accounts and internal client–contractor relationships. The Labour government of 1997 promised to replace CCT with 'best value' requirements and pilot schemes were introduced in 1998. But the Labour government stressed that this did not mean a return to the 'municipalisation' of services, since a mix of providers would be required and quality and consumer satisfaction would remain the prime criteria.

The emphasis on quasi-market mechanisms in Conservative policy was also expressed through the mandated delegation of education budgets from the local authority to individual schools and their governing bodies, and the 'opting out' of schools from local authority control by giving them Grant Maintained Status with direct funding from the national government. While the Labour government has removed grant maintained status, schools will retain considerable autonomy. Alongside the market and surrogate market forms for implementing urban policy, the Conservatives stressed consumer choice and quality control as integral to service delivery. To this end 'Citizen's Charters' – setting out what standards could be expected in a particular service – were devised by the Major government in the early 1990s. At the same time, the government required that local authorities should monitor outputs of the services they provided through performance indicators and publish the results in 'league tables', for example of school examination and test results. The successor Labour government supported the Citizen's Charter provisions and placed even greater emphasis on the use of performance indicators and other measures.

For Thatcher and Major the use of the market, of Quangos and of consumer choice, were not just about efficiency, they were also about power. Their governments in the 1980s and early 1990s sought overtly to reduce local authority bureaucracies, limit what they saw as unaccountable trade unionism and increase the influence of parents, consumers and the private sector. These perspectives reflected the anti-statist, new right philosophy of Conservative governments and changed the foundations of policy. The judgement has been that, overall, the supply-side, 'trickle-down' policy, while it ameliorated did not solve urban deprivation and decline.

## Competing for funds

In the 1990s urban policy became increasingly based on competition between areas for the available funding. This began when in May 1991 the government announced the City Challenge regime in which bids for funds were put together by partnerships of local authorities, business groups and voluntary organisations. The focus was not on the most deprived areas *per se*, but on projects which could demonstrate a capacity for improvement – a focus that was changed when Labour came to office in 1997. In Whitehall, City Challenge widened the involvement of other departments beyond that of the Department of the Environment. At local level it gave community groups more involvement in the decision-making process and provided a more prominent role for local authorities in regeneration partnerships, in contrast to the anti-local council thrust of previous policy.

City Challenge was suspended after only two rounds of funding, but the principle of competitive bidding was continued, when City Challenge was incorporated into the Single Regeneration Budget Challenge Fund. The Single Regeneration Budget (SRB) system was introduced in April 1994 to bring together in one budget 20 existing economic regeneration programmes from 6 Departments and to wind down the former Urban Programme. In addition a statutory Urban Regeneration Agency, known as English Partnerships, was set up as a property agency to assume responsibilities for City Grant and for Derelict Land Grant and English Estates, two former programmes that aided site clearance and physical redevelopment. The Urban Regeneration Agency was a kind of 'roving Urban Development Corporation' which operated through six regional offices in England.

These regional responsibilities were transferred to the new Regional Development Agencies from April 1999. At the same time as the introduction of the SRB system in 1994, it was announced that the three major conurbations of Birmingham, London and Manchester would take part in City Pride, a 10-year programme for each city. The programme was later extended to seven other cities and continued under the Labour government. The City Pride projects were promoted to give a shared vision for regeneration, fostering a more corporate approach by local councils and their partners.

The Conservative government argued that the SRB system would overcome the 'patchwork quilt of complexity' of previous regeneration efforts criticised by the Audit Commission and replace it with a more coherent strategy (Audit Commission, 1989). But the programme did not expand regeneration efforts: rather the reverse. The overall SRB allocation in 1994–95, at £1.4 billion (out of a total DOE budget of nearly £40 billion), was £300 million less than the combined amounts contained in the budgets from the 20 programmes being replaced in the previous year (Cm 3207, 1996). And while the SRB met Urban Programme commitments which had arisen from project approvals in 1992–93 and earlier years, the UP itself would be phased out at the end of March 1997 (in practice, as Chapter 7 shows, it was reprieved by the incoming Labour government). The SRB Challenge Fund element was equally modest: £125 million for bidding partnerships in 1994–95, rising to £600 million in 1998–99. Under the Labour government's July 1998 Expenditure Review and the move from annual to three-year spending programmes, £3 billion in additional money was added to regeneration for the years 1999–2000 to 2001–2002. As a result the total regeneration budget would rise from £1.352 billion in 1999–2000 to £1.75 billion in 2001–2002. An important part of the system is that bids are required to show that they can lever in matching funds from sources outside the SRB, both from the private sector and from European Union Structural Funds.

By the mid-1990s, competitive bidding for government funding had become the dominant element of policy. Governments continued to insist, however, that this was an effective way of making sure that funds went to those projects that could demonstrate their efficiency. The SRB system was also defended as addressing the problem of coordination. This was achieved, the government argued, by managing it through the regional offices of Whitehall set up in 1994. In April 1994 10 new regional offices were set up in England, the Government

Offices of the Regions (GORs). The new bodies, the government believed, would manage the SRB in a more coordinated way since each GOR would bring together the regional offices of four Departments: Environment, Trade and Industry, Employment (now Education and Employment) and Transport. The government also claimed that greater coordination was being achieved within the SRB bids themselves, given that local authorities were working jointly with the Training and Enterprise Councils to ensure that their enterprise and skills objectives were incorporated into the projects.

**Judging outcomes**

The review of the framework of urban policy provided by this chapter must also consider what the programmes and projects achieved. It is clear that the development of urban policy over the 1980s and early 1990s was marked by ad hoc responses to particular issues and crises. In so far as there was a coherent and evolving policy, it was one of the increased targeting of deprived areas, insistence on private investment and enlarging the role of business in local projects. How successful has this policy evolution been? Since 1979 assessments have been published by a variety of bodies, including reports from the Audit Commission, the House of Commons Environment and Trade and Industry Committees and studies commissioned by the Department of the Environment itself. All point to a number of shortcomings. These include: the problems of departmental coordination; the lack of an overall strategy; the size of targeted funding compared to that of mainstream programmes; and the effectiveness of managerial oversight, guidance and bid processing on the part of sponsoring Whitehall Departments.

It is not just the case that the programmes and projects have formed a 'patchwork quilt' rather than a uniform and coherent pattern, but that these initiatives have been numerous and successive – eight different national programmes to rehabilitate the most disadvantaged areas between 1969 and the early 1990s. Within the programmes themselves, much of the attempt to evaluate success relied on output-based monitoring which in turn used short-term measurement. What is also needed is a consideration of outcomes – what has changed and what makes a difference – to view the process of change itself over a longer time period. A further judgement is that while gains have been made they have been excessively modest, as Table 2.1 Challenge Fund outcomes shows:

*Table 2.1*    City Challenge: actual and forecast outputs

| Key outputs | 1995–96 actual | 1996–97 actual [1] | 1997–98 forecast [2] | Five-year outputs [3a+b] |
|---|---|---|---|---|
| Dwellings – completed/improved | 26, 038 | 28,989 | 12,114 | 102,191 |
| of which dwellings for sale | 2,876 | 3,786 | 1,539 | 10,520 |
| Jobs created/preserved | 35,251 | 43,924 | 31,503 | 153,030 |
| Land reclaimed/improved (hectares) | 902 | 758 | 430 | 3,744 |
| New/improved business and commercial floorspace (sq m) | 700,904 | 857,275 | 881,0753 | 3 391,045 |
| New business start-ups | 2,114 | 2,162 | 1,345 | 8,525 |
| Private sector leverage | £798,706 | £1 402,705 | £1 106,300 | £4 503,450 |

*Notes*:
1  Source: 1996–97 final reports (pacemakers); 1996–97 annual reports (Round 2s).
2  Source: 1997–98 decision letters (Round 2s only).
3  Source: a) annual/final reports 1992–93 to 1996–97 (Pacemakers – actual outputs);
           b) 1997–98 decision letters (Round 2s – forecast outputs).

*Source*: Department of the Environment, Transport and the Regions, Annual Report, 1998

The achievements of City Challenge between 1995–96 and 1997–98 have been positive but limited: some 66 000 dwellings completed or improved, 111 000 jobs created or preserved, land reclaimed and business space created or improved and some £3.3 million in private investment attracted in.

In 1994 research commissioned by the Department of the Environment, led by Brian Robson and colleagues from the Universities of Manchester, Liverpool John Moores and Durham, revealed that policy outcomes had been uneven. In Whitehall there was no common definition of the inner-city or agreement on the degree to which government's policy instruments target inner-city areas. In the urban projects studied, public resources had had some impact, with relative improvement in unemployment across all the 57 targeted Urban

Programme Authorities (UPAs) as compared to untargeted authorities with similar social and economic profiles. But the impact of these resources had to be weighed alongside the extensive cuts during the 1980s in mainstream funding for inner cities, especially Rate Support Grant and Housing Investment Programme monies. A further issue was the unevenness of the outcomes from the specialised targeted projects. In the most deprived areas, particularly in conurbation cores and areas of high unemployment, policy had made little impact and conditions had actually worsened in relative terms. In the largest cities, 'inner-city' conditions had become more extensive (Robson *et al.*, 1994). Elsewhere, Robson himself commented on the obstacles that would have to be overcome to achieve improvements; in his view, 'the impacts of the urban policy of the 1980s have proved at best modest and at worst ineffectual' (Robson, 1994: 216). This is not to argue that all outcomes were negative. Many neighbourhoods benefited from physical refurbishment, subsequent programmes improved in the light of successes and failures and more effort went into examining how problems such as housing and crime were linked. But in spite of the continued refinement of programmes in the light of experience, the condition of many of the worst affected areas has not improved. In some cases, it has actully worsened: it is this that continues to give most cause for concern.

The era from 1979 to the mid-1990s was thus one in which approaches to urban problems were a mixture of ideology and pragmatism. The aims of policy shifted over time in reaction to events, the results fragmented and the outcomes uneven. The Single Regeneration Budget system introduced in 1993, however, marked a point at which regional and urban policy began to converge, a process taken further by the Labour government after 1997, as Chapter 7 shows.

**Convergence around a new consensus?**

The Labour government elected in 1997 promised new directions in housing, education and the contracting out of services to the private sector. To tackle the ravages of unemployment a 'New Deal' was launched to bring together measures to improve training and skills and prepare people, especially young people, much more adequately for work. The emphasis in these endeavours was on a new way between capitalism and socialism, on the need to seek shared values not sterile conflict and on the need to steer an approach between castigating government as the problem and seeing government as the solution. The approach focused on the requirement to match individual opportunity with responsibility (in welfare to work for example), on new forms of accountability of service providers to consumers and voters, on citizenship as fulfilling obligations as much as claiming rights and on the virtue of community. This 'return to Beveridge' puts work at the centre of citizenship and social inclusiveness.

To solve urban problems, power would not be held exclusively in town halls, but must be shared with other agencies, groups and communities, in order to empower individuals and meet changing demands. Wider regional groupings were essential to meet economic and social needs effectively and to provide structures to which decisions could be devolved from the centre. The 'physical determinism' that had long marked British urban policy would give way to economic and social programmes working across boundaries and sectors. More consultation of local groups and communities would be required and voluntary organisations encouraged to play a major part in taking decisions and implementing programmes. Subsidiarity and community are the linked themes of these proposals, though ones which are accompanied, as subsequent chapters show, by strong centralist tendencies.

Thus the framework of policy that dominated for the 30 years after 1945, with its twin planks of land-use planning and the universalist philosophy of the welfare state, has disappeared in its original form. In its place has emerged a new framework in which planning and universalism have a less dominant place and the emphasis is on a mix of public and private provision of services. In this mixed provision business, local councils, communities and voluntary organisations are the main political actors. That this has now mutated yet again into a totally new approach, a 'Third Way', is yet to be convincingly demonstrated. What is certain is that local authorities will not return to their pre-1979 multipurpose status nor be the sole actors in promoting the wellbeing of cities. Everyone is agreed that there are no easy solutions. Issues are interrelated and if regeneration is to work then the problems of education and health inequalities, youth crime and the negative picture of run-down areas that reinforce exclusion have to be addressed in comprehensive ways (Shaw and Robinson, 1998).

The incoming Labour government of 1997 was committed to remain largely within Conservative budgets for the first two years of its administration, though additional monies were announced in 1998 for allocation after 1999. The government did give a higher profile to urban policy and designated a leading Cabinet member its political supremo. Deputy Prime Minister John Prescott was given responsibility for a merged Department of the Environment, Transport and the Regions (DETR), which also took over regional development responsibilities from the Department of Trade and Industry (DTI). The merger produced a very large department with a wide policy remit and a heavy legislative agenda of reforms affecting regeneration and the regions, transport, local government and including the establishment of a new strategic authority and elected mayor for London. One of the key goals of the new DETR is to create an integrated transport and environment policy, though energy policy remains with the DTI.

Urban policy became a major task – and potentially a more coherent and integrated one – for the new superministry. As part of this concerted approach, DETR Secretary of State Prescott announced new proposals for Regional Development Agencies (RDAs) to come into operation from April 1999. This was to be a prime strategy in regeneration policy. On entering office Labour set out guidance for Round 4 of the SRB Challenge Fund (1998–99) to bring regeneration bids into a regional framework. From 1 April 1999 the RDAs themselves have responsibilities for the SRB Challenge Fund and took over the regeneration programmes and funding of English Partnerships and the Rural Development Commission. The remaining national capability of English Partnerships, together with the Commission for the New Towns, would be merged after April 2000 to form a single organisation, though its precise role has yet to be laid down. The RDAs are statutory bodies led by nominated boards. Alongside these are voluntary regional chambers though a possible long-term move to elected regional chambers remains problematic (see Chapter 7). But the competitive requirements of the bidding process remain.

The Labour government has stated that its regeneration policy objectives are to enhance economic development and social cohesion through effective regional action and integrated local programmes. What we are seeing at the end of the 1990s are policy-makers looking for an urban renaissance by which families will want to live in revitalised, 'sustainable' cities because they see them as welcoming places offering good education, health care and a quality environment (Rogers, 1997). Achieving such a renaissance is a major challenge. Reversing the trends to out-of-town shopping and leisure and the flight of business and home-seeking to the outer suburbs and rural areas will be a huge task. It is likely that the 'return to the city' on any scale will be limited to a small group of supercities offering the best housing, schools, transport and leisure: in the United Kingdom outside London these are likely to be Cardiff, Glasgow, Edinburgh, Manchester and Leeds. This is not to downgrade the positive efforts in other towns and cities to achieve 'the good city' which offers services and hope to its citizens.

## Conclusion

Just as urban ills are multidimensional, involving poverty, crime, physical decay and economic stagnation, so too are the solutions brought to bear on them. But it is too simplistic to view cities as being debilitated or urban policy as solely concerned with the management of decline. Cities provide the setting for creativity and innovation and are essential to fostering social cohesion. Cities are dynamic, not static places; they offer opportunities as well as presenting challenges. It is not just the poor, or run-down areas, that benefit from special attention. The quality of life of all city dwellers improves when urban policies succeed in overcoming environmental and social degradation.

That urban policy has come to be primarily associated with the deprivation of the 'inner-city' reflects a combination of Britain's industrial history and the 1960s recognition of the apparent paradox of poverty within the welfare state. Over the following decades of the 1970s and 1980s many initiatives were introduced to remedy inner-city problems. By the late 1990s the prime objective was to find more coherent and long-term strategies that would bring together economic and physical development, community inputs with region-wide perspectives and to foster multiagency partnership working.

The purpose of this chapter has been to structure these approaches within an historical overview of how policy has expanded and mutated since 1945. This provides the necessary setting for later chapters in the book. Only by understanding why policy has come to have a particular shape and direction can we judge the promises of the present agenda. The review began with the framework set in the late 1940s: land-use planning, regional economic incentives and the universal services to national standards of the welfare state. While the landmark planning plank of this policy remained, albeit in modified forms, the other elements underwent significant changes. This chapter has shown how these changes began with the impact, in the late 1960s, of issues of poverty and racism in the most run-down neighbourhoods of towns and cities. Ideas on how to deal with these challenges came from both America and Britain and emphasised very localised projects and disadvantaged groups rather than the former welfarist approach which delivered services to everyone wherever they lived.

By the mid-1970s these projects were becoming specifically inner-city in intent. They also took on a more economic as opposed to social focus, seeking to tackle the declining employment and business and employment opportunities of the old industrial areas. Government intervention and economic and physical planning, were still the principled and pragmatic responses. This chapter's review has shown how this response changed, in many ways radically, after 1979. A different philosophy of the relation between state and markets, of governments and intervention in the economy, was introduced by Conservative governments. Deregulation, new local agencies, the greater involvement of business in regeneration projects, all highlighted the Conservative governments' determination to reduce planning in favour of market solutions. At the same time, following the riots in London and Liverpool in the early 1980s and in other cities in the middle of the decade, the government had to make direct responses to urban crises. Governments were also determined to replace what they saw as the bureaucratic delay and inflexibility of local authorities and the entrenched self-interest of trade unions, with new structures that were business-led or with services provided wholly or partly by the private sector.

By the late 1980s competition had become the driving force of these policies. The chapter showed how policies moved from targeting deprived areas on the basis of need as judged by Whitehall to a system which required local authority regeneration projects to compete for funds from a defined central budget. In the early 1990s a series of reports were published which enabled judgements to be made about the strengths and weaknesses of urban policy. The judgements were relatively harsh. Whilst gains had been made, they were uneven and poverty remained concentrated in much the same areas as they had always been. More than this, initiatives did not amount to a coherent strategy but a piecemeal succession of interventions, operating for a limited period of time, to be followed by other schemes.

This overview is then in a position to consider where the post-1997 developments may be leading. The enterprise ideology of Conservative governments between 1979 and 1997 with its emphasis on markets, quasi-markets, efficiency, consumer choice and quality standards effected real changes in both the objectives of services and their delivery. Though the Labour government argues from a different set of premises, much of these changes remain in place. The system may still have local authorities as lead actors but programmes are now a mix of public, private and not-for-profit action and will continue to be so. It opens up the question of whether this means that urban policy is coalescing around a new consensus of mixed provision by multiagency partnerships. New programmes to redirect resources and attention to unemployment and skills training, to combat the alienation and worklessness of the worst housing estates, to turn around 'failing schools', all demonstrate a philosophy of 'what works' pragmatism. Such a philosophy is clearly a long way from the government intervention beliefs of the late 1940s. It demonstrates the ways in which the political agenda has, since 1979, been transformed by the end of the Keynesian welfare state in its original form and the shrinking of the public sector under successive Conservative governments. In inheriting this legacy Labour's determination to forge a more inclusive society clearly has both strong continuities with the recent past and claims for implementing new ways of improving opportunities and alleviating poverty.

In this shifting arena of policy, understanding the principles that inform and drive government action is crucial to making sense of the efforts to reinvigorate cities. The theoretical debates that underpin such action are the subject of Chapter 3.

# 3

# Debating the Issues: the Ideas that Underpin Policy

The principles that guide decisions are often implicit rather than openly acknowledged. Examining these principles, however, is important to an understanding of the changes that have taken place in urban policy in recent years. In the 1980s the terms of the debate became more explicit and focused, as Conservative governments sought to make radical changes in public action at both central and local levels.

The re-evaluation of the state and the economy in the 1980s originated in the New Right: those strands of neoconservative and neoliberal beliefs whose common concern was with state–market and state–individual relations. 'The free economy and the strong state', in Andrew Gamble's familiar phrase, sums up a key aspect of their approach (Gamble, 1988). But the focus on state-economy relations goes much wider than this. The changing forms of international capital and its relation to labour markets have impinged on national economies. The end of Keynesianism, and of the post-war welfare state settlement, has revolutionised social institutions and the individual's relations with the state. The guarantee of 'cradle to grave' collective protection has ended. This section of the chapter, then, looks at the many aspects of debate based on political economy: regulation theory and post-Fordism; public choice; neo-Marxism; 'social movements'; and regime theory. Urban policy and politics, embedded as it is in the operation of post-war welfare capitalism, has been a major element of this shift in political economy. A related intellectual discourse challenges the continued relevance of the modernist project itself. Social theorists point to the fragmented nature of contemporary society and question the acceptance of any one overarching theory. In cities, this fragmentation is reflected in competing life styles, interests and objectives. Thus theory too is necessarily heterogeneous, and there is no one valid truth with all-encompassing explanatory power.

Although frameworks drawn from political economy have been a

41

major element of recent debate, social theory has also played an important part. In particular, there has been a resurgence of interest in the
analysis of social cohesion and attachment to place. This has taken two
related forms: the concern for community and the enquiry into communitarianism. These raise issues of identity as well as social relations
and further stimulate interest in the locality and the urban policyscape.
This chapter also shows how the theoretical debate has been informed
by feminist perspectives. These contemporary concerns inform a more
orthodox debate on the justification of local government. Normative
theories of local government centre on the three key values of liberty,
participation and efficiency. The perspective of normative theory helps
to draw conclusions on the grounding of urban policy and politics in
democratic structures and values. In the late 1990s this focus on democratic values has been reinvigorated by the Labour government, with
an emphasis on the obligations of citizenship, on widened consultation
and accountability, on community and participation, and on the inclusive society. As later chapters show, these developments are having a
direct effect on how policy is being developed and on the local politics
that drive their implementation.

Box 3.1 helps our understanding of the range of ideas that inform
policy by summarising the main theories that have underpinned urban
policy over the past two decades. These will now be considered in
turn.


## Neoliberalism, neoconservatism and the limited state

In the 1980s urban policy was no longer based on the governmental
intervention and collective action of Keynesianism. Instead, a New
Right ideology was promoted as a radically different approach. The
term New Right embraced both neoliberal and neoconservative strands.
The former stressed the relations of the individual to the state, the latter
the individual's place in the moral order. The key is individual responsibility, supported by a state system which provides the basic legal
framework. This legal framework protects both the rights and responsibilities of individuals and families, and regulates and underpins the
operation of the market. It is the market which fosters individual
choices and provides goods and services through processes which are
flexible, efficient and transparent. Beyond these framework provisions,
the role of the state is limited.

*Box 3.1*    Key approaches underlying policy

1. Neoliberalism, neoconservatism and the limited state:
   - The enterprise culture;
   - Individual choice in the market;
   - Individual and family responsibility in the state.

2. The political economy discourse:
   - Regulation theory and post-Fordism;
   - The post-welfare and post-Keynesian state – from collective public provision to flexibility and consumerism;
   - Public choice theory: public bureaucracies and rational choices;
   - Marxism and neo-Marxism: the hegemony of state capitalism versus local state processes;
   - Social movements: from class interests to consumption interests.

3. Alternative accounts:
   - Modernism;
   - Postmodernism;
   - Feminist Theory;
   - Community and communitarianism.

4. Elite, pluralist and neopluralist frameworks:
   - The elite versus pluralist debate;
   - Regime theory: politics and urban entrepreneurs.

*Key values*: liberty, participation, efficiency;
Urban theory and intergovernmental relations.

*Beyond 2000*: *A Theory of the 'Third Way'? Community, opportunity, responsibility, accountability* (CORA).

The neoliberal component of new right Conservatism rests on individuals exercising choice in the free economy. Supply-side measures of deregulation and low taxation are preferred to Keynesian demand-side intervention supporting consumption and investment. Supply-side economics promotes competitive restructuring and market discipline. The new right's neoconservative strand, by contrast, was socially authoritarian. While it shared the neoliberal belief that questions of social justice are politically irrelevant or at best marginal to the operation of the market, nevertheless the state had to act to ensure law and order, individual market freedoms and traditional and family values. Neoconservative thought, that is, emphasised the 'strong state' over local diversities. Local councils had to be prevented from promoting groups and causes which were perceived as threats to core family patterns and relationships. Local government had also to be restrained in its provision of welfare services, notably housing, in order to reduce the long-term dependency of individuals and families on the state. Thus a greater freedom or autonomy for local government as neoliberalism might suggest was rejected by neoconservative thinking in favour of strong central state direction.

These issues were widely discussed on both sides of the Atlantic and there was a significant US influence on British thinking (for a resumé, see: Hoover and Plant, 1989). The new right position challenged Keynesian state welfarism. Collective provision of tax-based services, to standards set by state bureaucracies, was rejected in favour of individual liberty and choice. That the outcome may be inequality was justified by the opportunities which the market provides. To this end, markets were deregulated, services privatised and, where public sector provision continued, market surrogates imposed. These processes, together with the emphasis on individual and family responsibilities, replaced public action with that of the private sector, voluntary organisations and families. In addition, the public sector was attacked by the neoliberal new right who saw public bureaucracies as hierarchical, autocratic and inflexible structures, antithetical to consumer choice. Nor did democratic elections necessarily provide effective control. Periodic elections, it was argued, could only set the broad framework. Making changes then becomes a slow and overregulated process which only consumer sovereignty could remedy.

'Rolling back the frontiers of the state' and returning freedom of choice to individuals were key themes of Conservative governments between 1979 and 1997. 'Thatcherism' described the new radical approach, combining neoliberal and neoconservative elements within a populist platform. Its implementation, however, had a strong element of pragmatism and there were continuities as well as distinct breaks with previous policy. Nevertheless, though neoliberal beliefs were never those of the majority of society, the long period in office of successive Conservative administrations meant that new right influences played a major role in setting the agenda and determining the shape of urban policy.

Prime Minister Thatcher's forceful condemnation of the 'nanny state' and drive to deregulation strengthened, rather than weakened, the role of central government. If for government the ideal urban policy was no urban policy, legislation had to be used to curtail local authority powers and enable government to create new bodies to promote enterprise. These moves were aided by Britain's position as a unitary state, with its lack of a formally encoded Constitution. As a result, the definition of local government's role is dependent on convention and tradition. The outcome was that the claim for a strong autonomous role for local government succumbed to the Conservative government's assertion of its national mandate, backed by strong financial controls. The replacement of Margaret Thatcher by John Major in November 1990 marked a change in manner but not of ideology. Individuals as consumers, not citizens as voters, were at the heart of this theoretical approach.

The Labour victory in the General Election of 1997 brought new directions, in which decentralisation and empowerment were strong themes. But the emphasis remained on a mix of public–private–voluntary provision, not a return to a collectivist or neo-Keynesian approach.

## The political economy discourse

The power of central and local governments to solve urban problems has been questioned by analysts who see the changes in national and international economies as determining what solutions are possible. Theories drawn from political economy are used to describe these analyses. Under this broad heading will be considered a number of theoretical frameworks which look at changes in contemporary capitalism. The approaches considered here are: regulation theory and post-Fordism; public choice; neo-Marxism; and two sociopolitical frameworks, those of social movements and regime theory. Importantly, this theoretical discourse has been influenced by the debate on the 'globalisation' of capital and labour markets. The place of the global in the local is thus considered in this context.

### Regulation theory, post-Fordism and globalisation

The 'Fordist' stage of capitalism refers to that set of economic arrangements which depends on the mass-production of goods and services for a mass consumer market. In Britain this period lasted roughly from 1945 to the early 1970s. Under Fordism, mass-production of manufactured goods was matched by mass-consumption, operating in a world of nuclear family households, separate spheres for men and women in the workplace and home and standardised public services delivered through the bureaucratic state. In the Fordist period after 1945, the Keynesian welfare state had a crucial role in maintaining consumer demand and in underpinning the reproduction of the labour force through the collective provision of education, health and other social welfare services. But, it is argued, developments within capitalism – the crisis of Fordist mass production and its replacement with niche markets and widened consumer choice – have swept away these certainties. We are now in a state of post-Fordism (or 'after Fordism' for those who argue that we are in a stage of transition, not a new era) where both mass-production and the welfare state have been eroded by pluralism in production, markets and welfare.

Regulation theory seeks to understand these changes by analysing relations between the economic and the social, particularly how work and production (accumulation) are related to reproduction (consumption). This relation between production and consumption is the *regime of accumulation*. Capitalism is by its nature unstable, going through swings of overproduction, inflation and deflation and fluctuating investment. Its inherent contradictions can only be stabilised by a range of institutions, practices and norms which regulate the regime of accumulation; these form the *mode of social regulation*. This mode of social regulation governs customs and norms, laws, and family and civil institutions. Under the Fordist mode of social regulation, the local state delivered welfare services (housing, transport, education, social services) and provided the planning framework to support economic growth (Painter, 1991). This system broke down in the 1970s as changes in the economy brought a shift from demand-side to supply-side activity and an emphasis on innovation, entrepreneurship and labour market flexibility. The former settlement of the Keynesian welfare state became what Jessop has called the Schumpeterian (entrepreneurial and innovative) workfare state (Jessop, 1995).

These changes in capitalism demanded a new form of social regulation. The workfare state shifted the emphasis from universal social rights to flexible labour markets and consumer choices, with social policy subordinated to economic policy. At the local level the result was a shift from public, collectivist solutions to a more privatised form of service delivery and from political alliances based on major producer interests (trade unions, business) to a broader, networking regime of urban politics (Stoker and Mossberger, 1995). The hierarchical, bureaucratic organisation of standardised local services gave way to decentralisation and diversity, flexible working practices and consumer choice. Planning gave way to deregulated markets. The question of whether this is a new post-Fordist regime rather than a late stage of the existing capitalist era remains a contested one. Nevertheless, the analysis itself still offers a means of understanding economic changes of the past two decades and of the role of the locality in this transition.

A major premise of the new regime is that, in today's globalised markets, individual nation-states can no longer control their economies. Instantaneous electronic financial transactions, the mobility of capital and the new international division of labour drive decisions. Economic and financial systems are increasingly integrated into one international order (if one which is markedly asymmetric between rich and poor countries). This thesis has been challenged by those who point out that it undervalues the ability of governments to influence pan-capitalism and the rootedness of multinationals in particular countries and cultures (Hirst and Thompson: 1996). Here, however, we are primarily concerned with the implications of global markets on urban action. This arises in three main ways: the investment decisions of transnational corporations; the effect of the Information Technology (IT) revolution on the globalisation of production and consumption; the impact of the international financial markets. The effect of these changes, it is argued, is to reduce the nation-state's capacity for economic management in favour of supranational, and subnational, interventions. The state becomes 'hollowed-out' from its previous role as the principal site of social and economic activity. There is a double movement of globalisation on the one hand and decentralisation on the other which has been termed 'glocalisation' (Peck and Tickell, 1994).

The outcome of these 'globalising' forces for urban politics is new and demanding social and economic responsibilities. New relationships between the public and private sectors have to be forged and resources, local voters and interests mobilised in support of changed policy goals. These changed goals emphasise growth over distributive services and economic policy over social policy. From this perspective, though cities as the site of action become more important, the ability of local leaders to take autonomous local decisions becomes more limited. As competition between places for mobile capital grows, so locally autonomous social and economic policies diminish. Thus place as a policy arena becomes both more important and more circumscribed (Preteceille, 1990; Clarke, 1993).


*Public choice*

By contrast to global economic changes, public choice theory draws attention to the self-interested behaviour of officials as suggested by classical economics, a perspective made famous by Buchanan and Tullock's *The Calculus of Consent* (Buchanan and Tullock, 1965). Public officials are assumed to be rational utility maximisers, who defend and expand public services to reflect their own interests as producers, not those of consumers (Niskanen, 1971). In the same way elected politicians retain power by maximising votes for expanded public programmes; the result is a potentially ever-growing public sector and state 'overload'. The remedy, once again, is to reduce public sector activity in favour of the market by cutting bureaucracies and budgets. Where market alternatives are not feasible, then surrogate market disciplines must be imposed.

Public choice analysis is thus concerned with the operation of markets in situations where governments produce public goods. 'Public goods' are those goods and services which have to be produced and consumed for society as a whole and where no individual can be excluded from enjoying the good whether or not they paid for it. Where people could not be excluded from enjoying a good (for example clean air) then they become 'free riders', getting the benefit without paying. The issue here is that state provision encourages both the free riders and the vested interests who boost public expenditure. Together, these undermine the free working of the market. In addition, state provision distorts political life by preventing the allocation of resources to the most efficient programmes and by raising the potentiality for corruption.

In the case of British urban politics, public choice theory was a major influence on government thinking in the 1980s. In particular, the argument was that there was a need to restrain local public officials and political leaders in order to prevent Labour councils, in collaboration with the trade unions, from maximising services which benefited their supporters and inflated local expenditures. Indeed, Madsen Pirie, of the Adam Smith Institute, claimed that public choice theory had changed local government fundamentally through privatisation, the bolstering of consumer choice through the Citizen's Charter, and the internal market, purchaser/provider split in services (Pirie, 1992). Such public choice reasoning has been criticised on both its hidden value preferences and the soundness of its premises. Its values are anti-collectivist (especially towards trade unions) and individuals are viewed primarily as consumers with preferences, not citizens with needs. But these public choice premises of self-interested individuals ignore the complexities of behaviour and the altruistic – and often non-rational – sources of action.

Often subsumed within public choice theory, but based on a less ideological value system, is rational choice analysis. Public choice theory has its roots in economics; it is particularly associated, as has been noted, with the work of Milton Friedman and Buchanan and Tullock. Public choice has been tied to right-wing prescriptions for freeing the market from regulation and preferring private over public solutions to problems. John argues that it is necessary and helpful to distinguish rational choice explanations from public choice theory. Rational choice does not advocate any one political form, but seeks to show how strategic choices affect action (John, 1998).

Rational choice analysis has been used to examine the changes in the central British state in the 1990s by which former core functions were hived-off to executive agencies. It has also been used to look at the choices people make on where to live and work. Individuals are seen as rational, self-interested maximisers who will move location to seek the lowest taxes and most favourable areas: from inner-city to suburb, from high spending local governments to minimalist regimes. As a result, cities become segregated into different class (and ethnic) areas and local councils compete to attract investment. Tiebout (1956) advocated small, fragmented local government units within metropolitan areas since this facilitated individual choice of area, regime and provision. From this perspective local authorities offer a market of choice for services and taxes such that individuals can choose the mix of the two that best suits them. But critics of Tiebout argue that competition is always imperfect. In practice there are tax and other cost constraints on individuals which outweigh the advantages of moving to low tax municipalities. Other writers on rational choice (Dowding, John and Biggs, 1994) have suggested that the approach can explain residential mobility based on the attraction of lower council tax areas (for example in London) and also point to the link between the Tiebout model and the community charge or poll tax of the early 1990s, given the Conservative government's argument that the poll tax increased choice and mobility in precisely this way. As a result, contemporary theorists argue for individual preferences matched to outcomes through the market, rather than through mobility from one area to another (John, 1997b). As local authorities attract investment to their areas, make their service more efficient (including increasing choice through alternative private and voluntary provision), then individual interests will be maximised in ways which demonstrate public choice rationality.

*Marxism, neo-Marxism and social movements*

If public choice theory sees bureaucrats and politicians as utility maximisers, Marxist analysis places urban politics as a part of the capitalist state. In the Marxist framework the capitalist state apparatus sustains production, and the reproduction of social relations, through the legal system and economic and political institutions. The state maintains law and order in order to manage conflict in society, itself an inevitable outcome of the class divisions within capitalism. Difficulties arise, however, about the nature and role of the locality within the capitalist state and Marxist writers are divided about the degree of autonomy which local institutions do or can hold. Those writers who view the state as the extension of the ruling class see urban political institutions as an integral part of the state and thus lacking any autonomous power. Local policies reflect dominant national interests and local political participation is a substitute for, not a reflection of, real power. Structuralists, by contrast, argue that state institutions can be seen as separate from the ruling class. There are divisions between the 'fractions' or elements of capital and state institutions play an important role in reconciling conflicting groups and managing the demands of the working class. From this perspective, local political institutions do have a degree of autonomy (Pickvance, 1995).

The first of these two perspectives, that which takes the view that the local arena is part of the state *per se*, is reflected in Cockburn's study of the London Borough of Lambeth, *The Local State*. This asserts that the state is a single unified system in which all the parts work *fundamentally* as one (Cockburn, 1977). The local state is not the same as local government, but includes all state functions carried out at the local level, including health, water (then a public utility) and public transport. Local government, for its part, is neither autonomous constitutionally nor in practice. More than this, Cockburn argued, Lambeth showed that the real power struggle was dominated by a propertied class of developers and their business partners for whom the local arena was marginal or irrelevant. From this perspective, the function of the local state is the subordinate one of sustaining the reproduction of the labour force through housing and other services. A wider view of the local state's role is taken by Duncan and Goodwin's *The Local State and Uneven Development*. This sees the local state as in part subservient, and in part oppositional, to the central state. The local state both responds to central state interests and reflects local needs and interests. Their study focuses on the extent of the local state's freedom to promote these local interests against the central state (Duncan and Goodwin, 1988). From both these perspectives, urban politics is dominated by struggles between capital and labour, centring on particular issues such as housing and the expansion or cutting back of public services.

Structuralism, by contrast, argues for the autonomy of state processes as against the ruling class. It gained prominence with Manuel Castells' work which emphasised the state's distinctive role in organising the reproduction of labour through its role in 'collective consumption' (Castells, 1977; 1979), that is, it is the state that organises the provision of those services which we consume collectively rather than as individuals. Collective consumption includes state regulation of social relations (especially property, labour and family laws) and the provision of services which maintain the labour force (health, welfare, housing and education). The political struggles surrounding these state services Castells defines as 'urban' politics (this refers to the conflicts over services and is not a geographical definition as such). Castells' analysis of urban politics, however, does not focus on parties and electoral democracy but on social movements – that is the interests, groups and activism that surround a particular service, such as tenants associations and the housing service – and on their role in bringing about change through their challenges to state action.

Castells' later work has been criticised by Ira Katznelson, who argues that it has abandoned Marxism for what is in effect a relativist, pluralist position. By contrast, Katznelson argues, there is a viable neo-Marxist explanation of the use of urban space which classical

Marxism, with its focus on the division of labour, had neglected. The way cities are laid out is the result of the residential locations of different classes. The outcome of nineteenth-century urbanisation was to concentrate workers not just in factory workspaces but also in their home communities; this in turn affects how people take part in urban politics (Katznelson, 1992). While the development of the working class in the United States separated work and community, in Britain by contrast the two were intimately related, making for a different outcome. The British class structure was more complex, such that urban political conflict arose from issues of city space, local services and other 'non-class' sources. The overall impact of structural Marxist analysis, however, has been to sharpen the definition of urban studies and give it a more theoretical thrust (Lefebvre, 1971; Castells, 1977; Harvey, 1973; 1985).

The importance of Marxist studies to urban policy lies in the focus on economic interests and their political advantages, instead of concentrating solely on elections and the relations between officials, politicians and voters. Throughout these writings the issue is the conflict between classes, interests and movements and the extent to which the state, both centrally and locally, can act autonomously. There is also debate as to whether analysis should concentrate on conflict between classes, or on more broadly based 'social movements' centred around public services, or on the differences arising from the position in city life of non-class defined groupings such as ethnic minorities and women.

It is these social movements, centred on services such as housing, welfare, the environment and transport, that have been the main concern of structural neo-Marxists. This kind of urban analysis was highlighted by Castells and others who pointed to the importance of the politics of collective consumption, expressed in the active protests of affected groups – social movements – who were fighting to protect public services (Castells, 1977; 1983; Pickvance, 1976). For urban inhabitants, the locality has use value (the enjoyment of present facilities and services), not merely exchange value (the potential price of assets on the market). For residents, housing, health, the physical infrastructure, transport, are consumed collectively and must be protected. Hence the close affinity between urban politics and the politics of collective consumption. But as British studies reveal, the movements which coalesce around services are not necessarily homogeneous. There are divisions between different 'sectors' or 'cleavages': parents concerned with schools; council tenants and rent increases; home-owners and planning permissions (Saunders, 1984). As a result, people's political positions also differ and, it is argued, are centred on their direct interests in these services, not their assumed class interests and their party manifestations (Dunleavy, 1980). But the role of social movements as a catalyst of change is limited. While they may influence politics (breaking down the old hierarchies and organising around use values) they may be unable to change society: 'They are a reaction, not an alternative' (Castells, 1983: 327). Moreover, as Dowding and Dunleavy have noted, it has become increasingly hard to distinguish between 'collective' and 'private' consumption (Dowding and Dunleavy, 1996). Public–private consumption is blurred as the division between public and private provision is blurred, with public money subsidising market provision and the plethora of partnerships through which services are delivered.

Nevertheless, social movements in the broadest sense remain important in local politics, for example those movements based on lifestyle, gender and race issues. A neo-Marxist, structuralist approach, however, has been judged inadequate to account for these phenomena (see below) and Castells himself appears to have moved away from a Marxist to a relativist, essentially pluralist, position.

### Alternative accounts

*Modernism, postmodernism and feminist theory*

In the late twentieth century confidence in ideas of modernity – that inheritance of the European Enlightenment, with its core beliefs of scientific rationality, progress and all-embracing theory – gave way to a heterogeneity of explanations. We now live in a postmodern age, a postindustrial, informational society dominated by electronic media. The reaction against the 'modern', in literary criticism, in architecture and then in the arts generally, became widely known from the works of critics such as Lyotard (1984). In urban politics, the postmodern city is seen as the site of the crisis of late capitalism. More disturbingly, it could also become the site of an incivil future where neighbourhoods are segregated, dividing the enclosed, gated communities of the prosperous and the ghettos of the deprived and lawless. At its most futuristic, the postmodern city is a place of 'tribalist fragmentation' of diverging communities, fenced off from one another and embedded in a wider world through electronic superhighways (Keil, 1994; Davis, 1990). There is no public realm, no jointly used public space, no trust in civic loyalties.

While postmodernism has not played a major part in theoretical explanations of British urban politics, it cannot be ignored. Its reasoning contrasts the modern and postmodern eras of city life. Under modernism, urban politics centred on divisions in cities derived from their industrial base, the large commercial and civic core, growing suburbs (which allowed the middle class and new business to distance themselves from city problems) and an inner-city of increasing deprivation. By contrast, the postmodern city is not defined by its industrial base but by its consumerist environment of malls and museums, characterised by revivalist architecture and 'heritage' refurbishment. At the same time the suburban shopping mall and motorway network make nonsense of the idea of the city as a unique and defined space: we inhabit, rather, a 'placeless' world of interchangeability. Modern communications transform our perception of place, such that we live in a world of space defined by images and communication networks as much as within physical locations (Soja, 1989; Harvey, 1989). The city is also the place where difference can be expressed: of gender, ethnicity, lifestyles and beliefs which pose a potential challenge to the dominant power structures and demand expression in political life.

A major criticism of this approach is that if postmodernism's claims that there can be no grand theory, no metanarratives, is true, then discourse on social justice, equity and equality, becomes meaningless. Theorising becomes no more than a fragmented subjectivity; there is no one 'truth', no single framework from which explanation can be derived. Not only are there no universal truths, there can be no valid claims for universal services. Postmodernism claims that difference and diversity make claims for universal welfare standards and services redundant. A different criticism is that, far from being distinctive, modernism and postmodernism are intertwined (Cooke, 1990b). There is yet a third critique, which seeks to establish within postmodernism a radical position associated with the feminist challenge of (implicitly male) rationality as the ultimate standard of judgement in favour of difference and the equality of groups and cultures. As Laws has put it, feminist and postmodern writings are applicable to many oppressed groups who reject their given status in the built environment and urban politics (Laws, 1994). The feminist concern is that urban politics is shaped by these gendered social and economic relations. Democratic theory has been in danger of ignoring group difference; the remedy is to increase greater grass-roots representation of oppressed groups (I. Young, 1990). Feminist contributions to urban theory thus emphasise new organisational forms and specific (family; 'carer') issues. At the same time there are attempts to move away from earlier neglect of differences *between* women (arising from class, race and culture) to examine how these affect urban politics (Clarke, Staeheli and Brunell, 1995).

Though the claims of 'postmodernity', like 'post-Fordism', remain problematic, postmodern discourse does provide insights into what are essentially the contradictions of late modernity and its democratic forms. Feminist theorising, for its part, relates to this questioning by challenging received wisdom on the nature of urban power relations and policies.

*Community and communitarianism*

Community as an essential element of urban politics has a long history. With the advent of a Labour government, debate on its meaning and relevance has taken on a renewed vigour. Critiques of community point out that definitions cannot be based on mere propinquity. There are communities of interest not constrained by physical boundaries. These include minorities (as in 'the Asian community') and professional, leisure and other interests. One difficulty arising from this approach is that these groupings serve as labels imposed by others. Labelling a neighbourhood, an ethnic or a lifestyle group as a 'community' can then give them a false cohesiveness.

From the 1950s onwards, the sociological analysis of community focused on two main elements. The first element was that of community studies' research on family and kinship networks, stemming from Ferdinand Tönnies's distinctions between *Gemeinschaft* and *gesellschaft* relations. In premodern society social relations were based on personal interaction and mutual obligation: *Gemeinschaft* (Tonnies, 1955). This is 'community' based on customary rules, authority and family and kinship. Such a pattern implies stability and cohesion. By contrast in modern industrial, urbanised society relations are based on association: *Gesellschaft*. *Gesellschaft* depicts contractual relations characterised by impersonal legal rights, separation between public and private life and associated with the values of liberal individualism. Community studies showed how *Gesellschaft* had replaced *Gemeinschaft* and become the defining feature of urban life. The second element of sociological analysis was the flowering in the 1950s and 1960s, in the United States, of local community power studies. The debate on community power engaged in a long and ultimately unresolved struggle over the measurement of power and the definition of community. The answer to the question: 'Who Governs?' diverged among elite theory (which held that certain kinds of business and political leaders did so), pluralist accounts (no one ruled) and neo-elite explanations (for whom the issue was: who set the agenda and why they were not challenged) (Harding, 1996).

Other analysts emphasise that community is not synonymous with homogeneity. In practice individuals identify themselves as members of different networks and communities of interest, some of them place-centred and others not. The places of community themselves vary from the immediately local, the neighbourhood, to the citywide, that is, people's attachment to place and its investment with meaning exists alongside networks of social relations. Not all such communities are inclusionary. Some communities define themselves as against the Other and exclude those seen as non-members. This can be particularly evident where out-groups are defined in terms of lifestyle, ethicity, religion, or even deprivation. The result may be a local politics of rejection and conflict, rather than cohesion and mutuality.

The modern communitarian movement – some might say crusade – fostered by Amitai Etzioni's *The Spirit of Community: Rights, Responsibilities and the Communitarian Agenda* seeks a turning back from the impersonal relations of *gesellschaft* to a moral universe of *gemeinschaft*. It places self within society, with the aim of strengthening parenting and families, supporting schools that promote a moral education and stressing the responsibilities as well as the rights of citizenship (Etzioni, 1993). Communitarianism views community not just as the object of analysis but as the true source of values, particularly of self-reliance and self-help. Communities 'congeal' around their local institutions, from local schools, churches, museums, to community policing. Social justice comes from mutuality of family, neighbour and kin, not from state action: indeed, the welfare state has contributed to the disintegration of family life. In relation to physical spaces, communitarianism sees communities as a series of Chinese boxes in which families and neighbourhoods are nested into villages and towns, in turn situated in national and cross-national ones (like the emergent European community).

Communitarian ideas have been widely debated. Tam is much less authoritarian in his approach. He rejects market individualism because of its corrosive effect on community life, encouraging political apathy and discouraging community commitment. Tam's communitarian perspective, in contrast to Etzioni, rejects both authoritarian practices and individualism, pointing instead to the need for a new agenda promoting a much more inclusive form of political and social community (Tam, 1998). Common values – agreed through deliberation not imposed – should form the basis of mutual responsibilities and the encouragement of the participation of all as equal citizens. This will then be the truly inclusive community. This formulation of the communitarian perspective is heavily dependent on deliberative discourse (in citizen juries and other fora), requiring major change in current political practices to promote active citizen involvement in both decisions and action. It also calls for far greater decentralisation than currently exists. It aims to go beyond the old left–right divide, favouring instead an approach based on community, social capital and a vibrant civil society. Communitarians deny that the inclusive community so achieved is hostile to rival groups or claims, arguing instead for 'layered loyalties' that build on interaction and respect between and among constituent communities.

Communitarianism's claim that community, rather than the individual or the state, should be the focus of analysis, is contested, as is the lack of a clear definition with its familiar confusion over 'community of place' and 'community of interest'. In addition, while many feminists believe community remains important, some radical feminists reject community and family as authoritarian and hierarchical and communitarian arguments as reactionary and inegalitarian. There are also difficulties over community–individual relations. Communitarianism articulates a common good based on shared values. This raises the question of how those who resist inclusion, and define self-identity outside assumed 'shared values', can be accommodated. The claims of individual liberty and rights versus the claims of community raise difficult issues of the common good, the public interest and of notions of justice and exclusion. And there can be no return to nostalgic views of community; rather, social inclusion is now more likely to be formed from friendship and friend-like relationships arising from work and neighbourhood ties (Pahl and Spencer, 1998). Whatever perspective is favoured, community as an ideal and as an organising principle has an active part to play in urban politics, as Chapter 5 shows.

## Elite, corporatist and pluralist frameworks

The principles examined so far have become important parts of the theoretical debate in recent years. By contrast, elite and pluralist accounts have a long history in urban analysis.

### The elite versus pluralist debate

Urban theories show a tension among structuralist, elitist and pluralist/neopluralist frameworks. For example, while in neo-Marxist accounts it is the structure of capitalism itself that determines the dominance of business, for elitists it is the power to act – human agency – that is crucial. It is elites themselves who are the major force in urban politics. The early elite theorists of the late nineteenth and early twentieth century were highly critical of democracy and what they saw as its incipient 'mob rule'. Normative elite theorists, by contrast, favoured elites who, while having power to rule, were responsible to mass democracy. But it was the restatement, in the 1950s, of elite theory by C. Wright Mills (Mills, 1956) and others which raised questions of the reality of democratic pluralism. The few, not the many, actually ruled, with the power of the mass electorate limited to periodic support of governing elites. Locally, attention turned to alliances through which business, property developers and civic leaders and associated groups dominated urban growth and change. These alliances had a more permanent form than the political coalitions of the earlier community studies and came to be described by scholars as 'growth machines' (Harding, 1994) (see below).

Pluralism itself has long claimed prime place in the analysis of British urban policy and politics. In the pluralist model the state is independent of any one section or group in society, public policy is the outcome of discussion and compromise and power is dispersed rather than concentrated. This dispersal of power is itself seen a desirable feature of democracy (G. Jordan, 1990). The application of pluralist analysis to local politics is most famously associated with the work of Robert Dahl and others in the study of American cities in the late

1950s and 1960s (Dahl, 1961; 1986). The urban pluralists characterised power as dispersed (polyarchic) and contained within a democratic framework of society based on a (largely) shared popular
consensus over procedures and processes. In Britain, pluralist
approaches have ranged from the case studies of decision-making of
the 1970s and early 1980s (Newton, 1976; Saunders, 1983; Dearlove,
1973) to more recent neopluralist studies focused on a broad range of
groups, including those centred on ethnic, gender, environmental and
specific issues. Urban analysis has always noted the closed nature of
local politics and power networks in which business and labour interests play a major part. What is now acknowledged is a situation in
which local authorities are downgraded in favour of non-elected agencies and business and property interests are major actors in promoting
growth. Thus, the dominance of the pluralist framework has shaded
into a neocorporatist concern with local elites.

*Regime theory*

A particular concern of elitist and pluralist accounts has been with the
way in which local entrepreneurs may shape urban politics. Closely
allied to the notion of urban regimes has been that of growth machines:
the constellation of political and economic interests whose objectives
are investment and physical and economic development.

What is central to these analyses is the strong link between politics
and markets. Political and business leaders form complex bargaining
alliances or coalitions to manage the urban system and promote development. Within this approach, Logan and Molotch's work has been
seminal (Molotch, 1976; Logan and Molotch, 1987). Those local businesses which are most place bound and place conscious – who cannot
easily move their investment elsewhere – will, it is argued, be at the
heart of the growth machines. But owners seeking to maximise profit
and growth are opposed by neighbourhood organisations and other
groups whose primary concern is to enjoy and defend their home areas,
that is, they are concerned with using the facilities and opportunities of
their neighbourhoods, their use value, not their value as an investment.
These analyses differ from the former community power studies in that
the question is not so much 'Who Governs?' but an exploration of the
power of particular groups to determine outcomes, particularly development.

While the growth machine thesis can be seen as a reworking of elite theory, regime theory has its roots in neopluralism (Harding, 1996). Regime theory holds that the growth machine model is but one type of regime. For regime theory in general, politicians are not the dominant actors but have to use their limited controls and incentives to forge relationships with business interests. While elected politicians preside, they may not rule: only coalitions which can amass and control resources can do that, establishing leadership and, crucially, the *capacity* to govern (Stoker, 1995b).

The development of regime theory and the analysis of growth coalitions has taken place primarily in the United States, where the government of conurbations is fragmented and where local authorities lack comprehensive governing powers (Stone, 1989). By contrast British urban politics has been much more independent of business. Business elites had a strong position in the nineteenth century but have largely withdrawn from civic life, leaving the governing of cities to parties of the centre-left. But the approach is seen as having salience, with the emergence of urban development coalitions to promote economic growth. Such coalitions of private and public interests have been stimulated into being, however, not by developments within local capitalism but by national government promotion and public incentives. Central governments have given powers and functions to autonomous public–private bodies and encouraged partnerships between local councils and business to promote urban regeneration. Now, concern over economic development covers a wide area of urban policy, including infrastructure, crime, and effective services, particularly education. The result is that business is acutely sensitive to the need to cooperate in public decision-making to protect and foster their markets.

The importance of regime theory to the analysis of urban policy and politics in Britain is, then, that it alerts observers to the interaction between politics and markets and the exercise of power (Stoker and Mossberger, 1994; Stoker, 1995b). In the late 1990s, the climate of urban policy is favourable to governance through collaboration between private and public elites that goes outside the formal structures and parties and bureaucracies. The result is, as John and Cole show, that governance in major cities has regimelike qualities (John and Cole, 1998).

## Normative and intergovernmental theories

The present chapter has examined the main elements of contemporary theoretical discourse on urban politics. Much of this debate appears detached from the traditional perspective which focuses on local government as the framework for local democracy. Such an assumption is misguided. The traditional justification for local government, centred on the three key values of liberty, participation and efficiency, remains relevant in two main ways. The first is that the traditional theory is in fact believed in: the system operates as though the values dominate. The second way in which normative theory remains relevant is as justification: the values ought to dominate if democracy is to work effectively. They should act as benchmarks against which to judge the outcomes of the changes of the past 20 years.

The three core values of normative theory, liberty, participation and efficiency, are concerned with the distribution of power in the state, between levels of government and between individuals and institutions. Liberty is advanced by the existence of multiple centres of power and local government thus guards against a tyranny of central domination. Participation, in the Artistotelian and J.S. Mill tradition, is the foundation of citizenship and legitimises local government action. Efficiency arguments point to the need to take decisions, and provide services, as close to users and citizens as possible and to be responsive to local demands and needs. As will be seen in subsequent chapters, these elements of normative theory are in practice open to question. There are many other local organisations which contribute to the pluralism of political and civic life, with local councils becoming strategic and 'enabling' bodies. Much participation remains a middle-class, middle-aged activity and electoral turnout in local elections is low.

The orthodox debate still has value, in both its *is* and *ought* dimensions, but needs recasting if it is to meet new challenges. The local authority must become the voice of the community. The participatory element, for its part, needs augmenting with new forms of involvement, as considered in Chapter 5. Local councils must become more transparent and responsive to changing demands. As Stoker puts it, 'A more participatory, involving and reflective politics' is required (Stoker, 1996b: 23), an emphasis which can be seen in New Labour philosophy.

Normative theory is also concerned with the distribution of power in the state. Though the nation-state may have become 'hollowed out' by globalisation, relations between central and local state levels remain crucial to urban action. The relations between the two levels determine urban politics in practice and Stoker claims that the study of intergovernmental relations is at the leading edge of urban theory (Stoker, 1995a). There are four dimensions to intergovernmental theory: rational choice; organisation theory; dual polity; and state theory. The way that rational choice influenced policy in the 1980s has already been examined. Organisation theory, by contrast, examines the network of bargaining relationships between national and sub-central government, including local authorities, notably in Rhodes' power-dependence model. Thus central–local relations take place within known rules and conventions which draw on the power bases of different organisations (Rhodes: 1988). Dual polity and dual state theories, for their part, explore two aspects of the same contextual setting of central–local relations. Dual polity theory is based in historical and constitutional analysis while dual state theory places relationships within the wider economic, political and social context. Bulpitt's work on the nature of the dual polity considers the different perspectives and functions of central and local government. Central government's perspective is strategic, that of local government the immediate and detailed; central government has a hierarchical supremacy over local government which is close to that of principal and agent (Bulpitt, 1983). The dual state concept put forward by Saunders, by contrast, argues that the locality (the local state) cannot be seen merely as an agent or functioning part of the centre. In practice, there are two distinct arenas of state activity (Saunders, 1986). That at central and regional level is focused on economic and social policy strategy for the whole society. The other operates at local level and is characterised by pluralist and localist actions determined by local variations and demands. The result is diversity, and potential conflict, between the two levels, not the hierarchical control of the one over the other.

## Guiding principles for 2000 and beyond

The Labour government elected in 1997 argued that a radical set of principles was needed to take policy in new directions. A new direction was needed to enable individuals to cope with the impacts of globalised capitalism while rejecting 'big government' solutions and putting 'no rights without responsibilities' at the heart of Labour principles.

The American parallels are instructive. President Clinton in his State of the Union Address of January 1998 referred to a Third Way beyond the sterile debate between those who said government is the enemy and those who said government is the answer. In Britain as in America the view is that individuals need help to deal with the risks that come from globalisation while recognising the public's growing distrust of 'big government'. Certainly the buzz words of welfare to work, tough attitudes to crime and on the causes of crime, and action beyond left and right, have become commonplace on both sides of the Atlantic. So too have service delivery processes through partnerships between local authorities, business and voluntary agencies. In his first major speech as Prime Minister Tony Blair stressed the inclusive goal of his government's agenda, recreating the bonds of civic society and community in ways compatible with the more individualistic nature of modern life. Both Blair and Clinton see the 'Third Way' as their legacy, not just of a political programme but of an alternative philosophy for the twentyfirst century. Critics such as J. K. Galbraith, however, dismiss it as a purely political concept. In this criticism, the Third Way is not a philosophy but a pragmatic response of centrist governments to the demands of their middle-income key voters. These voters are opposed to any increases in taxation while supportive of specific public services such as education and health. In spite of these criticisms of the authenticity of the Third Way's claims to be a distinctive and coherent body of thought, its position as an organising explanation of government action commands attention and is a means of judging policy.

The debate over how new the new ideas are and its exact definition, was widened by the explanations published by Prime Minister Blair in a Fabian Society pamphlet. The pamphlet defined the Third Way as a 'modernized social democracy'. The vision for that modern democracy was to reconcile themes wrongly judged antagonistic – patriotism and internationalism, rights and responsibilities, the promotion of enterprise and the attack on poverty and discrimination. The Third Way, in Blair's view, unites the two streams of left-of-centre thought – democratic social and liberalism – in ways which marry values with pragmatism. The crux was that 'what matters is what works to give effect to our values' (Blair, 1998b:4). Three of the four policy objectives (the fourth is international cooperation as the basis of foreign policy) have important implications for urban policy: a knowledge-based economy where governments enable not command; a strong civil society with strong communities; modern government based on partnership and decentralisation. The difficulty is, as critics have argued, that the concept of a 'Way' calls for a strategic direction of its own not just a space between existing forms or a hybrid between them. As Thompson puts it, 'It requires, in other words, a coherent and substantive framework of goals and values from which a distinctive story can be fashioned to guide policy and action' (Thompson, 1997: 7). The extent to which these are principles that guide action is considered in Chapter 7.


## Conclusion

Consideration of the principles that underlie policy reveals how dynamic urban political analysis is. Debate has centred on changing state–economy and state–individual relations over the past two decades. The new right critique of the Keynesian welfare state was at the heart of Conservative policy between 1979 and 1997 and led to a reassertion of market and individual freedoms. A Labour government from May 1997 promised new priorities and directions, but there was to be no return to the all-providing local authorities of the Keynesian era.

The discourse of political economy examines urban politics from a number of different perspectives. Regulation theory and 'post-Fordism' sought to understand the changing relations of capital and labour from mass-production and consumption to mobile, niche markets and flexible workforces. Relatedly, universal welfare services to national standards have given way to selective, private and public–private provision. The ending of the Keynesian welfare state is also the topic of public choice theory and its rejection of bureaucratic public sector solutions to problems. By contrast, Marxist analysis of urban politics focused on the nature of the local state and its autonomy within capitalism. Neo-Marxist analysis moved on to consider urban conflict centred not on classes but on social movements, that is on groups clustered around particular issues such as housing. Regime theory and the focus on growth coalitions are similarly concerned with the divisions within the urban economy and polity. Developing from the community power studies of the 1960s, contemporary regime theory encapsulates both elite and pluralist approaches. Though developed in the United States, it has become of increasing interest in Britain where it is part of the renaissance of urban theory.

Theories of the urban have to meet the challenge, as this chapter has shown, of two externalities. One is the issue of 'globalisation' and its effect on national and local economic action. The other is the question of the duality of nation-state and local state and the relation between them. At the same time, urban theory has also had to acknowledge the alternative perspectives presented by postmodernism and feminism. If these are new elements to the debate, concepts of community and the communitarian refer back to some of the oldest ideas of democracy. Both community and communitarianism are disputed definitions. Both draw criticism of their nature and relevance to modern urban politics, but their status as dominant values has been enhanced under New Labour's 'Third Way'. Historically, the justification of local government was that it fostered democratic participation, countered state power and provided efficient services. This has been the province of normative theory. Now, this orthodoxy is challenged by an approach which emphasises the need to find new ways of encouraging participation and to recognise the changed ways in which local councils work with other actors and agencies to promote wellbeing in their areas.

What this chapter has demonstrated is that tackling urban problems is underpinned by a serious and complex theoretical discourse. This debate intensified in the 1980s when Conservative governments challenged long-standing assumptions about what the role of governments should be. Instead of state provision, new right theorists argued, individuals and families should take greater responsibility for their needs, markets should be deregulated to increase choice and local bureaucracies should be replaced by new bodies to deliver services. These beliefs did not go unchallenged. A rich variety of theoretical explanations all made a contribution to understanding why urban politics operate in the way they do. The analyses showed how different perspectives reflected the effect of both economic changes and the demands of different groups for recognition of their needs.

If principles have an important part in guiding decisions, so too does the legal and political framework. It is to the context of decision-making that Chapter 4 turns.

# 4

# Providing the Framework for Action

The present chapter examines the forces that shape urban affairs by putting policy into its legal, institutional and political framework. The elements of this framework are varied and complex. It includes: the local government system; the political alliances that influence council decisions; the growing regionalisation of policy; the relations between central and local government; the managerial culture in which services are delivered; and the impact of the European Union. Legislation and funding for local services are determined by central government, but local authorities have an important input into policy and a leading part in its implementation.

The chapter begins by showing how the present system of local government has come about. Major changes in the 1970s provided the basic institutional framework of local government, but one which was modified in the 1980s and again in the early 1990s as the political and strategic objectives of government changed. The current system is the legal setting for regeneration and service delivery. The powers and duties of local authorities are laid down by central government but the system is more than an administrative structure delivering services determined by the centre. It remains an elected system of local councils accountable to their local citizens: it is a *democratic* structure of urban action. However, councils are influenced not just by their electorate but by a wide range of interests and groups, notably by business and increasingly by voluntary organisations. The chapter considers how these influences affect local councils and the decisions they take.

In the late 1990s the system changed again as the Labour government strengthened the regional dimension. Finding an effective system of regional administration and government is beset by technical, political and boundary problems. In England, important regional offices were brought in by the Conservative government in 1974. Labour's commitment to devolution and decentralisation in Britain took these changes further, though a fully democratic structure for the English regions remains problematic.

The operation of the local government system is itself embedded in a wider constitutional and political structure of central–local relations. The way that these relationships operate have become a key theme of urban analysis. As the chapter shows, the extent to which central government had extended its powers of control and direction became a contentious issue in the 1980s. The contemporary situation, however, has not seen a reversal of those trends. On the contrary, although the Labour government emphasises decentralisation and empowerment, it is determined to improve education, reduce endemic unemployment and tackle the most deprived urban neighbourhoods. This has led to an emphasis on raising standards and inspection and could mean actual intervention where local authorities or their specific services are deemed to have failed. Central control of funding also remains a contentious issue.

Concerns over the potential legacy of the conflict of the 1980s between the centre and localities led to an extensive analysis by a House of Lords committee. Its 1996 report, significantly entitled *Rebuilding Trust*, made important proposals for strengthening good relations and reaffirming the democratic responsibilities of local councils. As this chapter shows, the Labour government has taken these proposals forward in large measure, through still denying that councils need greater financial autonomy if they are effectively to control their own decisions. These issues are important to the future of urban regeneration and social inclusion, raising questions of the extent to which local variations subject to local demands can be reconciled with the agendas of radical governments.

These constitutional and political questions will continue to be important as Britain moves towards a more devolved structure. The managerial revolution has had equally important influence on how local councils actually make decisions and implement them, and this chapter considers the implications. The chapter considers the implications of 'reinventing government' for local services. The search for quality, standards, consumer choice and influence has moved from the private into the public sector. The hope is that this will revolutionise how councils tackle physical and economic decline, foster greater consultation of groups and community and promote greater openness of decision-making.

These developments are still evolving. The relationship between local councils and central government and the impact of the new public management are changing yet again as the Labour government targets resources and puts pressure on standards. These are issues that operate in a wider European arena. Increasingly, urban projects are affected not only by the funding that comes from the European Union but also by the moves towards wider objectives of sustainable growth, lowered unemployment and the increased influence of cities and regions in such planning. The chapter concludes by setting out this wider framework and its implications for urban programmes beyond the year 2000.

## The democratic structure

Urban politics takes place within a structure of local government that has evolved over a long period. The modern system has its roots in mid-Victorian reforms aimed at overcoming the worst effects of industrialisation. Beginning with the Municipal Corporations Act of 1835 and the Local Government Acts of 1888 and 1894, county boroughs, counties and districts were set up as democratically elected bodies with specific powers and duties. The resulting system remained virtually unchanged in the first half of the twentieth century, though the powers and duties of local councils increased after 1945. With the coming of the welfare state, the duties of local councils expanded (though they were not health authorities and the nationalisation of public utilities removed some of their former powers). The result was that local authorities became multipurpose bodies and prime providers of education, housing, personal social services and leisure and other facilities.

In the 1960s, the development of modern communications and changes to work and residential patterns resulted in the size and responsibilities of local authorities being reconsidered. The London Government Act 1963 changed the government of the wider London region, creating the Greater London Council and the London Boroughs. In the 1970s, under pressure to increase efficiency through enlarged local units and to provide greater strategic coordination in the conurbations, the local government system was reformed. The 1972 Local Government Act, which came into operation in 1974, abolished all the county boroughs (the multipurpose authorities of the cities and major towns) and reduced the 58 county councils in England and Wales to 47. Separate legislation set up a two-tier system of regions and districts in Scotland. In the English conurbations 6 metropolitan county councils were estalished together with 36 metropolitan districts; a similar two-tier structure operated in the shire counties with county and district councils. In the conurbations these changes lasted only a decade, when the 1985 Act, effective in 1986, abolished the metropolitan counties and the Greater London Council, devolving their powers to the metropolitan districts and London boroughs. The separate Inner London Education Authority (ILEA) came to an end in 1990. Equally important to the working of the local government system were the changes introduced in the 1980s to the powers of local councils. Other agencies were set up alongside local councils to carry out certain tasks, such as urban regeneration, and councils saw some of their responsibilities passing to schools or to the private sector.

In the early 1990s Conservative governments reformed the local government structure, outside the conurbations, yet again. In England, Unitary Authorities were established for major towns, with a revised two-tier system elsewhere. The reforms of the 1992 Local Government Act were designed to secure effective local government while reflecting the identities and interests of local communities: goals which were hard to determine and proved controversial. Initially, the government anticipated that unitary authorities, modelled on the former county boroughs and responsible for all services in their areas, would prevail over the existing two-tier county/county district system. As the reform progressed, however, the Local Government Commission for England proposed the retention of the two-tier system for much of England (a review and critique of the reform process is given in Leach and Stoker, 1997). In Wales and Scotland there was no review Commission: unitary systems were imposed by the respective Secretaries of States, with the abolition of the top-tier councils.

The present pattern of local authorities is summarised in Box 4.1.

The reformed structure has meant a reduced number of local authorities and fewer elected councillors, particularly in Wales and Scotland and sharpened still further the contrast between British and European levels of representative institutions and members. As Box 4.1 shows, the new unitary authorities are large, some ten times the average size of municipalities in Europe. These were not seen as important factors by the Conservative government that introduced the 1992 changes. The Conservative argument was that, as local authorities were increasingly 'enabling' bodies, setting strategies for services provided by the private sector, public–private agencies and voluntary organisations, size was only of secondary importance.

*Box 4.1*   The system of local government

---

- England    34 county councils; 36 metropolitan districts; 238 shire districts;
             46 unitary authorities; 32 London boroughs; the Corporation of
             the City of London.
- Wales      22 unitary authorities; 12 of the largest authorities are served by a
             number of decentralised area committees.
- Scotland   32 unitary authorities; very localised Community Councils were
             retained and unitary councils encouraged to devolve powers to
             them.
- Size       Average population of unitary authorities: 185 000 in England;
             132 000 in Wales; 174 000 in Scotland.
- Elections  To unitary authorities on a three-year, whole-council basis; other
             councils retained their existing periodic cycles. Labour proposes
             moves to annual elections for most councils.
- London     Greater London Council abolished by the Local Government Act
             1985 and the Inner London Education Authority in 1990. The
             1985 Act established the London Residuary Body (work ended in
             1992) and the London Planning Advisory Committee. A number
             of other quangos exercised functions in the capital. From 2000
             London is governed by an elected Mayor and a London-wide
             Assembly with strategic powers.

---

The Labour government of 1997, pursuing its agenda of devolution, established a Parliament in Scotland and an Assembly in Wales. In England, the structure of local government was left largely in place, but two important new features were brought forward. These were the proposals for an enhanced regional dimension (see below) and the introduction of elected mayors and changed committee structures within local councils (see Chapter 7).

The present system remains, in spite of the changes to structure of the 1980s and 1990s, a democratic one where decisions are taken by elected councillors responsible to local voters. But how realistic is this picture, given that local governance now depends on collaboration between different agencies and bodies? Local democratic politics is essentially a matter of alliances, which raises further questions of who actually has power over decisions.

## Alliances for action

For urban policy to be successful, action must fit the circumstances and demands arising locally. Variations between authorities arise from local needs and from local party regimes. Response to need is reinforced by criteria laid down in national standards and constrained by government funding decisions. But local policymakers still have discretion to decide within these guidelines. Such decisions are largely determined through party politics and in particular through the ruling party group on the local council (Sharpe and Newton, 1984; Boyne, 1996).

Explaining decision-making in this way, however, leaves open the extent to which local authorities can act autonomously. In practice, they operate in conjunction with other local public bodies, the private sector and interest groups. This does not necessarily mean, however, that there is a dominant business-led coalition which drives urban decision-making. In 1992 the business rate was removed from local authority control, so removing any direct business interest in local budgets, a situation that may change again as Labour reforms require consultation with business where councils are allowed to levy a small additional rate. Collaboration is also required between local authorities and the private sector to qualify for Single Regeneration Budget grants and other funding. Businesses are also deeply involved in the Regional Development Agencies and in the new 'action zones' for health, employment and education.

As Chapter 3 showed, growth coalition interpretations of urban politics have shifted the focus from public sector-led regeneration to the patterns of public–private agencies and networks of collaborative working. These 'growth coalitions' are not necessarily always dominated by private interests but may in some cases be led by councillor/officer elites within local authorities (Cole and John, 1995; Stoker, 1995b). Research shows that business involvement is largely a pragmatic opportunism to make the local state more friendly to the private sector (Peck and Tickell, 1995). The judgement on the role of the private sector is that while business groups are influential and are drawn into partnerships in other services besides regeneration, they do not exercise the degree of sustained and integrated influence that can be found in cities in the United States. Business nevertheless does express a broad interest in local politics. The urban riots of the 1980s and the growth of such groups as Business in the Community (founded in 1981 and which has stimulated involvement in local partnerships) demonstrate that business interest goes beyond questions of economic growth to a concern with crime, civil peace and stability. Business is also being drawn into educational and anti-exclusion measures. Two results of local alliances between councils and business are that all the mainstream parties favour such collaboration, and that competition has increased between cities rather than between business and other classes within them (Keating, 1991).

As well as business, collaboration in pursuit of regeneration and a more inclusive society increasingly draws the voluntary sector into local alliances. Making a contribution to resolving problems of decline and exclusion is a challenging task for voluntary groups. They have found it difficult to assemble the resources to build the necessary capacity for action: helping people to take an informed, active and sustained part in decision-making. Nevertheless, the voluntary sector remains a dynamic contributor. Its major input is not just to provide services either autonomously or under contract with local authorities, but to act as a catalyst in finding new ways to overcome problems. Currently, the voluntary sector is also helping to alleviate deprivation by using the talents of individuals as 'social entrepreneurs' or 'civic entrepreneurs' to create the resource/information/people capacity that being involved demands. Such local activists use community-based organisations to help to revitalise disadvantaged areas (Thake, 1995), creating 'social capital' to create greater social cohesion and rejuvenate public services (Leadbetter and Goss, 1998).

Political alliances and multiagency collaboration are now the key to the successful delivery of regeneration and other programmes. But, it is argued, trying to solve problems of run-down neighbourhoods and economies cannot be taken solely within the boundaries of individual towns and cities. A much wider, regional strategy is urgently needed. There are two ideas at work here. One is to decentralise more decisions from the centre, the other to plan urban strategies over areas wider than individual cities.

## Moving to a regional dimension

The pressure to bring a wider regional strategy to bear raises, as Box 4.2 shows, many questions of boundaries, functions, power and overlapping responsibilities.

*Box 4.2* Issues in the regional debate

- The need for a regional dimension: strategic links over wider areas than individual cities; to make administrative regions more accountable; EU pressure for a regional basis to funding applications.
- A confusion of administrative areas, with some 100 regional structures of diverse scope and scale. These include the 10 Government Offices of the Regions; 8 Standard Regions; regional offices of the NHS, the Housing Corporation, the Further Education Funding Council, the Arts Council and the Sports Council.
- Problems of the configuration of regions: geographic and technical boundaries; political and community identities.
- New moves to strategic regionalism: the Labour government's Regional Development Agencies and voluntary, appointed Regional Chambers.
- The need for democratic regional government.

In Britain, administrative regions have existed since the 1940s. As Box 4.2 stresses, their scale and scope are complex, with nearly 100 regional structures and more than one set of regional boundaries (Hogwood, 1996). The regionalisation of the central state was given a boost by the establishment of the Government Offices of the Regions in 1994, but this move strengthened the presence of central government in the regions rather than enhancing devolution (Mawson and Spencer, 1997). It is difficult to define a regional level of governance given these complexities, but there is general agreement that the present system of making decisions at regional level is opaque, difficult to understand and imperfectly accountable (Stoker, Hogwood and Bullman, 1996). The debate will continue to be a lively one because of the demands for a greater democratic voice in some English regions, countered by doubts that regional identities in other areas are both weak and territorially ambiguous (as in the large South East region for example). In addition, there are strong voices calling for strategic links over city regions, somewhere between cities and the existing standard regions, to reflect both planning realities and parallel developments taking place in the European Union.

These different pressures for a wider and more democratic regional dimension to policy are already reflected in the collaboration that exists between local councils. All the English regions have organisations which bring together local authorities, for example in regional associations, based on standing conferences or regional planning fora and increasingly concerned with economic development. The London and South East Regional Planning Conference is the longest established of the regional planning bodies. A rather different body is the North West Regional Association, set up in 1992, which incorporates three counties and their districts and was in part a response to new regional groupings in the business community. Regional Assemblies exist in both the North of England and Yorkshire and Humberside regions. These bodies form the pressure for addressing the democratic deficit at regional level. This pressure is growing: the North-East Constitutional Convention, a non-party political group, was launched at Westminster early in 1999, and the Commons standing committee on regional affairs in England was revived.

It has been the Labour Party, however, which pursued the issue in the 1990s, when in opposition, and which acted swiftly to set new bodies in train when they came to power in 1997. On entering office, the Labour government moved rapidly to introduce a regional development agency system, rather than an elected tier of government, to oversee regeneration strategy. The Regional Development Agencies Act 1998 established the bodies that came into operation on 1 April 1999. The main provisions are summarised in Box 4.3.

The RDAs have their own budgets, drawn from the bodies they are replacing. They work alongside the Government Offices of the Regions (GORs), on whose areas they are based (with Merseyside incorporated into the North West region). London has a separate Regional Development Agency and, uniquely among the regions, a Greater London Authority, set up under separate legislation and which is composed of an elected Mayor and Assembly. At the same time as the establishment of the RDAs, there was a parallel merger of the Countryside Commission and the Rural Development Commission as the Countryside Agency, with the RDC's rural regeneration work being handed over to the new RDAs. As Box 4.3 shows, the RDAs are managed by business-led Boards whose members are appointed by the Secretary of State, taking into account suggestions for nominations from a wide range of regional interests. The 1998 act also established voluntary regional chambers – advisory assemblies – appointed by the Secretary of State from among nominees of local authorities and other public, private and voluntary organisations.

Under the objectives listed in Box 4.3, the first task of each RDA

*Box 4.3*   Regional Development Agencies Act 1998

---

Established a Regional Development Agency in each of the 8 English Regions plus London with effect from 1 April 1999

- Five objectives:
  (1) Foster economic development and social and physical regeneration;
  (2) Promote business efficiency, investment and competitiveness;
  (3) Enhance the development and application of skills;
  (4) Help to maintain and safeguard employment;
  (5) Contribute to the achivement of sustainable development.

- Core functions to achieve these aims:
  (1) Produce strategic regional economic plans;
  (2) Responsibility for Single Regeneration Budget (SRB) Challenge Fund; regeneration functions of English Partnerships and Rural Development Commission;
  (3) Take lead on European Union Structural Funds;
  (4) Coordinate inward investment; market the region;
  (5) Reclaim and prepare factory sites;
  (6) Contribute to policies on: transport; land-use; environment; further and higher education; crime prevention; public health; tourism.

- Management:
  (1) 12-member Board drawn from business (6), local authorities (4), voluntary sector (2);
  (2) Must consult with voluntary Regional Chambers consisting of business, local authority and other regional interests;
  (3) Government Offices of the Regions (GORs) remain; some staff transfer to RDAs.

---

was to prepare a regional economic strategy that determines many of the future activities both of the RDAs themselves and of other organisations involved in regional development. The input of the voluntary regional chambers into these strategies will be a crucial test of their real influence and that of the regional stakeholders they represent. One of the duties of the voluntary chambers will be to contribute to the government's regional planning guidance – a role that local authorities have traditionally taken and which will be continued through these new bodies. This is a key element of the new system, since Regional Planning Guidance (RPG) will provide the strategic planning and communication blueprint through which the RDA will operate. In some regions the work of the existing regional planning conferences might be integrated with that of the chambers. A central issue will be the relation between the RDAs' duty to prepare economic strategies for their regions and the wider strategic plans relating to land-use produced under the planning guidance system. The wider questions of how these regional duties and responsibilities fit Labour's agenda for modernising democracy are examined further in subsequent chapters.

The hallmark of present urban policy is thus the way solutions are being sought at both city and regional levels. This raises the question of what the power of the central government is and how the relations between centre and localities affect what is achieved.

**The power of the centre**

These issues of decentralisation and empowerment in the Labour agenda highlight the continuing debate on how urban policy is sustained within the unitary British state and on the power of the centre. The relations between centre and locality are a key element in the framework of urban policy and its implementation. Central–local relations are structured in four main ways: through statute law; through financial provisions; through administrative oversight – rules and regulations made under statute law, ministerial guidance through Departmental circulars, notes of guidance (as in planning for example) and other advisory directives; and through informal processes and policy networks. Under statute law, the powers of local government are defined by mandatory (local authorities must carry out a function) or permissive (local authorities may act if they so choose) laws laid down by Parliament. To act outside these powers is illegal or *ultra vires*, that is, there is no general competence power for local government, by which local authorities could act for the general wellbeing of their areas or citizens. There is a limited competence, under s. 137 of the Local Government Act 1972 (as amended by the 1989 Local Government and Housing Act), that allows local authorities to incur expenditure which is in the interests of their area or its inhabitants, under an annual limit set by central government. The 1989 Local

Government and Housing Act provides that local authorities can carry out local economic development for which they had previously used s. 137 powers. The issue of a general competence power for local authorities, however, remains and will be explored further in later chapters.

Parliament is sovereign and local authorities are the statutory creations of Parliament. But, as the Widdicombe Report of 1986 pointed out, that sovereignty is underpinned by custom and convention on how it should be exercised (Cmnd 9799, 1986). Bogdanor stresses the special status of this position: local authorities, like Parliament, have the power to tax, possess democratic legitimacy and provide those potential constraints on governmental power which in other democracies are enshrined in formal constitutions (Bogdanor, 1996).

In the 1980s this largely consensual 'dual-state' system (see Chapter 3), whereby the central state set policy and economic parameters and the local state was a major provider of services, began to erode. Central governments sought to curtail what they saw as overly rigid local bureaucracies, increase consumer choice (for example in education) and reduce expenditure. New institutions, including the Audit Commission (established in 1982), regulatory bodies such as Ofsted, and local quangos were established precisely, as Loughlin puts it, to alter the 'rules of the game' and to challenge the informal rules of traditional policy networks in order to replace them with a more formal, rule-based regime established by legislation (Loughlin, 1996b). In this 'juridification' of central–local relations, conventions are replaced by positive or jurist law, that is, instead of traditional and accepted understandings of how the two levels of government relate to each other, legislation lays down ever more rigid rules and courts have a role in mediating the situation. The result is that legislation establishes the norms and regulated central–local relations rather than, as heretofore, laying down a flexible legal framework within which norms could evolve. Judicial review applications have increased as councils attempted to challenge government financial controls. The result is that whereas legislation used to be facilitative, it is now regulatory (Loughlin, 1996a).

In practice, centralisation has primarily affected the local policy process in three ways. First, there has been the increasing domination of the centre over finance, such that by the late 1980s only some 15–20 per cent of local expenditure was raised through local revenues. The second aspect of central control has been the imposition of national standards and targets for services, a trend that has increased rather than diminished in the change from a Conservative to a Labour government. The third area of central influence has been the requirement that local services be delivered through a mix of public and private provision and that local authorities forge partnerships with other agencies to promote regeneration. Central government, that is, not only has power to change the structure of the local government system, it can also control how local councils go about their work of delivering services to local people. Central government has used these powers to alter the processes of how policy is implemented, changing local councils' previous role of providing the bulk of local services through their own departments and committees, to one where they share this task with other bodies. The result is a change from local government, where councils provide services and are accountable through the ballot-box, to local governance, whereby partnerships and networks facilitate service delivery, accountable to citizens, consumers, clients and users.

The unease over the power of the central state became more widespread in the 1980s. But it was the issue of financial control which led to a crisis in central–local relations. Central oversight increased following the 1980 Local Government, Planning and Land Act. Over the next few years the government increased its powers, setting the Standard Spending Assessments (SSAs) on which local authorities' needs were based and the share of grant that each authority should receive. The Rates Act 1984 introduced 'ratecapping', which allowed central government to set severe penalties ('capping' budgets) on those authorities deemed to be overspending. This raised important issues of local autonomy and local democracy. Traditionally, governments had set a national sum for local government grants which was then divided up between authorities according to national formulae and after a process of consultation. Where individual local authorities felt that, in order to deliver services, additional sums had to be found, this could be done (within limits) by raising the level of local rates. As elected councils, this could be justified on the grounds that local voters had the opportunity to express their views on such actions at election time. Conservative governments believed, however, that local expenditure had to be reined in, and that their national mandate to manage the economy overrode any claims to local differences. By the early 1990s government had reached a position where they decided both what each individual local authority should spend (through the SSAs) and what they should raise in local revenues (through the universal capping regime imposed on all authorities in 1992). In 1996, the House of Lords inquiry concluded that capping distorted local finance and contributed to the confusion over accountability (House of Lords, 1996). After 1997 there was some relaxation of the regime, though not its reversal, with the Labour government affirming that while universal capping would be removed, the government would maintain a reserve power to restrict local budgets. And the government comprehensive spending review of July 1998 still put the direction of funds to services in the hands of the Chancellor, not local authorities.

In the 1980s the way in which local taxes, the rates, were raised was also changed, as Prime Minister Thatcher fulfilled a long-standing promise to reform the rating system. These reforms led first to the contentious and ill-fated Community Charge (the 'Poll Tax', introduced in Scotland in 1989 and in England and Wales in 1990) (Butler, Adonis and Travers, 1994) and finally to the Council Tax introduced in 1993. The traditional rates had been a property tax based on dwellings and business premises. The Community Charge was levied on all eligible individuals not just heads of households. Local authorities also lost control of local business rates, which were set and distributed nationally. Controversy over the fairness of the Poll Tax, and widespread resistance to its imposition, lead to its abolition in 1993. The Council Tax which replaced the Community Charge was a reversion to a property tax (based on capital value not assumed rental value) with an element of individual levy. At the same time, continued control over revenues was matched by tight controls over capital budgets.

The changes to the financial system over the course of the 1980s, and the attempts by local authorities to circumvent its controls, increased central–local conflict. This was most notable in Labour-controlled councils in the major conurbations and large cities, pursuing what has been termed 'municipal socialism' objectives to expand local services in the face of government restrictions (Gyford, 1985). Though vigorous in the mid-1980s, rate capping controls and the abolition of the GLC and the metropolitan counties in 1986 defeated what government believed was a form of organised opposition to a mandated Conservative government and removed much of the friction. When the whole period of 1979–1997 is considered it is clear that there had been a major change in central–local relations. The traditional 'partnership' model had given way to a complex pattern of relationships to accompany the move to a restructured and deregulated welfare state in which a significant range of public provision moved to the private sector and to non-elected quangos. The outcomes were profound, increasing centralisation in both financial and administrative spheres and raising questions of what degree of autonomy remains to elected local councils (Goldsmith, 1995).

Thus the questions of autonomy and agency remain central to urban affairs. The success of urban policy depends on how central and local governments see policy, how these aims diverge and what freedoms remain to localities to pursue their own initiatives. In a landmark report the Layfield Committee of 1976 set out the dilemma of responsibility and accountability clearly. Accountability was diffused between central and local government and needed to be more precisely defined and located. The choice was between a centralised system in which local authorities were virtually agents of the centre and more decentralised government which fostered genuine local discretion. Layfield believed that an increase in the autonomy of local authorities depended on a reduction of financial reliance on central government and an increase in the amount of money they raised locally. As it crisply put it, 'The role of local government is to enable decisions to be taken democratically to cater for local needs and purposes . . . How effectively local authorities will be able to discharge [this role] in future depends on how much responsibility governments are prepared to let them have' (Cmnd 6453, 1976: 284). But the growth of centralisation feared by Layfield continued. By the 1980s governments had tightened financial controls, prescribed more specifically the priorities of expenditure and capped spending limits. The way services were delivered was also prescribed. In the late 1990s, however, Labour stated its commitment to a new partnership and a new trust, a view reinforced by the inquiry carried out in 1995–96 by the House of Lords.

### Seeking new trust

In 1995 the House of Lords appointed an Ad Hoc Select Committee, chaired by Lord Hunt of Tanworth, to consider all aspects of the relations between central and local government. The report *Rebuilding Trust*, published in July 1996, concluded that the relations between the two sides was unsatisfactory (House of Lords, 1996). Its main recommendations are summarised in Box 4.4.

*Box 4.4*   The recommendations of *Rebuilding Trust*

---

- Abolish the routine capping of local authority budgets.
- Relax Treasury controls.
- Give councils a specific power of local competence to act to act in the interests of the local community [but not a power of general competence].
- Set up a permanent parliamentary committee to oversee central/local relations.
- Return business rates to local councils.
- Review Compulsory Competitive Tendering (CCT).
- Set up a new *concordat* defining the right of local authorities to be consulted on policy.
- The government should sign the Council of Europe's 1985 European Charter of Local Self-Government.

---

In response to these recommendations, the Conservative government acknowledged that trust had broken down in the 1980s and needed to be rebuilt. It rejected, however, the report's central proposals that the UK should sign the Council of Europe's Charter of Local Self-Government, to abolish rate-capping except as a reserve power and return the business rate to local control.

On entering office in May 1997, the Labour government responded to the Hunt Report as part of the rebuilding of good relations between central and local government. A *Framework for Partnership* document, setting out the working relationship between the LGA (Local Government Association representing English and Welsh local authorities) and the government, was signed. A Central–Local Partnership Meeting was established, bringing together Cabinet ministers and senior local leaders, under the aegis of Deputy Prime Minister John Prescott. This body holds regular meetings and acts as a forum for collaborative working. As part of this collaboration, a national group including government departments, the LGA, the CBI, TECs and the voluntary sector was formed to support new integrated approaches to social and economic integration. The Local Government Association, which represents English and Welsh local authorities, set up its own Improvement and Development Agency (IDA) to provide advice and help to members, while 22 'pathfinder' local authorities with innovative programmes were set up to act as an example to other councils and feed into national policy.

The Labour government's White Paper on modernising local government set out the parameters within which the new central–local cooperation would work (Cm 4014, 1998). It also stressed that strong relations between local businesses and councils were vital. There is already a statutory requirement to consult business on the local budget; largely formal, this will be strengthened and expanded. While retaining the national non-domestic rate, councils would be given a measure of variation over the business rate, allowing local authorities discretionary power to levy a 1 per cent (and up to 5 per cent over time) supplementary local rate. 'Beacon authorities', those with a leading record of good practice (chosen by ministers guided by an independent panel), would be able to levy a 2 per cent additional business rate per year up to a maximum of 10 per cent. In setting a local rate, local authorities would be required to consult with local business on its use – in effect a negotiating position, though business could not veto the levying of a local rate. Crude and universal capping of local budgets would be ended, but the government would retain reserve powers to intervene. In addition, where councils set what are considered high levels of council tax, the government would make more of the cost of subsidy to people entitled to council tax benefit rest on local councils; what commentators believed was a reintroduction of capping by indirect means. The annual review of SSAs would be replaced by a 3-year process.

The government subsequently took the view, however, that local autonomy was not to be equated with financial independence (a decision which significantly moves away from the Layfield position of 20 years earlier), believing that there was no case for the return of the business rate to local control; a position many in local government remained unhappy with. Analysts are also concerned over the constraints on local choice and variation and the implications that this has for local democracy. Over a decade of research on central–local relations published by the Rowntree Foundation concludes that it is essential for local councils to be able to exercise 'freedom to do things differently', acknowledging that this has to be within recognised limits. From this perspective the British system, with its very high reliance on central government grants, is unsatisfactory. It is argued that a much higher proportion of local expenditure should be met from local sources if local democratic responsibility and accountability are to have any meaning.

The government's commitment to a new era, however, was demonstrated by its move, at the time it entered office, to sign and ratify the

European Charter of Local Self-Government. The Charter lays down, among other principles, that: local self-government be recognised in domestic legislation; that local authorities have the right to manage public affairs under their own responsibility, in the interests of the local population, with adequate resources of their own; these rights shall be exercised by councils of elected members (Council of Europe, 1985). In addition, the Labour government stressed that the new partnership was part of its overall commitment to decentralisation, shown in its devolution and regional policies. Its more positive approach gave local councils an enhanced role in regeneration and community leadership and promised more powers to the best councils.

The problems of 'partnership' versus 'agency' models, however, still remain. The 1996 House of Lords report had recognised that the days of local government as direct provider of the majority of services had gone, in favour of a role as community leader whose legitimacy lay in its democratic mandate. This still leaves open to question the issue of national standards and local discretion. While those who receive services demand levels of quality which are not dependent on where they live – that is, national standards – it is not clear how far they wish to see local variation. Local authorities have traditionally been noted for policy innovations which later become part of standard professional practice. And part of the rationale for locally elected councils is their democratic mandate to reflect their constituents' needs and wishes. The Labour government's emphasis on partnership and decentralisation has not completely quietened anxiety that, in the details of provisions, localities are seen as helping central government achieve its objectives in a continued top–down perspective. There is also growing disquiet over the government's intervention powers, with the reliance on private entrepreneurs and the market as the solution. The Department for Education and Science's advertising campaign inviting profit-making companies to join a list of other organisations which could take over the services of failing local education authorities goes beyond anything Conservative governments contemplated and appears to critics to set dangerous precedents.

The evolution of urban policy between centre and localities is determined not only by the relations between the two levels but by important changes in the way that modern governments deliver services. These new methods reject complex bureaucratic hierarchies in favour of managerial flexibility and consumer choice. The ideas arose in private management practice and have been reinforced by governments' search for greater quality control and openness about results that has transformed public services.

## Urban policy and 'reinventing government'

The international trend towards the 'reinvention of government', to use the famous phrase of American authors Osborne and Gaebler, emphasises the injection of entrepreneurial ideas into the public sector. In this model, public bodies should be 'steering' (i.e. enabling) rather than 'rowing' (providing) services (Osborne and Gaebler, 1992).

The new ethos of service delivery is marked by five main concepts (see Box 4.5).

*Box 4.5*   The 'new public management' ethos

---

- Deregulation; efficiency; accountability to customers and clients; performance measurement; quality control.
- Introducing market procedures into public services.
- Encouraging local authorities to adopt new working practices both internally (including the committee system and management hierarchies) and externally with other agencies.
- Measuring outputs through performance indicators and Citizen's Charter codes.
- Devolving decisions to cost centres and neighbourhoods.

---

These concepts brought private sector procedures and styles into public services and are central to what is known as the 'new public management' (Lowndes, 1999). The key ideas in the new public management are decentralisation to accountable managers and quality-driven services responsive to consumer needs and demands. The aim is to maintain overall strategy at the centre of the authority while decentralising implementation. As a result there have been changes to patterns of working in local councils, particularly to committee and departmental structures and in the decentralisation of decisions to neighbourhood-level committees. The result of these developments was that local authorities were encouraged to work more collaboratively, both internally and through interagency working in public–private partnerships.

Emphasising quality and consumer needs and demands, for their part, was fostered through two main projects. The first programme was the Citizen's Charter regime (introduced by Prime Minister John Major in 1991) and its successor Service First, launched by Labour in 1998. This aims to set standards of service, improve complaint handling and improve administration generally. The second was the measurement of output and quality through performance indicators and comparator data ('league tables'). A system of performance indicators was established by the Local Government Act 1992, administered by the Audit Commission, and with results published in the press. These developments, it was argued, would improve efficiency by making service delivery 'consumer' driven. By these means the paternalism of traditional bureaucracy is rejected and managers are expected to incorporate consumer criteria into performance measures. Local authorities, for their part, are increasingly putting procedures in place to improve service quality. But effective management in the public sector is still motivated by more than individual consumer satisfaction: it is management for public purposes, for the quality of city life and for democratic ends not private profit. Output measures, while important, are not the whole story. The evaluation of *outcomes* – the extent to which needs are met, problems overcome and permanent improvements gained, still awaits longer-term judgements and more in-depth research.

Labour, however, has maintained the output measurement approach, with a new set of broader-based national performance measures to be introduced by the year 2000. These include a number of 'general health' indicators reflecting the capacity and performance of local authorities as both democratic institutions and as spending bodies. Each major service will have key indicators reflecting the effectiveness and quality of local services, set by the government and validated and published by the Audit Commission. 'New partnership' clearly still involves considerable central oversight.

The trend to 'reinventing government' reflects a more fundamental shift in the dominant paradigm by which the state no longer delivers services but regulates private sector or quasi-private suppliers. A major example of this paradigm shift in the 1980s was the 'contracting out' provisions of the Compulsory Competitive Tendering (CCT) regime. Though this has now been replaced by Labour's 'Best Value' model of service delivery, the key emphasis remains that of plurality of provision, in which the local council is a strategic and enabling, not all-providing body. CCT required local authorities to place contracts for the delivery of services out to tender (from the private sector or in-house bids). First introduced in the 1980 Local Government, Planning and Land Act, it was extended by the 1988 and 1992 Local Government Acts to a wide range of services, made compulsory and further extended to core professional functions. CCT ceased to be politically controversial as the Labour government proposed that although compulsion would be abolished, services would continue to be delivered through whatever provider could give the best service: by the late 1990s it was being taken for granted that councils' priorities were to get the best deal for residents.

The Labour government's 1998 White Paper announced that over the longer term CCT would be abolished (Cm 4014, 1998). In November 1997 secondary legislation had already been amended to simplify procedures and councils were encouraged to pursue voluntary partnerships with the private sector. The Local Government Act of 1999 laid down that instead of CCT a new 'Best Value' system would place a duty on all councils to prove that they were providing high quality, value-for-money services. Universal capping of local authority budgets will be replaced with reserve powers to limit council tax increases, with effect from April 2000. There is a general duty laid on councils to secure continuous improvement in its functions. Targets for service improvement would have to be published annually in Local Performance Plans through which councils would be held accountable for the quality and efficiency of their services. Local authorities would have to agree a programme of performance reviews of all services over a 5-year period, to a 4-point agenda of Challenge, Comparison, Consult and Competition. These reviews, from which the agreement of performance plans embodying the targets will be the principal outcome, are at the heart of best value. Local authorities compare their performance with that of other councils ('benchmarking'). Councils have a duty to consult with service users, local taxpayers, and businesses, and show evidence of community involvement both in the review of services and in overall service evaluation. Competition continues to be a criteria of securing improved services. Services can be provided in-house, in public–private partnerships or privatised and have to comply with new performance targets. Observers believed that the government's general presumption was that services would be privatised.

The government made it plain that these changes would be backed with enforcement powers, underpinned by the local government inspectorate attached to the Audit Commission. If services fell below the new national standards then the government would require some functions to be handed over to other bodies, including neighbouring councils or other agencies. Government intervention can be triggered by failure to consult, to produce a best value performance plan or agree a review programme, to set or publish performance targets or set the targets too low. In addition, intervention could come where councils failed to meet nationally set standards or locally set performance targets, where there were persistently high unit costs and where there were failures either of standards or to improve services. Even though government will only intervene where there is clear evidence an authority is failing either to discharge its functions adequately or to meet its statutory obligations, these are draconic powers.

The Local Government Act 1999 also laid down that the Secretary of State could issue orders specifying the performance indicators by which the improvement in local authority functions as a result of best value could be measured. When the full regime is in place, a new Best Value Inspectorate will be established, working under the aegis of the Audit Commission. The Commission will play a central role in judging whether best value has been achieved, moves which raised concerns that this could give the Commission too powerful a role. The agency will become a new super-Audit Commission, in effect the Inspectorate of Local Government. The Commission will have the lead responsibility in coordinating the work of other inspectorates, including the Social Services, Ofsted (education), Housing, Police, Benefit Fraud and Fire inspectorates. Some of these bodies, notably Ofsted, Police and Social Services, are powerful operators and ensuring collaboration between them, and overcoming problems of duplication and competition between all of the inspectorates, presents a major challenge. But the overriding conclusion must be that the government's determination to push its agenda is being accompanied by strengthened, not relaxed, central oversight.

The driving force of 'reinventing government', looking for a plurality of providers and emphasising quality and consumer satisfaction, now operates within a European as well as a national framework.

**The policy impacts of the European Union**

The European Union has two significant influences on urban affairs. One arises from the influence of membership of the EU on relations between central government, local authorities and the institutions of the EU. The other is the direct impact of funding for urban projects. Membership of the European Union has changed the former central–local relationship into a triangular one of EU–central–local institutions. The extensive networks which mark the relations of local authorities and local and sectoral interests with the EU make the old central–local hierarchy porous, since the 'tiers' of the hierarchy coexist with the interlocking 'spheres' of policy arenas made up of representatives from different countries. There are tensions within these European–central–local relationships, particularly over EU funding and the issue of additionality. Rather than treating European money as extra funding which allowed 'additional' spending, the Treasury in effect clawed back the money by making an equivalent reduction in a local authority's approved capital programme, thus reducing the amount the Treasury needed to raise to meet spending plans. Though this system was relaxed in 1992, full additionality has still not been achieved.

At the level of specific projects, European funding is an important resource. A 1994 survey found that for 85 per cent of county councils, 62 per cent of districts and no less than 93 per cent of metropolitan authorities, European funding was significant to their activities (Pyecroft, 1995: 23). Most of the European funds were given to local

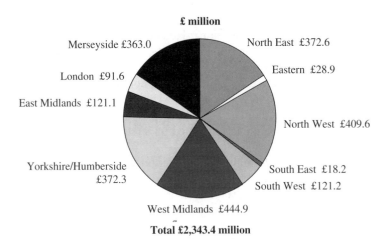

**£ million**

Merseyside £363.0

North East £372.6

London £91.6

Eastern £28.9

East Midlands £121.1

North West £409.6

Yorkshire/Humberside £372.3

South East £18.2

South West £121.2

West Midlands £444.9

**Total £2,343.4 million**

*Source:* Department of the Environment, Transport and the Regions, Annual Report, 1998

*Figure 4.1*    ERDF: allocation to English regions 1994–96

councils for infrastructure assistance and to employment and training initiatives. Between 1994 and 1996 the European Regional Development Fund (ERDF) allocation to English regions was, as Figure 4.1 shows, £2 343.4 million (Cm 3906, 1998).

These funds are of two main kinds: the large structural funds for regional development, social purposes and agriculture, ERDF; European Social Fund, ESF; and the European Agriculture Guidance and Guarantee Fund, EAGGF; and the smaller and more flexible funds for a wide range of Community Initiatives. The EU also has community employment initiatives to support women, the disabled, the low skilled and for vocational training, especially for young people, while the INTEGRA initiative makes more specific provision for migrants and ethnic minorities.

A full regional policy in Europe was instituted in 1975, following Britain's accession to the Community, with the creation of the European Regional Development Fund, ERDF, which initally emphasised capital projects. The 1988 reforms shifted the emphasis from projects to programmes and to partnership between the European Commission, national governments and affected parties (including local authorities). The Department of the Environment, Transport and the Regions coordinates ERDF programmes in the English regions. The programmes are carried out by the Government Offices for the Regions (GORs), in partnerships with local authorities, TECs, other local bodies and the European Commission. From April 1999 the new RDAs took a leading role in the administration of European Structural Funds. Since the reform of the structural funds in 1988 the more flexible Community Initiatives, which are growing in number, are directly funded by Brussels.

Box 4.6 sets out the five objectives of the EU funding system following the 1993 amendments to the Structural Funds. The restructuring of particular sectors has played a strong part in EU initiatives, notably in relation to the steel, coal, textiles and defence industries. Of the thirteen new Community Initiatives, accounting for 9 per cent of structural fund expenditure set up for the 1994–99 period, a number affected urban policy: URBAN (urban areas); SMEs (small- and medium-sized enterprises); KONVER (defence sector areas); RESIDER II (steel regions); ADAPT (of the workforce to industrial change); NOW, HORIZON, YOUTHSTART (all concerned with human resources development). The URBAN initiative in particular supports 50 projects targeted on major cities. URBAN has a social exclusion remit, empha-

*Box 4.6*    The objectives of the EU Structural Funds

- Objective 1: promoting development in those regions lagging behind [initially Northern Ireland was the only part of the UK to be eligible, with Merseyside and the Highlands and Islands added in 1994].
- Objective 2: converting those regions, seriously affected by industrial decline [including Clydeside, NE Egland, South Wales and small areas in south and east London].
- Objective 3: integrating those excluded from the labour market, including the long-term unemployed and young people.
- Objective 4: facilitating the adaptation of employees to industrial change.
- Objective 5a: adapting the processes of the Common Agricultural and Fisheries Policies to facilitate their reform.
- Objective 5b: rural development.
- Following the entry of Austria, Finland and Sweden in 1996, a new Objective 6 was added, targeted at areas of very low population in northern Finland and Sweden.

sising integrated approaches for deprived neighbourhoods, including action on employment, quality of life and the reintegration of marginalised groups. It reflects the European view that exclusion and marginalisation need to be addressed explicitly. While these Community Initiatives can be applied for by most councils, the Structural Fund monies themselves tend to be geographically targeted, restricted to those areas designated Objectives 1, 2 and 5b.

Following the Maastricht Treaty of 1992, Europe-wide links increased in strength. Local authorities increasingly seek to influence EU policy development through their membership of cross-border associations and pressure groups. British regions and cities have also established links with their counterparts across Europe, for example the Committee of European Cities, or Eurocities, the EIC Middle-Sized Cities network, the Commission des Villes of smaller towns and cities, and the Association of Traditional Industrial Regions of Europe. Local authorities' EU networks and their lobbying of Brussels have created what John calls a 'growing Europeanisation of UK subnational government' (John, 1994b). In addition, there are long-established peak local authority organisations, including the Council of European Municipalities and Regions and the Assembly of European

Regions. Added to this network by Article 198 of the Maastricht Treaty was a Committee of the Regions (CoR), which held its inaugural session in 1994. CoR is made up of representatives of regional and local authorites (the 24 UK representatives are local councillors) and has the right to be consulted on policy issues. Though only an advisory body, its input into policymaking will be increasingly important and its powers are likely to grow.

Some commentators have concluded from these developments that the period following the approval of the Maastricht Treaty in 1992 marks the formation of a 'Europe of the Regions' that will increasingly erode the role of central governments in favour of both Brussels and the regional–local levels. This, it is argued, will reinforce that 'hollowing out' of the state which globalisation and the use of private organisations for public purposes has fostered. On the other hand British governments have maintained that subsidiarity – the principle that decisions should be decentralised to the lowest appropriate level of government – is defined in Article 3B of the Maastricht Treaty to mean relations between member states and the Union, which justifies continued national control of policy and decisions. It is sometimes argued that local authorities' lobbying of European institutions, and their search for funds, are aimed at pursuing their own policy objectives by bypassing central government. In practice this is hard to achieve, since national governments act as gatekeepers for the distribution of European funding. On the other hand, Article A of the Maastricht Treaty implies that decisions should be taken 'as closely as possible' to the citizens. Ambiguity thus remains.

From the year 2000 this system will undergo its most significant changes since the 1989 reforms which accompanied the introduction of the single market in 1985. As the European Union expands to include central and eastern European states, these will become eligible for Objective 1 status under the structural funds. The result will be that funds to existing member states will shrink. The European Commission set out its reform proposals in the *Agenda 2000: For a Stronger and Wider Europe* (European Commission, 1997). These proposals cut back the eligible areas in the existing 15 member states. The number of priority Objectives under the Structural Funds, as well as the number of Community Initiatives, is to be reduced to three, with tightened eligibility criteria, more targeted projects and streamlined working. The new Objective 1 (lagging regions, with a GDP of less than 75 per cent of the EU average) guidelines will be more strictly adhered to and those areas likely to lose Objective 1 status (the Scottish Highlands and Islands) would receive transitional payments; South Yorkshire and Cornwall are likely to qualify for aid for the first time. The new Objective 2, which will integrate current Objectives 2 and 5b, would be extended from declining industrial areas to cover service sectors, fishing communities and deprived urban areas. Eligibility would be tightened and unemployment would be used as the main criteria. A new Objective 3 would help all areas not covered in 1 and 2, with an emphasis on lifetime learning, skills training and tackling social exclusion.

The outturn for the UK is likely to be that the assisted areas will be left with a patchwork of small localities eligible for structural funds (Armstrong, 1998). On the positive side, the EU proposals will stimulate UK thinking to produce new Regional Plans in the RDA context, as the bidding and allocation of European Structural Funds becomes regionalised. Currently, the EU is taking a greater interest in urban affairs, as its publication *Towards an Urban Agenda* reveals, and the proposals to incorporate funding for urban areas in mainstream Structural Funds. It also remains the case that British towns and cities recognise both the importance of EU funds and the need to maintain European links and networks to protect their interests.

**Conclusion**

This chapter has demonstrated the importance of the structures and processes that provide the framework for urban policy. As Chapter 2 showed, the problems that urban policy attempts to solve are long-term and complex. Solutions to these problems have developed and changed over the past three decades and, as this chapter has emphasised, have done so as government institutions and relationships between them also changed.

Decisions to meet economic, social and political objectives take place in the context of local, regional, national and European institutions and processes. At the immediate level of urban projects and services, the structure and powers of local government and the relations between the centre and the localities set the boundaries. Modern local government has its roots in Victorian reforms but the major growth of its duties came after 1945. The welfare state laid expanded responsibilities on local councils who became multipurpose bodies providing a wide range of services. Changes to the system in the 1970s increased the size of local authorities and reallocated their duties among different tiers of government, while those of the early 1990s re-established some of the features of the pre-1972 county boroughs. Now, this reformed system and the parallel changes to local council powers in the 1980s provide the legal and administrative framework of local action. Over the past two decades the pressure to solve urban problems over areas wider than individual cities has led to an increased focus on regions. The regional dimension includes both decentralisation of certain Whitehall responsibilities to the Government Offices of the Regions, and new Regional Development Agencies with strategic overview for physical, social and economic regeneration.

Changes in the structures and powers of local authorities have been matched by changed ways of working. Urban politics involves partnerships and alliances, which have become more extensive – and intensive – as governments promote cross-sector cooperation in delivering services. This raises questions about the role of business in decision-making: does it now have too dominant an interest in urban affairs? The conclusion of this chapter is that the relations between councils and the private sector are better described as networks rather than growth coalitions in which business dominates. The factors that influence decisions go wider than this. One such factor is the effect of new ways of managing services that have spread from the private sector into public services. The chapter showed how the new managerialism promotes the objectives of governments for public services: quality, value for money, consumer satisfaction and published data on outputs.

Local coalitions have to work within the realities of the constitutional and political power of the state. The chapter showed how increasingly centralisation led to tensions in the 1980s. This has been the subject of considerable debate over local autonomy versus increased central control. The title of the Lords' Select Committee report on central–local relations, *Rebuilding Trust*, is an eloquent testimony to the disquiet that had arisen. The Labour government's response to these concerns offers some hopes for greater partnership, but central control has not yet been significantly reduced. The issue is one of autonomy and agency: how central and local governments exercise powers and what freedoms for local variety remain. The forces that impinge on policy, finally, go beyond the nation-state. The chapter examined the influence of the European Union on both local councils and on the regional framework of funding. For individual councils,

European funds can have a significant effect. But the influence goes wider than this, since European rules require that bids for funding be organised on a regional basis, a factor that is part of the increasing regional profile of urban regeneration projects.

The conclusion of this chapter is that urban policy depends on a complex system of multi-layered relationships: between public and private; central and local; local–regional–national and international. But the traditional orthodoxy of policy and politics, that they operate within democratic structures which are responsive to local communities and afford citizens real participation in urban affairs, is thus open to question. It is these issues of democratic pluralism and accountability which are considered in the next chapter.

# 5
# Urban Politics: Democracy for All

Urban politics reflects the consensus, divisions and expectations of democratic society. At local level people express their views and demands through voting, standing for elections and working towards their goals through parties, interest groups – and protest. In this the local council, as the legitimate, democratically elected body, plays a pivotal role. Since 1979, however, urban politics have become more complex as governments have devolved decisions to a variety of unelected agencies. These bodies have been used to deliver services, as in the case of the National Health Service Trusts, to manage services delivered by others, as in the case of the Training and Enterprise Councils, and to emphasise partnership in problem-solving, as in the case of urban regeneration and in the Action Zones for unemployment, education and health established in 1998. What has characterised all of these bodies is that they are appointed, rather than elected, are funded wholly or substantially from the centre and have specific remits and terms of reference.

The late 1990s, however, have seen a renewed concern for the vitality of local communities and local democracy, highlighted by the Labour government's modernising project. The ideas of community and locality have been challenged in the debate over modern city life, and this chapter considers their contemporary relevance. The arena of urban policy involves a variety of political actors: elected representatives and their constituents; organisations of all kinds – business and other sectional interests; a multiplicity of voluntary bodies; and, in some areas, neighbourhood fora expressing sub-city needs. The local arena thus claims an important part in the plural state as a setting for the expression of citizenship and the opportunity for participation. But citizenship, as with other elements of the state over the past two decades, has been subject to vigorous analysis. From the Conservatives' 'active citizen' of the mid-1980s, through the consumer-orientation of the 'Citizen's Charter', to the obligations and rights of Labour's third way – debate has focused on the individual's role in political and civil society.

If urban politics are to flourish, then local democracy needs to be revitalised to overcome problems of apathy, division and exclusion. Currently, the reality is that local elections are marked by low turnouts, that those who participate in interest group and other action are middle-class and predominantly middle-aged, that citizens are poorly informed and that apathy about local institutions is the norm. This chapter considers these assertions. But the problem is more than apathy. There is now a sharp focus on the issue of social exclusion, that is, there are barriers to full membership of civil society which arise from poverty, long-term unemployment, a lack of educational skills and from discrimination on racial, gender or other grounds. The chapter ends by analysing the extent to which exclusion threatens to undermine democratic action itself. Can civility and the civic remain the rationale of the city, as political tradition from Aristotle onwards has held?

## Claiming democratic legitimacy

The advent of a Labour government committed to decentralisation, empowerment and the reform of local democracy has highlighted the need for effective processes to facilitate action on urban problems. Urban policy and politics have traditionally been seen as the remit of local bodies democratically elected and accountable to local citizens. Accountability has two aspects: responsibility *for* and answerability *to*, that is, giving an account for actions taken and being held to account for these actions. Traditional accountability through elections is under-pinned through the formal requirements of financial and administrative probity, by the Audit Commission's analyses of local authority services and its role in directing the production of performance indicators, by judicial review, and by the Local Government Commissioner (Ombudsman) that deals with complaints of maladministration.

The effectiveness of traditional accountability, however, has been called into question by public choice theory (see Chapter 3). Local public servants, it is alleged, are only superficially accountable to their local authority and through it to the electorate. In practice public services are marked by bureaucratic self-interest which protects and inflates budgets and programmes. The result is that bureaucratic hierarchies dictate service provision and elected members are poor protectors of effective choice. From this perspective representative democratic accountability is flawed. Elections are a necessary but not sufficient condition of local democracy. Elections do not offer real alternatives, since citizens will continue to vote for expanded services – particularly where, as at local level, it is the national taxpayer not the local ratepayer who picks up the largest part of the bill. By contrast, the political right believes, individuals are best protected through market accountability.

The Conservative governments' mistrust of public bureaucracies led to the setting up of alternative bodies to deliver services. In the 1980s local elected bodies had some of their functions transferred to quasi-nongovernmental organisations (quangos) run by appointed members. Research suggests that, by the mid-1990s, there were 6 424 executive and advisory quangos; of the 5 575 executive quangos 5 207 or 90 per cent operated at local level (Hall and Weir, 1996). At between 66 000 and 73 500 people, board members outnumber councillors by a ratio of nearly 3:1. Disquiet over the position of quangos centres on their accountability, secrecy, public probity, systems of appointment (including issues of patronage) and, relatedly, the fragmentation of decision-making of which they are a significant cause. The level of disquiet over these issues has led to the system being described by Morris (Morris, 1994), Stewart (Stewart, 1992) and others as a 'new magistracy', an unelected lay elite whose powers are insufficiently subject to public scrutiny. Public authority becomes privatised and the result is a 'democratic deficit' in public life. The objective of the Labour government in 1997 was to widen democratic channels, increase public involvement and consultation and improve electoral processes. But while the Labour government wants to see more women and ethnic minority members on appointed boards, it remains reluctant to allow local councils to conduct inquiries into quangos in their areas.

In general the public has a high level of satisfaction with the way local authorities run services. They also support elected bodies over unelected ones, though this is not the same as supporting local government. Dunleavy and Weir's 1994 research showed that, in relation to rented housing, education, health authorities, employment training and police service, only in rented housing did a clear majority choose councils as the right body to be in charge (Dunleavy and Weir, 1994). On the other hand there was little support for these services being run by self-governing oligarchies. But there is positive support for local councils as a good way to organise and control local services, highly rated in comparison with other agencies such as hospital trusts and TECs and satisfaction with councillors is at a comparatively high level (Miller and Dickson, 1996). In 1998 MORI figures, taken from the first national citizens' panel study conducted for the Cabinet Office, showed that the public were evenly divided on whether services were improving or not, but many local government services were still well regarded, notably schools, refuse collection, libraries and leisure services. Again, people wanted more information, especially on the details of local services, how money is spent, and projected improvements (Page and Elgood, 1998). The public and councillors also agree that on average quangos and the private sector are not a good method of delivering public services, with 64 per cent of the public and 73 per cent of councillors believing that local quangos should be accountable to local councils (Stoker, 1996a).

For democratic accountability to be effective in practice, standards in public life must be high, a theme which has concerned both Conservative and Labour governments in recent years. In 1995 the first report of the Committee on Standards in Public Life (the Nolan Comittee) drew up seven principles of public life: selflessness, integrity, objectivity, accountability, openness, honesty and leadership (CM 2850, 1995). In 1996 Lord Nolan's Committee published a second report, on Local Public Spending Bodies (including higher and further education bodies, grant-maintained schools, TECs and housing associations) and proposed a stronger new regime (Cm 3270-I, 1996).

Currently councillors' conduct is subject to the National Code of Local Government Conduct of 1975 (revised 1990) which covers declaration of pecuniary and non-pecuniary interests, representation on other bodies, relations with staff, dealings with the media and disclosure of information. Councillors also have a fiduciary duty to council tax payers and are the only elected representatives who can be surcharged, that is held personally responsible for a local authority's financial misdemeanours (a position that will change when surcharge is abolished, see below). Similarly, there are non-statutory codes which apply to officers, which cover conflict of interest, political neutrality, relations between officers and councillors, acceptance of hospitality, dual employment and disclosure of information. Statutory responsibility is split between the chief executive, the chief finance officer and the monitoring officer (a role which may be filled, and frequently is, by the chief executive). The monitoring officer, a post established by s 5 of the Local Government and Housing Act 1989, has a duty to report, to all members of the local authority, on proposals which have led or may lead to illegal acts, contravention of statutory codes of practice, or maladministration. The monitoring officer's role will become much more proactive and positive under the government's 1998 *Modern local government* white paper. Similarly under the Local Government Finance Act 1988 the chief finance officer has a duty to report any decisions involving 'unlawful' expenditure or financial loss or deficiency.

In July 1997 the Nolan Committee published its third report, a review of conduct in local government, including pecuniary and other interests, procedures relating to contracting out, safeguards against planning abuses, audit, the statutory role of officers and officer codes and rules, and the councillors' national code of conduct (Cm 3702-I, 1997). It proposed that a new offence of the 'misuse of public office' should replace the current system of surcharging councillors and officials. As well as other reforms, Nolan proposed that each local authority should have a standards committee to monitor behaviour and exercise disciplinary powers.

The Labour government response was positive, but went beyond the Nolan recommendations by adding external scrutiny. It proposed, in the consultation paper *Modernising Local Government – a new ethical framework* (DETR, 1998e) and the White Paper (Cm 4014, 1998), a new independent national body, a Standards Board, which would investigate all allegations of malpractice and would have powers to impose penalties ranging from public censure, through suspension (up to six months) to disqualification of councillors (up to 5 years). These measures became part of the draft Local Government (Organisation and Standards) Bill published in March 1999 (Cm 4298, 1999). The proposal that the surcharge powers of the Audit Commission be abolished, while not included in the March 1999 draft Bill, remained a possibility for the final legislation.

The Local Government (Organisation and Standards) Bill set down that the Secretary of State (in England) and the National Assembly (in Wales) could specify the principles governing members' behaviour and issue model codes of conduct consistent with these principles. Each local authority (and, in addition, Police and Fire Authorities) would be required to adopt a code of conduct, incorporating the mandatory provisions of the model code, make them available for public inspection, and send a copy of the code to the national Standards Board. Councillors have a duty to comply with the code (rather than the current requirement under s. 83 of the Local Government Act 1972 'to be guided' by the National Code of Local Government Conduct). The White Paper stresses that the code of conduct will cover: councillors' discharge of their representative function; conduct in relation to pecuniary and other interests; the relationship between councillors and officers; rules on expenses and allowances claims; and the use of council facilities. The White Paper also proposed a statutory duty on each council to maintain a public Register of Members' Interests.

The Local Government (Organisation and Standards) Bill also laid down that every council must set up a Standards Committee, to include at least one independent member, with duties to oversee the model code of conduct, advise members, and consider reports from the Standards Board. The government rejected the Nolan recommendation that these should have disciplinary powers, which would be given instead to the national Board. The Standard Boards (one each in England and Wales) would consist of members appointed by the Secretary of State as ethical standards officers or as ordinary members. The ethical standards officers investigate cases, following written allegations to the Board, and are required to produce reports. Where serious failures are established, these will be referred to an Adjudication Panel (one each for England and Wales), working through case panels, for judgement. There would also be a new Code of Conduct for council employees. Though not in the draft Bill, it is anticipated that the rules on political activity of senior officers will remain, but with an increase in salary thresholds at which posts are 'politically restricted', and more protection for 'whistleblowers'. In Scotland, a similar standards commission was proposed.

The conclusion on these moves is that a revitalised local democracy, pushing forward the regeneration and anti-poverty programmes, must be sustained by a local politics which rests on probity and high standards. These standards must be publicly demonstrated through a uniform system and independent scrutiny, if public confidence is to be sustained.

## Local democracy and local community

As Chapter 3 showed, local government as an integral part of the democratic state has its justification in tradition and ideology. The modern local government system embodies a number of assumptions.

First is the legitimation of local government as the creation of statute law, subject to parliamentary sovereignty. Within that framework local councils are elected bodies answerable to their electorates, responsible for raising local revenues (the rates) and delivering a wide range of services as multipurpose rather than single-function authorities. National governments lay down laws, exercise control over standards, give financial aid and have default powers. But a second set of traditional assumptions go beyond this politico-legal framework. From John Stuart Mill onwards, claims of local self-government have also been grounded in beliefs about the rights and duties of individuals to take part in local affairs, both as voters and as elected representatives. Locality and place are important factors in this involvement. The locality is the first arena of political action with which most people are familiar. The belief in community as the setting for obligations and rights goes back to the Greeks. A long tradition of civic republicanism from Aristotle onwards has conceived community as the public realm in which people achieve citizenship through the defence of and participation in community life. Following John Stuart Mill's promotion of civic participation as self-realisation and political education, subsequent writers have seen the participatory community as central to the development of individuals as political beings. Integral to this tradition is the idea of community as fraternity, that sense of common purpose, mutual respect and connectedness which is generally, but not exclusively, locality-based. Community, then, both acts as the arena for urban politics and invigorates it.

In the late twentieth century debate about this set of assumptions, including the realities as opposed to the myths of participation and community, intensified as the role and functions of local government changed. One challenge came from the use of markets as a major way of empowering people through fostering choice, views which were implemented progressively through the 1980s. On the opposite side, strong democracy at the local level continues to be defended on instrumental grounds (decisions and services are best achieved at the lowest level of feasibility) and on anti-tyranny grounds (dispersal of power is essential to a democratic state).

Local democracy in practice operates on the basis of party, which is an important channel of accountability. Political parties are often criticised as being inappropriate to local decision-making, on the grounds that what is needed is consensus and expertise, not party divisions. But local democracy consists of diverse and conflicting interests and political accountability in party terms can be defended as allowing informed choices. Informing choice and managing conflict are central to urban politics. Politics allows for that essential flexibility necessary to cope with ambiguity, crises and uncertainty, and local government should be valued as a site for political activity (Stoker, 1994). Nonetheless, while people vote the party label, voters' enthusiasm for political parties in local councils appears muted (Rao, 1998). Disquiet about the effectiveness of party politics in involving local people – especially where one party has been in power locally for long periods – has led to those proposals for democratic reform considered in Chapter 7.

In spite of these anxieties, local democracy matters. As Chapter 3 showed, community is an important concept in the theories that underpin local politics. In the late 1990s the Labour government took the view that for local democracy and accountability to flourish, community life must be strengthened. But the definition of community is open to debate. Communitarians of the right stress the need to return to traditional family, moral values and local institutions, building responsibility around core values which constitute the 'community as a moral voice' (Etzioni, 1993). Communitarians of the left believe community must revive collective public action and solidarity. Both sides stress the need to develop citizens who take their responsibilities seriously while respecting the rights of others. This theme is prominent in Prime Minister Blair's view of community and its members: 'Strong communities depend on shared values and a recognition of the rights and duties of citizenship' (Blair, 1998b: 12). Though in the past there may have been a tendency for people to take their duties for granted, now they would be positively encouraged and if need be enforced, for example reinforcing the obligation on parents to bring children up to be competent responsible citizens through 'home–school contracts' between schools and parents.

There is a real difficulty in how community can be expressed in modern, mobile societies. The separation of work and residence, and patterns of social relations based on professional and private interests rather than on kin and place, call into question the reality as opposed to the myth of community. It has long been recognised that no single type or size of unit is optimal for achieving the twin goals of citizen effectiveness and system capacity (Dahl and Tufte, 1974: 140). Research undertaken for the 1992 Local Government Review showed that people identify themselves in different communities for different purposes, including their home neighbourhood, where their work is located, where they shop and where their leisure interests are situated. The result is a difference between the 'objective community' and the 'felt community' and, as research shows, neither has corresponded particularly closely to actual local government areas. In practice, people do not have a unique sense of territory but a set of 'overlay maps' on a range of spatial scales. This attachment to place is strongest at the 'home area', typically smaller than the local authority area. But a significant minority have no strong attachment at any level (Young, Gosschalk and Hatter, 1996).

As well as attachment to place, people see themselves as part of communities of interest, sharing common outlooks and concerns with those in like circumstances (communities of identity) or of like views. The interests which people have are not necessarily territorial. Membership of groups and organisations can be based on a variety of attributes and aims, including individual characteristics (gender, ethnicity, religion, language) and pursuits (leisure, charitable action, professional solidarity) which expand beyond territorial jurisdictions. Combining place and interests gives rise to community as the expression of social networks, set in different physical scales from neighbourhood to city. Community is thus a social as well as a physical construct within which debate, taking decisions, public initiatives and public action – that is, politics – can occur (Mabileau, Moyser, Parry and Quantin, 1989). It is this actual network of social interaction which is important to participation, not whether people have a sense of community in subjective terms.

Despite the diversity of meanings of and values attached to community, there have long been attempts to give expression to it in urban politics. It is frequently seen as the opposite but complementary force to that globalisation of economic action which is now an important element of the framework of urban policy. The search for community has idealistic and practical objectives. At the ideal level the goal is the 'good community' of self-reliance, mutual help and public concern. Many would see this as a utopian vision, given that it remains problematic as to whether the locality is the primary basis for interpersonal relations for most city residents. Thus, while for some people neighbourhood-based social networks, services and political action are relevant, for others the neighbourhood remains the 'community of limited liability' (Janowitz, 1967) which fills certain pragmatic functions while not constraining individuals' choice of friends, schools and leisure and other activities. By contrast, networking by some groups themselves forms the basis for community. A good example is the networking of women, especially ethnic women in very poor communities, engaged in mutual assistance and campaigning for support from public and voluntary agencies (B. Jordan, 1996). At the practical level, neighbourhood organisations may channel inputs into council decision-making, be used by local authorities to deliver services, or provide consultation channels with local people; it is these features that have commended decentralised bodies to Labour's modernising project.

It is necessary to recognise, however, that 'community' is not neutral. Community can be criticised because of its defects: communities can be reactionary and oppressive, a labelling and exclusionary device to mark out ethnic, cultural and belief groups. There are divisions within communities and questions then arise as to whether membership is elective or non-elective and to what extent individuals have the opportunity to leave the community or to have voice within it (Frazer, 1996). Recognising these divisions is to acknowledge that Tönnies' (1955) 'traditional' community based on kinship, locality and mutuality (as opposed to the contractual relationships of *Gesellschaft* bound together by friendship) cannot be recreated. This does not preclude seeking a revived civic culture and the virtues of liberty, equality and fraternity. How this might be achieved is explored in the next section.

### Citizenship

Empowering people and communities and fostering a more inclusive society are the current objectives of government. Being a citizen in a more participative democracy underpins attempts to push forward the urban agenda. The rights and duties of citizenship, and its expression in Aristotelian civic *virtu* (only by taking an active part in the city republic do individuals realise their true human nature), have long been a matter of debate. Overall, though legally citizenship inheres in the nation-state, in practice individuals are citizens of the European Community and exercise citizenship in sub-national fora at county, district, parish and neighbourhood levels. Attempts to discern a 'local citizenship' specifically attached to locality and separate from national ties, however, remains inconclusive (Miller and Dickson, 1996).

Citizenship incorporates two major elements: that of human agency (humans have autonomy and engage in purposive action) and that of mutual community membership (the ties of social relations and political association), that is, active citizenship inheres in community membership and demonstrates *civitas* or civic virtue of fraternity and mutual obligation. But this is challenged on the grounds that it is an ideal rather than a reality.

In recent years the concept of citizenship has been subject to renewed interest. To those on the right, the obligations of citizenship are the reciprocal of civil and political rights and voluntary action – Douglas Hurd's call in 1989 to the 'active citizen' – has moral ascendancy over demands for collective state provision. To those on the left, following T.H. Marshall, citizenship includes social rights collectively expressed, and positive action to facilitate (including removing discriminatory barriers to) individual and group involvement in decision-making. Now, Labour seeks reform on the basis of an obligation-based conception of citizenship. Citizenship must be earned through work, with the labour market as the prime route to inclusion in society. These ideas are important in Labour's policies to achieve the inclusive society: in the New Deal and its obligations to take up work/training/voluntary agency placements or lose benefits; in the need for wider consultation and community involvement; in multiagency working to address problems of law and order, health and community care.

The differing emphases of right and left both incorporate ideas of citizen obligations and duties, as did Marshall himself (Marshall, 1950). Today, obligations are again at the centre of debate, as governments change the provisions of the welfare state and its reach. In this view citizenship is not a pre-existing legal status but rather something that is achieved by contributing to the life of society, most notably by work. Work is the passport to social and economic citizenship and the way out of social exclusion (Plant, 1998). Among the other duties, as opposed to the rights, of citizenship are the moral duty to vote and take part in civic life, to obey the law and pay taxes and for individuals to take responsibility for themselves and their families, reducing their dependency on the welfare state.

Exercising citizenship has also been critically scrutinised by feminist writers. The argument is that state structures are male-dominated and hierarchical and that equality of rights and power is played out in the private as well as the public domain, the family as much as the workplace or political arena. In other words, the symbolic spatial division of the male public sphere from the female private sphere is charged as illegitimate, requiring positive public action to challenge it. Ethnic minorities, and gay and lesbian groups, also claim difference and diversity, rejecting the assertion of a generalised, homogenised community and citizenry. Similarly, ecologists believe citizenship must be expanded to include consideration of future generations and of the natural world *per se*. One conclusion is that the concept of citizenship must be pluralistic: postmodern in its acknowledgement of the heterogeneity of contemporary allegiances and of 'a politics of difference'. This in turn highlights the tension between pluralistic concepts and the notions of universality and equality of rights found in the foundations of citizenship.

In the 1980s neoliberals attempted to redefine the citizen as consumer. This has been challenged on the grounds that people are not passive consumers but citizens with the constitutional and democratic rights by which they not merely purchase services but shape them. It is a citizen's right to be involved in decisions. By contrast to the neoliberal right, the Labour government's consulation paper *Local Democracy and Community Leadership* stressed that what was being sought was greater democratic legitimacy for local government and a new brand of involved and responsible citizenship.

## Participation

Getting people involved in decision-making, making them active citizens, must be more than mere tokenism, as Arnstein's seminal article of 1969 reminds us (Arnstein, 1969). In Arnstein's 'ladder' of participation, the first two rungs – Therapy and Manipulation – were effectively non-participation. Rungs three to five – Informing, Consultation and Placating – were degrees of tokenism. Only the top three rungs – Partnership, Delegated Power and Citizen Control – were effective degrees of citizen power. In the present British situation, what is needed for participation to be more than top–down information and public relations is for representative democracy to make a more vigorous attempt to reach out to citizens. This can be done by improved consultative procedures, being receptive rather than dismissive to protest or challenges, encouraging participation through referenda and civic fora, 'user control' through such methods as giving tenants' management organisations control over the delivery of a service and setting up neighbourhood/community councils. In this way participants are involved as stakeholders and contributors, not just as a passive audience.

The motivations behind action are similarly various. People take part for instrumental reasons, because they have an interest in outcomes. More widely, the motivation may be altruistic, taking action on behalf of the community. A further stimulus to participation arises from grassroots protest, often intense but shortlived, for example over development or environmental issues.

Participation, as is well known, differs among people according to their personal characteristics, life circumstances and attitudes. It is the middle-aged, middle-class and better-educated who participate most. Attitudes are also important: higher levels of political interest and of identification with party have a stronger impact on personal involvement than wealth or education (Mabileau, Moyser, Parry and Quantin, 1989). The relation between community identity and participation is, however, ambiguous. While a sense of community may demonstrate a positive attitude towards the local political environment, there is less evidence that this translates into high participation in local politics and community activity (Rallings, Temple and Thrasher, 1994).

The outcomes of these processes are that strategies may be 'top-down' and local authority controlled, or bottom–up attempts aimed at greater power sharing. At the formal level, participation has for 30 years been a requirement of the planning process. Public participation became a statutory obligation with the 1968 and 1971 Town and Country Planning Acts, with the Skeffington Committee on Public Participation in Planning Report of 1969 advocating a variety of techniques (Skeffington, 1969). At the same time, there is concern that while protest against planning decisions can command attention, other voices – those of the homeless and jobless, for example – go unheard (McCarthy, Prism Research and Harrison, 1995). And while access for the disabled has greatly improved, ethnic participation remains low. Local planning authorities, for their part, view public participation as a mixed blessing, time-consuming but, at least from some perspectives, a positive part of the democratic process.

A current proposal for broadening democratic input into decision-making is the use of citizen juries. These panels are a form of deliberative democracy, that is decision-making growing out of more open discussion, reflecting on the opinions of others and pursuing reasoned arguments. By this consultative mechanism a sample of local people form a panel of around 20–25 members which cross-examines witnesses, formulates views and makes recommendations (Stewart, Kendall and Coote, 1994; IPPR, 1996). They can be seen as a practical form of participation, allowing short but intensive involvement in an issue, which is potentially appealing to people who lack the time to become permanently engaged in public affairs. The idea has formed part of Labour's reform suggestions. Evidence from pilot schemes is that councils found they produced better informed recommendations, while jury members learned a lot from the experience, recognised the complexity of local authority working and realised that opinions could change (Hall and Stewart, 1996; Coote and Lenaghan, 1997).

Caution over public enthusiasm for involvement is still necessary. Parry *et al.* emphasise that for most people political participation means making contact with councillors and officials (Parry, Moyser and Day, 1992); as long as the council is doing its job people feel that they do not need or want to get involved (MORI, 1996). In spite of these views, the overwhelming majority of the public agrees that users do not get enough say in how public services are run (MORI, 1996) and do not feel that their council keeps them well informed (Page, 1997).

The key point is not the apathy or non-involvement of people but the need to reinforce and expand opportunities. Not to take part is a matter for individuals. What is important is that when people do wish to participate, the processes and procedures are there to be made use of, that they have the resources (individual or group) to enable them to take part, and that positive action is taken to discover the attitudes of the non-participants. It is these aspects – the opportunity structures for political and social involvement – which are receiving increased attention from policymakers concerned to spread participation to greater numbers of people and particularly to marginalised groups and communities. This means that local authorities must reach out to the public. If services are to be improved, and partnerships built with local people and groups, then councils have to find ways to engage citizens and promote participation and dialogue.

Significant numbers of people do play an active part in urban politics, as elected representatives, or pressure or self-help groups. It remains the case, however, that Britain has the lowest number of councillors per head of population in Europe (with the exception of Greece). The ratio is 2 605 inhabitants per elected member (Council of Europe, 1995). The Labour government's proposals for reorganising the work of local authorities will reduce the numbers still further, a question considered in Chapter 7. Representatives' roles have three dimensions: carrying out functions and services; representing constituents (by taking up a grievance for example); and representing a town's case to other bodies both nationally and in Europe. Labour's reform proposals are specifically aimed at separating executive and scrutiny and advocacy functions. Labour's view is that the backbench representative role is as meaningful as executive leadership. This advocacy role has long been recognised: councillors act as 'tribunes of the people', representing their interests, speaking for them and helping people exercise their rights. Councillors themselves stress their constituency roles (Rao and Young, 1993; Rao, 1993; Young and Rao, 1994). But in practice councillors spend the majority of their time (some 58 per cent) on council and committee meetings, preparing for them, and in meetings with officers. By contrast, dealing with the public and working in partnership with other organisations take up only 15 per cent of councillors' time. It is this situation that the Labour reforms are addressing.

Councillors' part in urban politics is significantly affected by their rate of turnover in office – around 40 per cent over a 4-year period – that raises worrying questions over the way council duties impinge on work and family life (Bloch, 1992). A disproportionate number of retirees are younger councillors, leaving after relatively short periods in office. Overall, while 40 per cent of councillors give personal reasons such as age, health and moving away as reasons for standing down, some 25 per cent cite work related reasons (Game and Leach, with Williams, 1993). These findings raise concerns that there is a trend towards long-serving, effectively full-time, members in committee and other leadership posts existing alongside a group of backbenchers with a high rate of turnover.

Active participation, however, does show an elite bias, with the stereotype of local councillors as middle-aged, middle-class, white, male and relatively highly educated largely correct (Parry, Moyser and Day, 1992). Currently, 55 per cent of councillors are over 55 years of age, 35 per cent are retired, only 27.3 per cent are women and 3.1 per cent members from ethnic minorities (Wright, 1998), a situation which Labour argues must change. Councillors are highly qualified educationally and more than 50 per cent are in paid employment (60 per cent of whom are in the private sector) (Wright, 1998). While membership of voluntary groups displays the same trends as for local councils, there are more women, younger adults, public sector tenants and people from manual working groups than among local councillors (Kearns, 1995).

An important question is what are the effects of these skewed participation rates on urban policy and outcomes. Councillor elites perceive themselves as being at the heart of the policymaking arena, seeing those outside, whether individual citizens or groups, as having much less – even if at some points significant – influence. Councillors are also confident that their own priorities are shared by their electors (Mabileau, Moyser, Parry and Quantin, 1989). This is largely true: the evidence is of a substantial degree of congruence between the priorities of the elite and local people, activists providing an essential link between the two (Parry, Moyser and Day, 1992).

Activists and groups play a major part in urban politics. Voluntary organisations are increasingly important as stakeholders in the community. It is estimated that there are about 200–240 000 organisations (Commission on the Future of the Voluntary Sector in England, 1996). Not all volunteers, moreover, fit the middle-class or mainstream group image. For example, inner-city groups operating under the broad aegis of the Citizen Organising Foundation (a movement derived from American ideas and the work of radical activist Saul Alinsky) focus on organising people to empower them, not to speak for them. The community organising movement, now some 10 years old, is based in east London, Merseyside, Sheffield, the Black Country, Wales and Bristol. It has drawn some 100 000 people into direct action, trained more than 100 local leaders, and is committed to community-based radicalism rather than 'politics as usual'. Some action groups cluster around 'faith communities', both Christian and other faiths, acting with tenant, residents and other groups (Marr, 1996), or with community and youth groups (Holman, 1997). From the 1970s onwards there have also been many new movements – gay and lesbian, black, women's, disability and environmental – which have tried to inject new forms of action into urban politics. A further set of participants are the not-for-profit organisations who run projects and provide consultation and advisory services. Self-help groups are burgeoning, for example local disablement groups and support networks, mostly formed by and for people who have been failed by the traditional services. There are, however, important questions to be asked about the nature of the many kinds of voluntary action and their place in urban politics. It is clear that local institutions, particularly the local council, are heavily involved in creating and moulding the voluntary sector in their areas – through grant regimes and what is termed the contract culture whereby the local authority purchases services from voluntary groups on the basis of formal agreements or contracts. What this means is that voluntary organisations operate within political opportunity structures – partnerships, joint working committees, service contracts, informal networks – that shape what groups are and do.

These moves are not confined to Britain. No civic leader in France, for example, could ignore local associations and in Germany such groups are a major link between citizens and councillors (Wahlberg, Taylor and Geddes, 1994). These trends will accelerate in Britain as Labour promotes linkages between rulers and ruled as essential to a more active community. Through the multiplicity of existing and proposed initiatives, it is hoped that the reality of involvement and power holding will move some way up Arnstein's ladder of participation from non-involvement, through tokenism to genuine decision-sharing.

## More active involvment: from neighbourhoods to deliberative democracy

The Labour government is actively promoting improved consultation and involvement through community decentralisation and other mechanisms. Currently, consultation is a requirement in certain aspects of urban policy, for example town planning, and as part of the conditions for Single Regeneration Budget funding, whereby bids have to include the consultation plans incorporated into the regeneration process. Local authorities must also have a community strand in bids for National Lottery money. In other areas, such as social services, the focus is on clients or users developing services as well as reacting to them, an objective also of community development work generally.

*Box 5.1*   The aims of decentralisation

- To deliver services to particular areas.
- To integrate services within areas.
- To delegate decisions to area managers.
- To delegate decisions to area committees of councillors.
- To encourage local views and local involvement.
- To strengthen democracy through elected neighbourhood councils.

As the summary in Box 5.1 shows, the aims of decentralisation are diverse. Over the past two decades decentralisation to a local area or 'neighbourhood' level has been used both to devolve service delivery and decision-making and to encourage residents to become involved in community life (Hambleton, 1992; Gaster and O'Toole, 1995). Decentralised approaches may reach down even further, where for example local authorities transfer management control to groups of residents for specific purposes, to tenants over estate management, or to the users of leisure centres in the form of management committees. User involvement also exists in social service provision, for example over community mental health centres or centres for disabled people.

Political decentralisation may take a number of forms. Area committees of councillors may cover one or more wards and have varying responsibilities for decisions, budgets and staff (Geddes, 1996). More fundamental changes, for example those in Tower Hamlets in the mid-1980s or Walsall a decade later, may take over the main responsibilities of the council's service committees, with the abolition, or greatly slimmed down versions, of council strategic committees at the centre (Lowndes and Stoker, 1992). The Walsall decentralisation experiment took on a third phase under a successful Single Regeneration Budget bid, when seven neighbourhood committees were established; in November 1997 these became elected bodies with devolved (if limited) budgets and functions. Other councils are experimenting with similar schemes, aimed at devolving decisions to wards and neighbourhoods, encouraging community-based planning, bringing councillors into closer contact with residents and re-examining the role of professionals in local working. The conclusion is that the place of community neighbourhoods in urban politics ranges from consultation to collaboration, from tokenism to activism. In general, decentralisation has been more successful in promoting access, information and influence and in allowing greater management discretion to officers, than in devolving political control over decision-making. There continues to be considerable ambiguity, as Geddes puts it, as to whether decentralisation is really a more participatory model of local democracy or merely consultation within a representative democracy framework (Geddes, 1996: 17).

Consultation and participation are not confined to neighbourhood decentralisation. Local councils are pioneering new ideas, including community plans, citizens' panels, local fora, surveys and focus groups and the use of the Internet, to foster working partnerships between policymakers and local people. In response to the Children Act, Local

Agenda 21 and children's rights, a number of local authorities are involving children in service planning and setting up Youth Fora or youth councils, while other councils have set up Equality committees, or committees for women and older people. All these innovations might be seen as more effective consultation, a step up the participation ladder. Overall, it is estimated that 83 per cent of local authorities have complaints procedures, 69 per cent regularly carry out customer surveys, 34 per cent hold neighbourhood fora, 59 per cent produce public service standards and customer contracts, and 27 per cent have user groups and user panels (Dawson, 1995). Some authorities open up council meetings to public questions and increasing numbers are using information technology to set up 'one stop shops' and call centres to provide service users with better access and information. These activities will become more important as 'best value' proposals require local councils to show evidence of community involvement in reviewing and evaluating services and reforms to local government require greater consultation.

If more active community involvement is to be boosted then, it is argued, low electoral turnout must be addressed. The reasons for low turnout are varied: the structure of local electoral systems, the restricted powers of local councils, the confusion over responsibilities of different agencies. Non-voting is particularly worrying among young people: 52 per cent say they never vote in local elections and 36 per cent are not even registered to vote. In addition, nearly a third of all potential voters in a MORI sample believed that voting cannot make much difference (Game, 1998). In London, 24 per cent of the African and Asian population fail to register to vote, as compared with 6 per cent of the white population; Operation Black Vote was set up in 1996 to address what was seen as a 'black democratic deficit' (Bryant, 1998).

A further criticism is that local elections are merely a form of referenda on national party performances. But while local voting may indeed reflect the state of the parties nationally, people still vote for a particular candidate or policy, or on the record of the local council, even where this was at variance with their national allegiance (Miller, 1988). It is true, however, that turnout in local elections in Britain is notably lower than that in many European countries and it is suggested that this is because of the greater powers councils in those countries enjoy. What is evident in Britain is that party activity stimulates turnout: higher levels of voting depend on the marginality of the contest, heightened political awareness (due to controversial local issues for example), or more intense party campaigning (Rallings and Thrasher, 1995).

A different argument, however, challenges these perspectives on the roots of 'apathy'. One perspective takes the position that only by the direct representation of particular sections of society – the disabled, women's groups and minorities – on decision-making bodies will their interests be defended. The second perspective looks for justification to deliberative democracy rather than the traditional claims for participation on instrumental, self-interested grounds. Deliberative democracy rests on the giving and taking of reasons in discussion. As a result, citizens relate to each other not simply as bargainers defending their self-interest but as participating in reasoned debate from which new positions and understandings – and better decisions – will emerge (Stoker, 1997: 166).

## Urban politics and the informed citizen

Taking part in urban politics demands information and, in respect of complex matters such as planning, a degree of expertise. Both the amount and credibility of information provided by local councils has increased over the last ten years (MORI, 1996). Improved awareness is fostered through the print and broadcast media and by electronic communication and information technology, for example videoconferencing which enables customers to have face to face contact with a range of services through an enquiry booth. The new information and communication technologies can be seen as offering access to political, social, economic and cultural opportunities, strengthening inclusion. These technologies are thus becoming the conditions for participation in the information age (Percy-Smith, 1995; 1996). It remains the case, nevertheless, that the new electronic developments have been driven more by organisational and technological imperatives than by the needs of citizens and promote consumerist as opposed to democratic values (Bellamy, Horrocks and Webb, 1995). Nevertheless there are hopes that under the government's forthcoming 'Better government' proposals, public services will develop the capacity to be delivered online, with the sharing of information between services in 'one-stop' electronic government. But there are reservations as to whether the new information and communications technology will overcome problems of the exclusion of the poor and other groups without the necessary skills, time or resources. To have positive results, electronic advances need to offer skills and access training to promote participation and be combined with better delivery of public services – combining the citizen as consumer with the citizen as political actor.

On-line and interactive systems will continue to expand. But at present, the main avenues of public access to information are official information and public relations activities and local print and broadcast media. The main sources combine both local authority and journalist sources – local print and electronic media, civic newspapers and leaflets delivered door-to-door. The strength of local journalism is important: research indicates that people's knowledge of their elected representatives is influenced by the strength of the local newspaper. If councillors appear in a local newspaper which is a widely-read weekly, then they become well known (MORI, 1996). In the late-1990s the local print media were economically buoyant, with some 1 370 provincial newspapers and a dramatic slowing of the decline in sales. There is still tough competition from free newspapers (which now outnumber local paid-for publications and generally lack in-depth news coverage). The syndication of features and editorial material within media conglomerates has traditionally raised issues of independence. The concentration of media ownership of the regional and local press evident in the 1980s, however, is now diversifying, with companies concentrating on provincial newspapers. As a result there is evidence of re-establishing community news within the new groupings and improved editorial quality (Greenslade, 1998). There is also a growing interest in community newspapers and newsletters.

For broadcast as opposed to print media, radio plays a part in providing information, even though, outside the major conurbations, it is sub-regional rather than local in coverage, and consolidation and acquisitions have meant that ownership is concentrated in wider holdings rather than being purely local. Some 60 per cent of people listen to commercial radio each week and there are more than 200 local and regional stations; most have a legal obligation to provide news. The commercial sector has targeted ethnic minority audiences, something the BBC has followed, and identified new audiences and new formats for radio. While independent local radio stations (ILRs) attract 40 per cent of audience share against BBC local radio's 9.6 per cent, BBC local and regional radio increased its audience in the late 1990s. In addition, small-scale community radios are organised by a range of local groups to provide services for niche markets. Demand is growing for greater public access to radio, through the expansion of these small-scale radio services run by and for the community, funded through public money and private donations (Murroni, Irvine and King, 1998).

A new Freedom of Information bill is now in process. The Freedom of Information White Paper of 1997 proposed that duties should be laid on all public sector bodies, including councils. But there are still questions of whether there should be charges for information requested and the extent of exemption on grounds of commercial confidentiality. A major concern is that law enforcement will be excluded entirely from the provisions. For its part, local authority provision of information is governed by the Local Government (Access to Information) Act of 1985. This provides the public and elected representatives with statutory rights of access to information in relation to local authorities and some other public bodies and opened up council and committee meetings to the public and the press. The Act appears to have been effective in laying down standards for openness and accountability and four-fifths of local authorities go beyond the minimum requirements. There are still concerns, however, that the use of closed sessions by committees remains common and this forms a part of the rationale behind Labour's proposals for reforming local authority committee systems. New arrangements on openness will also be needed as a consequence of these reforms. Under the existing system access to information is tied to meetings of the council and its committees; opening up the mayor and cabinet structures will need new arrangements. Currently, there are also legal constraints on what councils may promote. Section 2 of the 1986 Local Government Act prohibits the publication of material which 'in whole or in part appears to be designed to affect public support for a political party'. Section 28 of the 1988 Local Government Act bans councils from intentionally promoting a positive view of homosexuality. The clause was also included in the Education Act 1993, a move criticised by the British Medical Association and others on the grounds of the need for more educational information in this area. The Labour government is pledged to repeal Section 28 in the near future.

Other findings show that the aims of local information policies have been mixed. Public use of the 1985 Act is mainly through attendance at meetings which, while important, remains limited (Policy Studies Institute/DOE, 1995). Print and broadcast journalists are more likely to make use of informal sources of information than official minutes and papers. The public still feels that it does not have enough information; those authorities which kept users of services informed tend to be more favourably regarded (Page, 1996).

## Inclusion and exclusion

Improved processes for consultation, increasing participation and generating information, all support the objective of a more vigorous and inclusive urban politics. The aim is to avoid concentrating power in the hands of a narrow elite. The fear is that by enhancing the direct involvement of activists, the disadvantaged and marginalised in society are overlooked. Talking to poor people, listening to what they say and involving them in making policy as well as in local projects, is a major challenge. And it is not just the domination of middle-class interests which raises difficult questions. In the 'third way' approach, questions must be asked about the degree of compulsion that 'revitalising the community' involves: the obligations of citizenship and the requirements to take up New Deal placements could, particularly if the voluntary programme of work for single parents is made compulsory, equate responsibility with conformity and obedience. There are also difficulties on the other side. Minority groups of all kinds may be demanding both equality in recognition and treatment *and* respect for difference. The two demands are thus in constant tension, for the inclusivity of citizenship and the need to acknowledge cultural and other differences.

A key argument in the debate about urban political life has been that there is a growing polarisation of life styles, income and employment such that a minority of people are not just uninvolved but socially isolated and effectively excluded from full citizenship. Thus exclusion refers not just to material deprivation but the accompanying barriers to the exercise of Marshallian social, cultural and political citizen rights. The severely disadvantaged live in a different world, experiencing 'otherness' not communality. Room's definition of social exclusion is instructive here: 'Social exclusion is the process of being detached from the organisation and communities of which the society is composed and from the rights and obligations that they embody' (Room, 1995). Equally important is Goodin's location of the analysis in the different terminologies of citizenship on the one hand and exclusion on the other:

talking in terms of citizenship fixes attention on what is common and central. It fixes attention on what all citizens share. Talking of 'inclusion' and 'exclusion', in contrast, fixes attention – and necessarily so – on boundaries and margins, on what differentiates one class of persons from another.

(Goodin, 1996: 356)

The charges that the term exclusion is merely a euphemism for poverty, or that it is used to disguise a move from redistributive policies to a moralistic agenda stressing self-help and anti-dependency, are part of the debate. So too is the criticism that it suggests a simplistic polarisation between 'included' and 'excluded'. The two dominant arguments, however, focus on the 'underclass' and on discrimination. The first argument states that there are now significant numbers of poor people whose long-term weak attachment to the labour market makes them an underclass, set apart from the rest of society. The second argument is that particular groups are shut out from participation by virtue of their gender, sexual orientation, disablement, or ethnic origin.

The definition of the term underclass, and its composition, is a contested one. At its simplest level, the term refers to that subset of the poor who have chronically low incomes persisting over time – and even generations. Other definitions, stemming from the work of Charles Murray, Lawrence Mead and others in the United States, emphasise personal behaviour or attitudes grounded in poverty, including long-term dependency on state benefits (Murray, 1984; Mead, 1986; 1991). On this basis, Murray claimed that an underclass was evident in Britain (Murray, 1990). Such attitudes and behaviours are often labelled as deviant and dysfunctional – in relation to family structures or school drop-outs for example – and become subject to moral strictures and victim blaming. In this sense, the underclass comes close to that *Lumpenproletariat* of Victorian fears, social and spatially segregated, workless and disaffected. An associated analysis focuses on areas rather than individuals, looking at deprived neighbourhoods where there are high levels of poverty, poor housing and crime. This spatial focus denotes an urban underclass and can carry connotations of racial and cultural difference, though this is not so dominant in British as in American discourse (W.J. Wilson, 1987).

By contrast, economic definitions of the underclass concentrate on long-term relations to the labour market, defining the underclass as those people and families who are detached from stable employment and dependent on state benefits over long periods (Buck, 1996; Smith, 1992). As such they are not part of the class system but a strata separate from it. Other reports have suggested that there is an underclass of up to 200 000 young people aged between 18 and 20 which has fallen through the safety net of education and training and which has little hope of finding work. Unsurprisingly such young people are at high risk of homelessness, drug abuse and of offending (Training and Enterprise Councils, 1996). In terms of attitudes and behaviour, research suggests that people on very low incomes are not guilty of feckless welfare dependency but aspire to a job, a decent home and money to cover bills in the same way as the rest of the population (Kempson, 1996).

The implications of these findings for urban politics are that long-term unemployment and persistent insecurity about jobs, family conditions, home and health combine with income inequalities to set people aside from community activity, both social and political. These factors may affect majorities of people in deprived areas, for example certain housing estates. The concentration of extreme poverty increased in the 1980s, as did that of minority ethnic groups within these areas. Thus space as well as social conditions become polarised so that different groups no longer use the same political fora or meet in the same public places. Cities become segmented into areas which are distanced from each other in physical, experiential and attitudinal terms. Taking part in civic life is severely restricted for those without work (whether lone parents or not), living in poor conditions (including isolation in run-down estates with poor access to transport and other facilities). The fear is that these conditions become a chronic phenomenon with the poor, especially the young, elderly and lone parents, marginalised in the political process. Political leaders are recognising that as well as the traditional explanations for poverty, including de-industrialisation, increased male unemployment and family breakdown, government itself has contributed to the problems of poor neighbourhoods. National policies have added to the difficulties through bad housing design, rent and benefit policies, the residualisation and 'ghettoisation' of social housing, the relative failure of urban initiatives and a lack of a national policy to deal with structural decline.

The concern for urban policy is that these trends reflect a disintegrating social fabric marked by long-term unemployment, growing numbers of lone-parent families, crime and drug abuse. Nearly a quarter of all families in Britain are headed by lone parents, the highest proportion in western Europe. Some 7 out of 10 of these families are dependent on income support. In Britain, these lone parents are likely to be younger, poorer, less educated and to have more dependent children than their European counterparts. In addition, there is a widening gap of ill-health and life-expectancy between deprived areas and the rest of Britain (Willmott, 1996), restricted opportunities for young people and rising crime and incivility. The gap between rich and poor makes it much more difficult to sustain a sense of shared citizenship. Exclusion of some groups from mainstream economic and social life can also pose a serious challenge to the legitimacy of the state and to social cohesion, as the urban riots of the early and mid-1980s appeared to testify. The Labour government takes the view that exclusion is a multi-faceted problem: the 8–10 per cent of people who stay poor, on benefits, leave school with no qualifications, have no work, live in areas where more than half of all crimes are committed and which are marked by drug abuse. A note of caution is needed, however, when considering how policies might reverse these trends. Programmes that equate inclusion with work and obligations raise issues of compulsion, control and enforcement which may add up to 'compulsory inclusion' rather than policies concerned with redistribution and rights. From this perspective it is membership of, and participation in, a democratic political system that makes for social integration, not membership of the labour market and work and family obligations.

It is impossible to speak of exclusion, however, without acknowledging that which arises from racial discrimination (both historical and current) in unemployment and residential patterns. A small proportion, 5 per cent, of all British people are from non-white ethnic minorities, of whom 50 per cent are South Asian and 30 per cent are Afro-Caribbean. Members of the minority population are to be found primarily in urban areas, particularly the major conurbations. London is home to 50 per cent of the ethnic population of Britain. Birmingham, Manchester, Leicester and Bradford also have large concentrations of minorities but there are also considerable numbers living in other urban settlements (Forrest and Gordon, 1993). This concentration has increased over the past decade. Pakistani and Bangladeshi families live in concentrated communities: 'ethnic villages', particularly in West Yorkshire, the West Midlands and east London. Concentration in space terms matters when it is replicated by concentration of disadvantage. On average, Pakistani and Bangladeshi households are twice as large as white ones, and 80 per cent of Pakistanis and Bangladeshis live in households with an income below half the national average. Afro-Caribbean groups have a more open and assimilated social structure, and single-parent households with dependent children are common (Peach, 1996). Within cities, residential patterns are highly clustered and segregated. Patterns of work and residence vary within the minority population. Large numbers of Indians and Pakistanis are owner-occupiers whereas nearly half of Afro-Caribbean and Bangladeshi households are in social housing. For all these groups, unemployment is higher than among whites and youth unemployment is almost three times higher (Church and Summerfield, 1996). Access to housing has both created and reproduced ethnic segregation – in some cases giving rise to what are effectively ghettos – and this has been reinforced by the workings of the labour market. This in turn is amplified, it is argued, by education, with schools in inner-city areas reflecting the segregation of their areas and the lack of choice that individuals have. The cumulative effects of these multifactor divisions is to constrain inclusion in social and political life.

Women, and particularly poor women, also suffer disproportionately from exclusion. Women form larger proportions of marginalised groups such as lone parents and carers, rely more heavily on public transport and are more likely to suffer from the fragmentation consequent on the privatisation of public services. To promote more effective and inclusionary citizenship, local government women's committees (LGWCs) have been established by a number of local authorities, but this remains a minority of councils. Nevertheless, the argument is that more involvement is essential (Phillips, 1996).

One response to these problems has been renewed interest in what constitutes social capital and how it can be strengthened. Most notably promoted by Robert Putnam in analysing social ties in Italy and in America (Putnam, 1993; 1995), social capital refers to that network of relationships, and interpersonal trust, which fosters cooperative working and community wellbeing. In the British context the argument is that economic regeneration flourishes best in communities where there is a high level of social capital, marked by voter turnout, membership in organisations and cooperation for mutual benefit. One anxiety, however, is that lower socioeconomic and less-educated groups have a low participation rate in voluntary organisations. Weaker networks in deprived communities may be the result. It is still thought relevant, nevertheless, to try to foster trust and participation. This is so even given the reservations about what power communities can actually wield when faced with that of business and other elites. A different kind of concern is that participatory involvement and social capital can result in ties between people that are neither benign nor civic minded, for example those gangs, groups and neighbourhoods that exclude on racist or other discriminatory grounds or whose self-interest goes against the well-being of the wider society. Once it is recognised that clarity is needed over what kind of networks and associations are needed to foster community wellbeing, then building social capital can be a positive achievement. It is also argued as a positive way forward for a revitalised set of trust-based values for the twenty-first century (Wilson, 1997).

## Conclusion

Urban politics takes place in a plural state that rests on legitimate political power at local as well as central level. In Britain the legitimacy of local democratic institutions derives from philosophical and administrative traditions inherited from the nineteenth century. In practice, policy is devised and implemented in a system of party politics that manages conflict between interests and groups, carries out a policy agenda and mobilises support for council actions. The public's interest in party politics within local authorities is muted, but there is a generally high level of satisfaction with local services provided by elected councils over those provided by unelected bodies. Since the 1980s the plurality of local power has changed and now incorporates a wide range of appointed bodies, quangos. The existence and work of these bodies has raised the question of democratic accountability and enlarged the debate on how representative governments can be made more responsive to their electorates.

Prime elements of urban politics are the issues raised by citizenship and community. Community, whether seen in locality and area terms or in relation to interest and pressure groups, is increasingly important in drawing in more people to decision-making. Understanding urban politics means addressing the twin aspects of citizenship and participation: what are the rights and duties of citizenship, and how might the duty to be a full member of civic society be fostered? In addition to the theoretical and analytical aspects of this question, the present chapter explored the mechanisms of involvement and their top–down and bottom–up participatory forms. Elected representatives are prime participants in local politics and see their role as leading the political agenda as well as being advocates for their constituents. Active local groups – from business and other interests to voluntary organisations and self-help groups – reflect the tensions as well as the cooperative opportunities in urban politics. As well as traditional representative democracy – elections, councillor and interest group involvement – there is increasing use of new organisations such as citizen juries and neighbourhood bodies. These moves are essential if getting people involved as active citizens is to go beyond tokenism. Consultation is also increasing through the planning system, the use of referenda and other mechanisms and greater and more effective information through a wider use of traditional and new media formats.

It remains the case that questions of democratic accountability and participation need to do more to address the problem of exclusion. The poverty of areas and individuals sets people apart from social and political life. The fear is that this social and spatial polarisation undermines a common public realm and a common allegiance. Though the definition of the underclass remains contentious, social and political exclusion make it difficult to sustain a shared citizenship. If urban policy and politics is to be truly democratic, the alleviation of exclusion is an urgent task, not just for those marginalised by poverty, but also on gender, ethnic and lifestyle grounds. Local democracy, that is, must be accountable to all its citizens.

# 6
## Meeting the Challenge: Reversing Decline and Improving Services

The urban agenda is a challenging one: economic and physical regeneration, civil peace and order, raising standards in education, housing and social services. Under a Labour government these issues have assumed a new urgency, with local authorities playing a major part in tackling social exclusion and in meeting the objectives of improving education, health and unemployment in the most deprived neighbourhoods. These endeavours draw in a variety of political actors, from the public, private and voluntary sectors. These different interests compete for resources and for influence over policy. Though local authorities play a lead role in these processes, they do so within a framework laid down by government, under standards set nationally and through a multiplicity of partnership arrangements.

Urban policy over the past two decades has addressed economic decline and the associated ills of physical and social deprivation. The chapter begins with these issues. Many of the individual projects of the 1980s had come to an end by the mid-1990s, but the philosophy of public–private collaborative action remained under the Labour government. A major criticism of regeneration efforts in recent years has been the extent to which they are property-, as opposed to people-, orientated. And, following from that debate, how social and community issues might be brought back into the renewal process. Bringing the social back in involves tackling decline and the marginalisation of different groups. Overcoming deprivation, facilitating improvements and delivering services all involve political conflict over issues of equality and fairness, and over private and public provision.

The key issue is how to improve an area and the lives of its residents by organising change. The difficulty is that changing the physical, economic and social aspects of poor areas demands action on several fronts. Bringing these actions together requires the cooperation of many agencies, with their own expectations, agendas and ways of

124

working. Frustrations have also arisen because local communities and, in particular, minority groups have not felt that they were a real part of these processes. Positive attempts to include communities in the improvement efforts have become a key element in change. Looking for ways to overcome exclusion goes beyond specific projects. Tackling the marginalisation of the poor in society and the economy is a major objective of the Labour government. It has set up a special Social Exclusion Unit and is promoting a more inclusionary society through its New Deal unemployment policy and through the programmes targeted at the most run-down housing estates. A major difficulty, however, remains. It is minority groups that suffer particular disadvantages in finding good homes and employment. This chapter shows how their disadvantaged position is made worse by discrimination and racism. To tackle these problems, additional resources and specific projects are being introduced.

The regeneration and other projects aimed at reducing poverty and exclusion sit within mainstream programmes that local authorities – increasingly in partnership with other bodies – provide. The chapter begins its consideration of these programmes with an examination of how civil peace is maintained. Combating crime and disorder is central to city wellbeing and local authorities work in partnership with the police to achieve community safety. In addition, the extent to which crime and poverty are linked and the relations between the policy and community groups remain major issues in the law and order debate.

If local authorities are being increasingly drawn into the strategies for community safety, their role in education is showing, it is argued, the reverse. Local education authorities (LEAs) once held the controlling position in providing public education. But the determination of central governments to raise standards has imposed duties on LEAs to meet national curriculum targets, devolve decisions and budgets to schools and, where schools are deemed to be 'failing', pass responsibility to new bodies. These changes raise questions of responsibility and accountability as well as opening new possibilities and opportunities for solving problems.

In housing, though the major responsibility for new build homes has passed to housing associations, local authorities are still major landlords. This is so even though many council houses were bought by tenants under 'right to buy' legislation in the 1980s. In the early twenty-first century the key question is whether 'social housing' is in danger of becoming a residual welfare provision, with increasing polarisation between rich and poor areas and with homelessness a seemingly intractable problem. To meet its objective of a more inclusionary society the Labour government is encouraging local councils to work with other groups to bring estates 'back from the edge' of poverty and despair.

Concerted action is also the government's strategy to deliver improved health services and to end the divisions between health and community care at local level. Local authorities will increasingly take part in health planning and health improvement programmes. In disadvantaged areas new Health Action Zones (HAZs) will offer opportunities for innovative schemes delivered through multiagency partnerships. Tackling health and social care are part of the effort to improve the wellbeing of city dwellers, especially the poor and those living in poor neighbourhoods. But all citizens are affected by the quality of life in town and cities. The chapter ends, therefore, by considering the increasing pressure to find the 'sustainable city', reconciling the needs for growth with protecting the environment. How to achieve sustainable cities is climbing the political agenda, as people become more concerned about pollution, traffic and transport and how present trends will affect future generations. Pressures to improve the quality of life in cities comes from national, international and European sources. Governments are increasingly trying to incorporate environmental targets into their urban policies, to be carried out in large measure by local authorities. Transport policy is a good example: the 1998 White Paper and the subsequent legislation depend on local plans and permit the proceeds of local congestion and other taxes to be ploughed back into improved public transport systems.

The sustainable city brings the question full circle: how do we reverse the physical and economic decline of our worst urban neighbourhoods?

## Local regeneration

Economic growth and physical development are at the top of the urban agenda. At the beginning of the twenty-first century the main thrust of regeneration policies remains the competition for funds within the Single Regeneration Budget process and the local public–private partnerships, which will work increasingly within the Regional Development Agency structures. The aims of regeneration are to improve areas both physically and economically. The government's objectives were set out in a policy statement in 1998 and are summarised in Box 6.1.

*Box 6.1*     The objectives of local regeneration

---

- Improve employment prospects, skills and education.
- Address social exclusion; improve opportunities through community development.
- Promote sustainable regeneration and improve and protect the environment.
- Improve quality of life and people's capacity to participate in regeneration activities.
- Achieve better integration of programmes through partnerships and community and voluntary group involvement.
- Support and promote growth in local economies and businesses.

(Department of the Environment, Transport and the Regions, 1998a)

---

These goals were reiterated in the SRB Round Five Bidding Guidance, with priorities listing education and employment skills; addressing social exclusion; sustainable regeneration; local economic growth; tackling crime and drug abuse. The new Single Regeneration Budget allocates £770 million in new money over the 3-year expenditure plan period 1998–2001, with a further £800 million for the New Deal for Communities (see below).

Promoting economic wellbeing involves production and distribution issues that can result in political tensions over priorities between development, property-led projects and social needs. These choices are made more harsh by the competition for funding, though the Labour government's refocused Single Regeneration Budget is targeted more closely on areas of severest social deprivation in 50 most deprived local authorities in England. Under the Guidance to Round Five of the SRB, and the DETR working paper *Community-Based Regeneration Initiatives*, local authorities must show they have involved their communities in the development of their SRB bids and regeneration programmes. In the light of these competing pressures, localities have understandably supported all approaches, from favouring inward investment and indigenous resources to emphases on places and on people, as strategies of survival.

As part of these policies local authorities engage in a wide range of economic activities and most have a local development economic strategy. The Local Government and Housing Act 1989 required local authorities to prepare economic development plans; Part V enabled them to set up trading companies, and Section 33 the power to promote the economic development of their areas. The Labour government's White Paper on modernising local government said legislation would lay a duty on local councils to promote the economic, social and environmental wellbeing of their areas, and strengthen their powers to enter into partnerships (CM 4014, 1998). This would be underpinned with a discretionary power to take steps which in their view will promote the wellbeing of their areas. But action goes beyond statutory requirements. Local authority economic strategies support businesses and community bodies such as credit unions, cooperatives and training workshops, or make premises or land available, or have a strategic and coordinating role (Association of Metropolitan Authorities, 1996).

Two concerns have emerged in these endeavours in recent years. One is the competition city improvements face from out-of-town parks for retail, industry and business. Both Conservative and Labour governments have recognised this problem but controversy remains over outer-urban development and over future housing demand (see below). The second and related concern is to attract business through arts, culture and leisure developments. At the same time, local political leaders recognise that any urban renaissance cannot succeed if attracting the affluent back to city centres increases still further the polarisation between successful and deprived areas. It is for these reasons that improved community safety, better transport and lower unemployment are at the heart of urban politics.

### Attacking deprivation and exclusion

Measures to tackle deprivation and exclusion reflect a growing anxiety that, as research for the European Commission put it, 'a two speed city on the American model' is becoming a reality in Europe (Ward, 1994: 1). The European Commission expressed its concern over social exclusion in 1988 and again in its 1993 Green Paper on Social Policy (Commission of the European Communities, 1993). The EU saw social exclusion as a social phenomenon, concentrated in particular communities, which was a threat to social cohesion and economic wellbeing.

A comparable focus is shown by the *Quartiers en Crise* ('Neighbourhoods in Crisis') project which was concerned with the cumulative impact of unemployment, poor housing and education and their links with crime, drugs and a degraded environment. Towns across the EU are part of the project, including Manchester, Paisley and Belfast in the UK.

In Britain, income data reveals the extent of the problem. In the mid-1990s the number of people living below half average income was 13.7 million (Department of Social Security, 1997). Although a 1998 Rowntree Foundation study suggested that the earnings inequality gap may be narrowing, overall inequality was greater in the mid-1990s than at any time since the late 1940s (Hills, 1998a; 1998b). This means that some 14 million people live in families whose income, after housing costs have been met, is less than half the national average and one in five children, 2.5 million, live in households where no one is in full-time employment.

The Labour government has given a high priority to making Britain a more inclusive society, bringing those who are on the margins of opportunities for work, homes and education back into the mainstream. These problems were so urgent, the government believed, that it set up a special unit inside No.10 and introduced new schemes to be carried out by local councils and others. Local councils, for their part, had already begun to see poverty as a wider and more complex challenge that went beyond separate services of housing or physical redevelopment.

In central government the Social Exclusion Unit, established in December 1997, is located in the Cabinet Office and reports directly to the Prime Minister. Uniquely in Whitehall its members are a mixture of civil servants and outsiders from social services, the police, voluntary services, the Church and business. The Unit links into a network of ministers and officials rather than into a formal Cabinet Committee. The Social Exclusion's objective is to meet the Prime Minster's call for 'joined up' solutions to joined-up problems, working across functional and departmental boundaries in Whitehall and encouraging more collaborative working at local level. Its early tasks were to examine the problems of school truancy and exclusion, rough sleepers and the condition of the 2 000 or so worst council housing estates.

The Social Exclusion Unit's report of 16 September 1998, *Bringing Britain together – a national strategy for neighbourhood renewal*, emphasised that mistakes had become ingrained in central and local government. The report offers no single definition of a 'poor neigh-bourhood', referring instead to poverty, unemployment, poor health and concerns over crime. The report does, however, locate poor neigh-bourhoods in terms of the 1998 Index of Local Deprivation and sees the objectives as addressing unemployment, homelessness, crime and drugs, young people, health, ethnic minorities and access to services. The cause of policy failure in the past, in the report's view, is that efforts were highly fragmented, with gaps where problems were not covered by any of the existing programmes. Future policy needed to be aimed at preventing poverty and social problems, rather than as in the past dealing with their results. This approach emphasises integrated strategies, improving employment prospects for tenants, support for those with mental health and other problems, improving community protection and developing neighbourhood management initiatives.

The Social Exclusion Unit's view of the problems and the strategy for overcoming them is set out in Box 6.2. These are complex and interrelated problems and finding solutions will be equally difficult. It is notable that the Unit reports directly to the Prime Minister, empha-sising the priority that the government gives to these issues. *Bringing Britain together* called for 18 special action teams, each headed by a lead minister and including civil servants from 10 Whitehall depart-ments and outside specialists. These teams, under the coordination of the Exclusion Unit, are charged with tackling the most intractable problems of deprived neighbourhoods, again highlighting the determi-nation to achieve a more integrated policy approach. The government's success in tackling social exclusion, however, will be judged on how it deals with the poverty and inequality it inherited, particularly on the basis of the numbers of people on incomes below half the national average, unemployment, the numbers of 16 year-olds without qualifi-cations and the differential health rates between those at the top and bottom of the occupational scale. There are already moves to judge how well or badly the government is tackling these problems. The Joseph Rowntree Foundation has produced a set of 46 indicators cov-ering aspects of housing, income, education, unemployment and health and has urged the government to adopt them as a means of monitoring its achievements on social exclusion (Howarth, Kenway, Palmer and Street, 1998). In February 1999 the government announced that it would produce an annual audit on poverty, with baseline indicators devised by the Department of Social Security; the first audit would be published at the end of 1999.

*Box 6.2*    'Bringing Britain together'

---

THE PROBLEM:
:   A more divided country than a generation ago with pockets of intense depriva-
    tion. In these areas problems of unemployment and crime are combined with
    poor health, housing and education. Such areas are not confined to council
    estates, but include areas of private renting and owner occupation.

WHY IT CAME ABOUT:
:   No simple explanation, but factors of major economic and social change, weak-
    ening family structures, defective planning and social policies, multiple initia-
    tives, often 'parachuting' in solutions rather than engaging local communities;
    poor coordination between Whitehall Departments.

WHY IT MATTERS:
:   The current situation marks a costly policy failure, which we all pay for through
    the costs of social benefits and crime and the indirect costs of social division
    and low achievement.

WHAT CAN WE DO ABOUT IT?:
:   The goal must be to reduce the gap between the poorest neighbourhoods and the
    rest of the country.

A NATIONAL STRATEGY FOR POOR NEIGHBOURHOODS:
:   Learning from these lessons to promote a strategy of:
    - (a)   investing in people not just buildings;
    - (b)   involving communities;
    - (c)   integrated approaches with clear leadership;
    - (d)   ensuring mainstream policies really work for the poorest neighbour-
            hoods;
    - (e)   making a long-term commitment with political priority.

(*Bringing Britain Together*, Cm 4045, 1998, pp. 9–10)

---

Local authorities have a part to play in tackling these problems,
including through the New Deal for the unemployed and the New Deal
for Communities programmes. Under the Labour government's New
Deal welfare to work programme, councils are playing a role in
helping young people into employment. The £3.15 billion programme

(financed initially from the 'windfall tax' on the utilities) requires unemployed 18–24 year-olds to attend an intensive initial period of guidance – the 'Gateway' – followed by six months in one of four options: a subsidised job, paid work placements with either the Environment Taskforce or in the voluntary sector, or full-time education or training (Department for Education and Employment, 1997a). A fifth, self-employment, option was subsequently added from June 1998 whereby DfEE funding, administered by the 50 local offices of the Prince's Trust, is used to create more young entrepreneurs. The voluntary sector option of the New Deal will include a particular emphasis on placements to provide 50 000 new trained childcarers in support of the policy of getting lone parents back into work. The New Deal for lone parents includes increased allowances for childcare costs, expanded childcare places, out-of-school clubs and childcare tax credit for working families. Lone parents, the disabled and other benefit claimants of working age will lose all benefits if they fail to turn up to job advice interviews. But they will not forfeit benefit if they refuse to accept jobs. Parallel changes to the tax and credit systems through the Working Family Tax Credit aim to give greater incentives for work (McLaughlin, 1998).

Funding for all the New Deal schemes is committed until the year 2002. Lone parents and the disabled must attend job interviews, but are not forced to take jobs; for the young unemployed, one of the four options must be taken up, with loss of benefit for those who refuse. The scheme was subsequently extended to long-term unemployed people between 25 and 50. The private sector is heavily involved in running the scheme in conjunction with the local Employment service, local authorities, TECs and other bodies. In the areas of highest unemployment the government also created multiagency Employment Action Zones where benefits, employment and career services are coordinated, to focus help on the over-25s, the disabled, the low-skilled, lone parents, ex-offenders and victims of large-scale redundancies (Department for Education and Employment, 1997b). There have been political tensions over the New Deal developments. Local authorities have been uneasy over the private sector's prominent role. Concern has been expressed over the quality and number of permanent jobs that will be available and the problems of breaking the cycle of unemployment-subsidised jobs/training-unemployment. In the early experience of the New Deal programme, job openings in the public sector – local authorities and the NHS – were few. This is a matter of concern, since the expectation is that many key areas of work in the future, such as social care, will primarily be in the public sector. In areas of high unemployment the private sector's capacity to produce jobs is limited and is likely to be constrained further in times of economic slowdown.

Local authorities are nevertheless playing a key role in the government's anti-exclusion programmes both in partnerships to plan the provision and in consortia to deliver the services. They do so not only in relation to the young and long-term unemployed, but also as part of the New Deal for Communities channelling £800 million over a 3-year period to neighbourhoods with the highest levels of deprivation and the New Deal for schools with its £1.3 billion for repair and replacement of buildings. Under the New Deal for Communities, each of the seventeen 'pathfinder' local authorities (see Box 6.3) will have to identify a neighbourhood of between 1 000 and 4 000 households on which to target the resources. It is important to note that at this very localised level the projects will not be led by local councils themselves but by

*Box 6.3*   The 17 Pathfinder Authorities

| |
|---|
| 1.  Liverpool |
| 2.  Manchester |
| 3.  Newham* |
| 4.  Hackney* |
| 5.  Tower Hamlets* |
| 6.  Southwark* |
| 7.  Newcastle upon Tyne |
| 8.  Middlesbrough |
| 9.  Nottingham |
| 10.  Leicester |
| 11.  Birmingham |
| 12.  Sandwell |
| 13.  Kingston upon Hull |
| 14.  Bradford |
| 15.  Norwich |
| 16.  Brighton and Hove |
| 17.  Bristol |
| |
| * London Boroughs |

community and voluntary groups, something which has been emphasised by Prime Minister Blair as part of plans to boost the voluntary
sector. The duty of the local authority will be to produce an overall
strategy which includes unemployment, education, health and poverty
criteria. Promoting access to services (reflecting concern over the loss
of shops, banks and other amenities) and working with children and
young people to counter the drugs culture, are also key features. The
initiatives will operate through Partnerships involving community and
voluntary organisations, public agencies, local authorities and business
in each eligible area, and include existing projects and community
leaders. The Social Exclusion Unit's report speaks of testing out a
concept of 'neighbourhood management', with a manager and a management board, whose job would be to identify local needs and work
with agencies to plan and deliver services. This takes the concept of
decentralisation into new territory, and emphasises how far local governance has come from the days when the local authority was the auto-
matic leader and provider. A further question will be the extent to
which the 'pathfinders' are replicated elsewhere. To be effective, a
wider expansion of the scheme will be needed beyond the 17
pathfinder projects.

As Figure 6.1 shows, 44 local authority districts have extreme problems: between them they contain 85 per cent of the country's most
deprived wards. Compared with the rest of the country this means two-
thirds more unemployment, higher teenage pregnancy rates and single
households, very low educational attainment, high mortality ratios and
above average levels of vacant housing. It is noticeable that the geography of poverty has also changed, with the poorest becoming more
concentrated in small areas of acute need: polarisation has become the
mark of our cities.

**Bringing communities back in**

If these problems are to be tackled effectively, ways must be found to
give hope and a sense of 'ownership' to those most affected by the projects. For local councils, this means trying to meet both differences
between groups and between neigbourhoods – something that is both
difficult in itself and raises again the issue of 'places' versus 'people'
as the target of policy, or in other words, patterns of exclusion reveal
class, race, gender and age differences. They also reveal spatial differ-

1. Liverpool
2. Newham
3. Manchester
4. Hackney
5. Birmingham
6. Tower Hamlets
7. Sandwell
8. Southwark
9. Knowsley
10. Islington
11. Greenwich
12. Lambeth
13. Haringey
14. Lewisham
15. Barking and Dagenham
16. Nottingham
17. Camden
18. Hammersmith and Fulham
19. Newcastle upon Tyne
20. Brent
21. Sunderland
22. Waltham Forest
23. Salford
24. Middlesbrough
25. Sheffield
26. Hull

27. Wolverhampton
28. Bradford
29. Rochdale
30. Wandsworth
31. Walsall
32. Leicester
33. Oldham
34. Hartlepool
35. Doncaster
36. Coventry

37. Blackburn with Darwen
38. Bolton
39. Blackpool
40. Leeds
41. City of Westminster
42. Kensington and Chelsea
43. Burnley
44. Preston

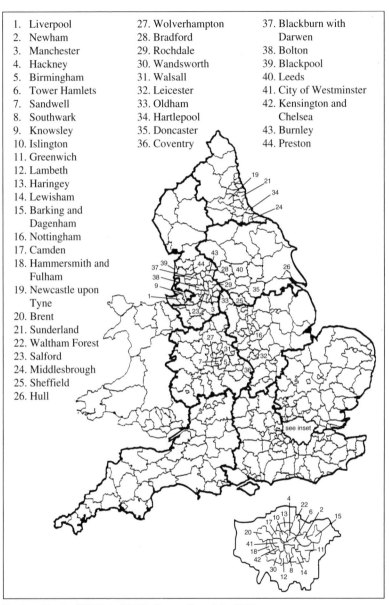

Produced by the GIS Unit, DETR. Crown Copyright 1998.

*Source:* Cm 4045, *Bringing Britain Together* (London: HMSO), 1998.

*Figure 6.1*   The 44 most deprived local authority districts according to the 1998 Index of Local Deprivation (in descending order of deprivation)

ences between neighbourhoods, access to services and participation in the workforce. Councils are seeking more cohesive and integrated strategies to address these problems. Progress in this direction was already occurring in the mid-1990s when the government published national guidelines to promote increased community inputs into regeneration programmes (Department of the Environment, 1995b). The DETR continues to stress the importance of these developments (DETR, 1997, 1998b). In particular, these initiatives include both those arising from local efforts, such as local exchange trading systems (LETS) and those in which communities join in partnerships to bid for SRB funds. Bringing local communities into regeneration has principled and pragmatic justifications: people have a right to take part and involvement enhances effectiveness. But in so doing it is important to recognise that local groups and interests are diverse, that ethnic minorities are not homogeneous, that managing conflict is as important as achieving consensus. Similarly, community involvement includes a variety of actions, from informing to acting together. To be effective community development must give people a sense of ownership of what is being done, and this then raises questions of where management and accountability should lie, that is, the degree of control that residents have remains problematic, as does the democratic accountability of different agencies.

Local authorities, in trying to bring the excluded and the marginalised back into the benefits of regeneration, continue to target particular areas of cities. The justification is that the long-term unemployed, lone parents, the old and the young unemployed are relatively concentrated in areas which also suffer from physical and economic decline. In addition, since poor people lack purchasing power and are thus marginal consumers in the market, they are both dependent upon, and likely to experience a lack of, easily accessed public services in their neighbourhoods. The quality of, and access to, public services (crucially, by public transport), is particularly important to women, including those with small children, the elderly and carers (Geddes, 1995). Concentrations of multiple deprivation are most marked in London but can be found throughout the country, with the divisions between rich and poor areas increasing over the past two decades (Gordon and Forrest, 1995). The result is that alienation and material hardship combine with drug cultures, truancy and crime in a cocktail of social problems.

In response, local authorities have gone further than the formal economic regeneration programmes. Over 200 local authorities have developed or are developing anti-poverty strategies (A. Harvey, 1998). These are directed at the labour market, small business, community enterprises, property development, inward investment and welfare rights (Geddes and Erskine, 1994). Others focus on neighbourhood projects, particularly for young people and ethnic minorities, that reflect the priorities of residents (Taylor, 1995). Nationally, the Local Government Anti-Poverty Unit provides research and policy development functions for local authorities, matched by the National Local Government Forum Against Poverty made up of councillors from member authorities. Much local authority anti-poverty strategy is based on a community development approach. The key ingredients include: defining areas that have meaning for local people; investing in funding and skilled community workers to support community groups; formal partnership agreements to encourage participants and stakeholders; a senior local authority officer to give coordination (Gregory, 1998). While all these efforts have made a positive contribution to poverty amelioration, local government is not a powerful engine of progressive redistribution (Bramley and Le Grand, 1992). Political tensions can also arise over a council's need to balance its anti-poverty objectives and funding services for all citizens and the need to avoid areas and individuals being labelled and blamed for their circumstances.

There is also concern that focusing on 'communities' implies that they are self-sufficient entities that can be left to regenerate themselves. On the contrary, it is vital that they are part of citywide urban strategies. But nor should local people be seen as passive recipients: effective self-help is growing. Self-help (individuals acting to help themselves or their families) and mutual aid (help between people) covers a wide range of cooperatives, care groups, literacy schemes and informal networks. One successful form of involvement operates through development trusts, non-profit enterprises with social objectives, accountable through their management boards to the local community (Wilcox, 1998). It is estimated that there are some 450 community enterprises in Britain having a collective annual turnover of around £18 million. An important part of this trend is the growing number of black and ethnic minority community enterprises seeking to play a bigger part in urban regeneration. Associatedly, community trusts, which are independent charities drawing down money into the locality, provide grants to voluntary and community projects. Two further examples are credit unions and LETS (Local Exchange Trading Schemes which allow local trade by creating an alternative to money) to provide financial services to those who are normally excluded from mainstream facilities (estimated as a quarter of adults) amid concern that banks, insurance companies and building societies are effectively black-listing entire communities. There are over 400 LETS schemes, and some local authorities are backing them as part of their anti-poverty strategies. Credit unions, which act as informal banks based on mutual saving and lending among people who cannot obtain credit elsewhere, are part of a wider community enterprise movement which, though marginal on the wider scale, is important to individual deprived neighbourhoods (Hayton, 1996a; Harvey, Jones and Donovan, 1998). Though critics have expressed doubts about the sustainability of LETS and credit union schemes, and stress that their impact has so far been very limited given the time and money invested in them, efforts to maintain these projects will continue. A similar example, which is attracting wider attention, is the work pioneered by the Wise Group in Glasgow. This gives individuals one year of trainee-employment, often in the 'intermediate labour market' of community projects, as the basis of launching them into the mainstream job market. This welfare to work programme is being franchised elsewhere, and its Intermediate Labour Market concept is being piloted through the government's new Employment Zones.

A question remains over the effectiveness of local anti-poverty efforts in the wider context of government urban programmes spear-headed by the Single Regeneration Budget Challenge Fund. Historically, these have run in parallel; the goal is to identify the link-ages and overcome the tensions between them. The government's emphasis on a rounded approach stresses the importance of the inter-face between local anti-poverty policy and broader national regenera-tion programmes. It is marked by the wider focus on social exclusion and social integration rather than solely on physical or economic devel-opment (Alcock *et al.*, 1998). Tensions also have to be resolved between the targeting of resources onto defined population groups or specific small areas. Achieving people-based targeting within geo-graphical targeting calls for linkages both between regeneration and anti-poverty strategies and with mainstream local services. From the perspective of those involved in community-based regeneration, the large number of initiatives that have been launched by the Labour gov-ernment in its first eighteen months in office – estimated in total to be around 30 – raises questions of capacity. While the initiatives are aimed at increasing partnership and coordination, there is a danger of increasing local complexity rather than reducing it.

## Disadvantaged minorities

Improving economic and social conditions has to recognise that ethnic minorities, both individually and as groups or communities, are particularly disadvantaged in their access to jobs, training and housing (Atkins *et al.*, 1996). The disadvantaged position of minorities is made worse by discrimination and exclusion. Unemployment rates among young ethnic men, particularly those from the Afro-Caribbean community, are twice those of white people while for adults generally black and Pakistani/Bangladeshi people have jobless rates three times those of white people (Office for National Statistics, 1996). Over 80 per cent of Pakistanis and Bangladeshis live in households whose income is below half the national average. Young black men are disproportionately likely to be without work, stable family life or qualifications and more likely to be in trouble with the police (Modood, 1998). Ethnic minorities suffer discrimination in housing and in London are four times as likely to be homeless as their white counterparts. Reported incidents of racial attack are still increasing. The overall picture is that ethnic minorities, particularly Pakistanis and Bangladeshis, suffer multidimensional disadvantage that amounts to social exclusion (Modood *et al.*, 1997).

Specific attempts to address ethnic disadvantage have been the inclusion in the Single Regeneration Budget of Section 11 grants aimed at minority adults and young people, the ethnic minority grant which supports training and enterprise projects provided by the voluntary sector, and the ethnic minority business initiative. The outcome remains mixed. Section 11 funding, originally established under the Local Government Act 1966, was primarily used for education (particularly English language support), but with some aid to youth and community work and other projects. Originally ring-fenced, the absorption of s. 11 into the SRB led to fears that it would atrophy. In 1997, however, Labour reversed the previous government's planned £40 million cut to stabilise it at £83 million annually. At the end of 1998 it was announced that funding would be increased by 15 per cent to £430 million over the following three years, with schools being given greater say in how the money was to be used. At the same time responsibility for s. 11 funding was transferred from the Home Office to the Department for Education and Employment and renamed the Ethnic Minorities Achievement Grant (EMAG). Judgement on the broad outcomes of SRB is that it has failed to address the needs of ethnic minorities adequately, with the first three rounds of the bidding process supporting only 4 ethnic minority-led bids out of 555 successful partnerships at a total of £4 million out of the £3 billion pool (Local Government Chronicle, 1998). The Labour government promised that future SRB projects would redress these imbalances.

Local authorities have tried to deal with these difficulties through specific programmes addressed at excluded groups. In anti-discrimination work, local authorities use a variety of mechanisms, including units, dedicated posts, committees and subcommittees, to cover their responsibilities under the 1976 Race Relations Act. Following the Race Relations Act 1968 local Community Relations Councils (CRCs) were established, funded by the Commission for Racial Equality and local authorities. Umbrella organisations with a coordinating role, they provide a broad-based platform for representing community views, support advice work and liaise with local authorities and other bodies. But internal divisions and conflict over control of the organisations means they have not fulfilled their potential to affect local urban policy. Questions also arise over CRC representation on area or regeneration committees, with different minority groups all pressing for their own voice in specific projects. Similar issues have arisen over access to local authority decision-making and over liaison with local police initiatives.

**The scale of local provisions**

Trying to bring minorities and other excluded groups back into regeneration has become a major element of the urban policy agenda. That wider agenda seeks to improve local services and to devise new programmes that cut across the old divisions between them. The key issues are maintaining civil peace, raising standards in education, giving people access to reasonable housing, ensuring cooperative working between health and social services, strengthening sustainable development and improving the environment.

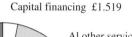

**TOTAL £48.04[1]**

**Main Service Block**

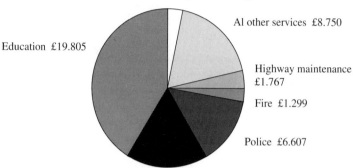

Capital financing £1.519

Al other services £8.750

Education £19.805

Highway maintenance £1.767

Fire £1.299

Police £6.607

Personal social services £8.293

**Main Service Block**

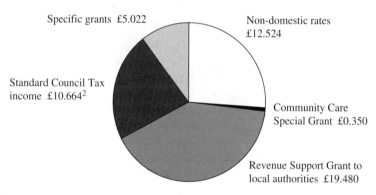

Specific grants £5.022

Non-domestic rates £12.524

Standard Council Tax income £10.664[2]

Community Care Special Grant £0.350

Revenue Support Grant to local authorities £19.480

*Notes:*
1   TSS excluding £120 million of restructuring costs, costs funded by supplementary credit approvals, £26 million for funding specified bodies and £7 million for the City of London Offset.
2   This includes £102 million which is funded by the SSA Reduction Grant, and £11 million funded by the Reorganisation: Transitional Reduction Grant.

*Source:* Department of the Environment, Transport and the Regions, *Annual Report*, 1998.

*Figure 6.2*   Total standard spending 1998–99 (£ billion)

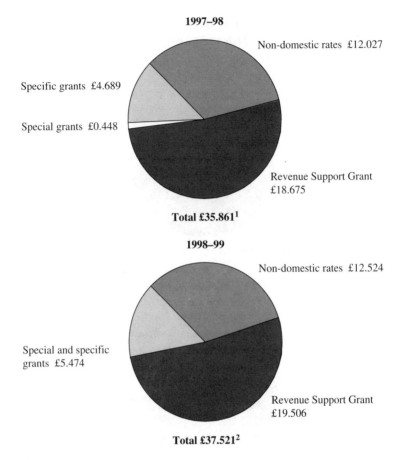

**1997–98**

Non-domestic rates £12.027

Specific grants £4.689

Special grants £0.448

Revenue Support Grant
£18.675

**Total £35.861¹**

**1998–99**

Non-domestic rates £12.524

Special and specific
grants £5.474

Revenue Support Grant
£19.506

**Total £37.521²**

*Notes:*
1  This includes £7 million for the City of London Offset, and £15 million for the Reorganisation:
   Transitional Reduction Grant (not shown in diagram).
2  This includes £7 million for the City of London Offset, and £11 million for the Reorganisation:
   Transitional Reduction Grant (not shown in diagram).

*Source:* Department of the Environment, Transport and the Regions, *Annual Report*,
1998.

*Figure 6.3*    Aggregate external finance 1997–98 and 1998–99
(£ billion)

As Figure 6.2 shows, the scale of local authority operations is large. Of the £48 billion service expenditure, education at some £20 billion takes by far the largest share, more than double the next largest share of just over £8.3 billion for personal social services. Police at £6.6 billion is also a large single item. Local authority spending is supported by government funding (Revenue Support Grant) which at over £19 billion is twice the income raised by Council Tax at £10.6 billion. Specific and special grants amount to some five and a half billion pounds: interestingly, the national 'non-domestic' (ie business) rates at £12.5 billion also exceed the amount raised locally. Figure 6.3 shows how, under the Labour government, totals increased by just under £2 billion, with the business rate proportion increasing less (some £500 million) than government grants (£830 million).

The scale of expenditure reflects the size of the problems facing local authorities, who must both deliver services to all their citizens and carry out specific projects for particular areas and problems. Of the five key areas identified, that of crime and disorder highlights the centrality of civil peace to city wellbeing and its links to deprivation. Crime and disorder, more contentiously, may be judged as evidence of the failure of policy to do more than contain, rather than solve, urban problems.

## Crime and disorder

Maintaining order and promoting civility is the basis of urban life. In institutional terms, the formal responsibility for order and safety lies with the 41 police forces in England and Wales, autonomous corporate bodies financed by a combination of central and local funding. Following the 1994 Police and Magistrates Courts Act and the 1996 Police Act, the concern has been that the new arrangements have changed the former basis of policing in England and Wales from one in which councillors and magistrates represented the community to one which incorporates independent lay members (predominantly from business, commerce and management) into the 17-member Police Authority, who need not necessarily represent any particular local interest (Walker and Richards, 1996; Jones and Newburn, 1997).

Police forces have, under the 1994 Act, a statutory requirement to consult with their local communities, particularly before preparation of the Local Policing Plan, LPP. To this end, community consultation fora, the Police–Community Consultation Groups, have been established, though their effectiveness is open to question (Harfield, 1997). The attempts to improve community safety have increased the collaborative working between the police and local authorities. Community safety partnerships between the police and local agencies have operated since the mid-1980s, focusing in particular on known problem areas and on drug misuse, car crime, violent crime, burglary, persistent young offenders and vulnerable groups. These collaborative approaches were strengthened by the 1998 Crime and Disorder Act. Stronger relations with local people also lies behind the drive to community policing, including neighbourhood watch and crime prevention projects, increased use of local beat patrols and the establishment of specialist community relations police divisions and Community Liaison Officers. Evidence for the effectiveness of neighbourhood watch is thin (Goldblatt and Lewis, 1998). A more worrying problem is where the line is drawn between neighbourhood watch and other community self-help and vigilante groups, particularly anti-racist vigilante groups which have sprung up in some inner-city areas. Anxieties are also raised by the proposals to expand the 'neighbourhood warden' schemes on council estates. Such wardens provide a mechanism of preventive action and someone to whom residents can turn for assistance. But issues arise of where the borderline with the police lies, and whether they are sufficiently accountable, given that they are taking on something of a surrogate community order role.

A contentious area of crime control and prevention has been the nature of the links between deprivation (of people and neighbourhoods) and crime. Crime statistics and victim surveys show that within towns, inner-city neighbourhoods, subject to rapid demographic change and transient populations and the most disadvantaged housing estates had risks of burglary and robbery several times the average. The British Crime Surveys, using ACORN ('A Classification of Residential Neighbourhood' based on a 17-fold neighbourhood grouping of social and housing characteristics as measured by the 1991 Census) differentiate between three kinds of high-risk area. The first two categories, the poorest council estates (including, but not confined to, the inner city) and multiracial areas which are usually at the city core, were prey to locally based offenders. The third category, that of high status areas where homes were left unoccupied during working hours or at weekends, were prone to property theft by outsiders (Mirrlees-Black, Mayhew and Percy, 1996). The 1998 British Crime Survey examines the question of locality further, in relation to burglary, vehicle-related thefts and violent crime, to demonstrate how risks vary both according to area and type of victim. Certain groups – single parent families, those who rent social housing – are at particular risk, as are inner-city and multiethnic areas and council estates. The burden of crime is thus markedly unequal on sectors of the population and areas of the city (Mirrlees-Black, Budd, Partridge and Mayhew, 1998). It is the case, however, that poor levels of social cohesion and social control appear as important as poverty *per se* in defining high-risk crime areas. In addition, deprived council estates with high unemployment and crime rates become stigmatised and their residents suffer isolation and social exclusion, with their young people at risk of falling into long-term delinquency.

Deprived areas and their links to crime have been at the forefront of attention in racial incidents and in the search for the causes of urban riots. In 1996–7 the number of recorded racial incidents reached 13 106, of which 58 per cent were damage to property or verbal harassment and 21 per cent were assaults (Maynard and Read, 1997) while the 1994 British Crime Survey, regarded as a more reliable guide than incidents actually reported to the police, put the figure at 130 000 (Aye Maung and Mirrlees-Black, 1994). Fear of violence among blacks and Asians is more than three times that among whites. Black, Indian and Bangladeshi/Pakistani people are likely to be victims of higher levels of crime than white people. Nearly half of South Asians and just under a third of black victims of attacks believed that these had been racially motivated (Church and Summerfield, 1996). It is estimated that over a quarter of racial harassment takes place on council estates (Home Affairs Committee, 1994). The 1997 Protection from Harassment Act created the criminal offences of harassment and causing fear of violence, giving courts the power to issue a Restraining Order to protect the victim and allowing civil actions against harassment. In 1998, Labour's Crime and Disorder Act added to offences against the person a category of 'racist intent' which requires racial motivation to be taken into account by the courts in passing sentence and gives an additional weapon for tackling racially motivated crimes by the use of antisocial behaviour orders.

In relation to police–minority relations, the situation continues to give cause for concern. Black people are nearly eight times more likely to be stopped and searched by the police than their white counterparts, while the national arrest rate is about five times higher than for whites. The differentials between whites and Asians are less. Complaints of racially discriminatory behaviour of police officers are increasing

(Police Complaints Authority, 1997), while 75 per cent of black people and 48 per cent of Asians believe the police treat people from ethnic minorities worse than they treat white people. Almost 60 per cent of young Afro-Caribbean men in inner cities said that they had been stopped or questioned by the police in the previous 12 months (Pool, 1997). Mistrust between urban minorities and the police has also been seen as one factor, together with alienated youth and drugs-related crime, in those severest cases of urban disorder, the riots in London and major conurbations of the 1980s and early 1990s (Cmnd 8427, 1981; Power and Tunstall, 1997).

The Scarman Report of 1981 (Cmnd 8427, 1981) highlighted the social and economic problems of inner-city areas but saw the immediate causes of the Brixton riots of April 1981 as local resentment of police behaviour in the large-scale 'stop and search' operations, perceived as targeting young black men. In July 1981 serious rioting occurred in Toxteth, Liverpool, followed by riots in some 30 towns and cities, as well as in parts of London. In 1985 riots again broke out, in Birmingham and London. Afro-Caribbean and Asian communities were involved in many of these disorders, again in conflict situations with the policy over specific incidents. The conclusion was that a major part of urban disorder arose from poor relations between the police and local communities. Further disturbances occurred throughout the early to mid-1990s, in peripheral housing estates as well as in inner-city neighbourhoods. The underlying problems were less those of ethnic minorities (though the riots in Bradford in 1995 involved Asian youths and policing policy) but did involve disaffected youth suffering high levels of unemployment. The disorder occurred in low-income areas, often traditional council estates and with long-standing social problems.

There is a growing determination of councils to address the problem of antisocial behaviour. Provisions in the 1996 Housing Act, implemented in 1997, make possession actions against council tenants for nuisance quicker and easier to prove. Councils can also operate introductory tenancy schemes whereby tenants have to complete a probationary period before gaining a secure tenancy.

The 1998 Crime and Disorder Act, as Box 6.4 shows, confers wide powers to tackle what are seen as the key elements of urban crime, including the new Antisocial Behaviour Order, a special form of injunction for use against both adults or children over 10 years of age. Breaches of the injunction could carry penalties of up to five years

*Box 6.4*    Main provisions of Crime and Disorder Act 1998

---

- Antisocial Behaviour Orders against harassment by anyone over 10, including nuisance neighbours and others.
- Duty on a local authority and the police, acting with probation and health agencies, to publish crime and disorder strategy.
- Parenting orders to compel parents of truants and criminal children to attend counselling sessions.
- Child safety orders for supervision of under-10s; curfew schemes for under-10s.
- *Doli incapax* (presumes child under 10 cannot commit criminal offence) abolished.
- Introduces racially aggravated offences covering assaults, public order and harassment.
- Lays duty on a local authority, police, probation and health, acting in cooperation, to provide youth justice services, and to establish Youth Offending Teams who coordinate the services and produce a Youth Justice Plan.
- Youth Justice Board monitors the youth justice system nationally.
- Other provisions of the Act include: changing the main aim of the youth justice system from a welfare role to preventing offending; speeding up court system for young offenders; electronic tagging; remanding children over 12 to secure accommodation or, if over 15, to prison; final warnings for young offenders with reparation for victims; compulsory drug testing and treatment orders for addicts over 16; sex offenders orders.

---

imprisonment. The policy is in large part a response to pressure from urban authorities facing antisocial behaviour on impoverished housing estates, often accompanied by a drugs culture. But there is disquiet about what this policy may mean for those who become outcasts, punished by the courts and losing their council tenancy – reinforcing social exclusion, not overcoming it. Already there is concern that council tenants are opting to put rebellious children into care rather than face eviction. The Crime and Disorder Act also allows local authorities to introduce curfew schemes for children under the age of 10; a number of pilot schemes have already been introduced, with some evidence that juvenile crime has been reduced. The various policies outlined in Box 6.4 aimed at reducing antisocial behaviour raise important questions for urban civility. What are the root causes of crime and how do you intervene to prevent them? Multiagency intervention, incorporating housing and education professionals, is one way forward, reflected for example in the Drug-Action Teams (DATs); community mediation is another.

The main element of the 1998 Crime and Disorder Act that fosters a multiagency approach is that which places a duty on local authorities to provide effective crime prevention, youth justice and community safety services. There is a statutory requirement on police and local authorities to prepare a crime reduction strategy and publish it. The inter-agency panels of local authorities, police and probation committees have to conduct a crime audit, including both reported and unreported incidents, and experiences, perceptions and fear of crime. An important element of this task will be collecting data from community groups and voluntary organisations, particularly in relation to racial harassment and racially motivated crimes. The legislation lays a duty on local authorities to ensure appropriate youth justice services.

Local authorities will have to formulate youth justice plans and set up Youth Offending Teams, involving police, probation, health and education personnel. These agencies will be required to cooperate to provide the youth justice services. The new structures will be operational everywhere by April 2000 and there will be a new Youth Justice Board for England and Wales – a new quango – monitoring and overseeing the system. Overall, the emphasis is on an integrated approach, drawing in health, social services, education, housing, police and probation into crime-prevention partnerships. The result is that community safety has become a key element in local urban policy.

The prime objectives in local policing are crime-control and prevention. Initiatives are broad-based, focussing on social as well as physical factors and promoting multiagency partnerships and community consultation, as for example in the Safer Cities initiative which ran in over 29 urban areas between 1988 and the mid-1990s. These schemes sought to reduce opportunities for crime through increased security of premises, environmental management, surveillance and general 'designing out' approaches. In 1993 the Safer Cities initiative became part of the Single Regeneration Budget process. In addition, two kinds of physical measures have been influential on local policies for crime prevention and community order. These are measures which are design-orientated (the 'defensible space' measures associated with the work of Newman (1972) and Coleman (1985) ) which link housing and urban design to crime levels. The main areas of expansion, however, have been in electronic surveillance. Electronic surveillance through closed circuit television systems, CCTV, is being increasingly used in town centres, car parks and shopping malls. There are civil liberties concerns, however, about this blanket oversight of individuals' movements, its impact on people's freedom to enter public spaces and its potential use for intrusive identification.

While surveillance measures are an integral part of community safety policies, strategy to address generalised antisocial behaviour is less easily focused. Local authorities, and the police, have tried a variety of tactics against vandalism, graffiti and what are seen as threatening situations of groups of young people loitering in town centres and on council estates. The police have looked at 'zero tolerance' responses, attacking minor crime to prevent more serious offences, an approach which is still being debated (Goldblatt and Lewis, 1998). Though the strategy can reduce crime in the short term, the Home Office's own research reveals a number of problems, not least the boundary between firm and harsh policing and the effects on police–community relations. Though contentious, the approach was boosted in September 1998 with the announcement by Prime Minister Blair that zero tolerance (or 'order maintenance' as it will be known) policing techniques would be extended to 25 crime 'hotspots' throughout Britain in a £250 million 3-year crime reduction strategy. Another development has been local council experiments with patrol forces and community safety wardens in their parks and streets. Certain police forces are also exploring with the government the possibility of private patrols licensed by the police. The use of private security services is growing – raising fundamental questions about the key nature of state responsibility for the civil peace.

If local authorities are being drawn more closely into community safety, their traditional role as the dominant provider of education is becoming more diverse.

## Education

Improving standards, and targeting the most deprived areas through special Education Action Zones, are prime items of the current political agenda in education. These follow on from the fundamental changes made to the education system in the 1980s, which devolved responsibilities from all Local Education Authorities (LEAs) to schools, boards of governors and parents. The Education (No.2) Act 1986 reduced local authority input into school governing bodies; the 1988 Education Reform Act's Local Management of Schools provisions required local authorities to devolve budgets to individual schools and their boards of governors; and schools were given the opportunity of Grant-Maintained status which took them out of local authority control completely. The aim of all these moves was to increase consumer, that is parental, choice in a marketplace of schools. In the case of Grant-Maintained Schools, where funding came from a national quango (the Funding Agency for Schools), LEAs relinquished all ties. The effect of the education reforms was to diminish the capacity of LEAs to control the system directly and reinforced the need to strike a balance between market forces and planning (Audit Commission, 1997c). Local education authorities have become enablers, providing overall strategy and certain services which governing bodies can purchase. At the same time a national curriculum and the testing of children at different stages in their school careers were imposed.

Parental choice was increased further through the establishment of City Technology Colleges (CTCs), under s 105 of the 1988 Act, aimed at attracting business investment (not wholly realised) into specialised technological, science and language schools with independence from the local education authority. The 1993 Education Act dropped the 'city' designation and broadened their remit; the colleges in effect reintroduced selective schooling, free of local authority control. Under the 1988 Act the polytechnics and higher education colleges were also removed from local authority control, followed by further education under the Further and Higher Education Act 1992. The higher and further education sectors colleges, including sixth form colleges, became free-standing corporations. In both cases financial responsibilities were transferred to national quangos.

The Labour government's White Paper of 1997, *Excellence in Schools* set out a prescriptive central framework for local action (Cm 3681), subsequently embodied in the School Standards and Framework Act, 1998. Soon after its election, the Labour government showed its determination to focus on education standards. In October 1997 a Qualifications and Curriculum Authority (QCA) was set up, bringing together the two national bodies responsible for vocational qualifications and for the school curriculum and academic qualifications. It sets national standards and a national curriculum, requiring the publication of examination results in 'league tables' and works with a range of other bodies in the education and business fields. A quango, its Board is apppointed by the Secretary of State for Education and Employment.

The School Standards and Framework Act of 1998 reaffirmed a high degree of school autonomy while laying duties on local authorities to improve education standards. The main provisions of the Act are laid out in Box 6.5. Among the key points highlighted in Box 6.5 are those forcing LEAs to empower parents, widen consultation and cede greater freedoms to schools. Local Education Authorities are required to appoint parent governor representatives to their education committees (as voting members, alongside existing coopted non-voting members), produce Education Development Plans to show how standards will be raised and enter into partnerships with the private sector to tackle the backlog of school repairs. The School Standards and Framework Act 1998 also abolished Grant-Maintained status, with the former opted-out GMS schools having the choice of becoming Foundation schools, Voluntary (like church schools), or Community schools under LEA control; special schools could become either community or foundation special schools. It was anticipated that most GM schools would become Foundation schools, which have greater freedom than local authority schools but would have to appoint local authority governors. The Funding Agency for Schools, FAS, which channelled funds to the opted-out sector, ceased to operate and funds for all schools routed through the LEA, though with requirements that 90 per cent of the monies are delegated to schools budgets.

The devolved budgetary arrangements for all schools have been strengthened further with the announcement in 1998 that £1 billion would be transferred from local education authorities to school budgets, allowing head teachers and governors to have direct control of repairs, meals and teacher salaries. These reforms give all state schools the same kind of financial independence that the former Grant-Maintained schools enjoyed. Local fora of LEAs, school governing bodies, head teachers, churches and others will agree and coordinate admissions arrangements, with a new independent adjudicator to resolve disputes. Selectivity for admission on ability grounds is abolished, though those 330 or so schools specialising in technology, languages, sports and arts (including the former City Technology Colleges) are able to admit up to 10 per cent of pupils on 'aptitude' grounds, a move seen by critics as reinforcing the expansion of selection. Under the 1998 Act, Voluntary (mostly church schools) and Foundation (previous GMS)

*Box 6.5*    Main provisions of School Standards and Framework Act 1998

- Duty on Local Education Authorities (LEAs) to raise standards, in line with code of practice drawn up by the Secretary of State for Education and Employment.
- Each LEA required to prepare three-year Education Development Plan, in discussion with schools and approved by the DfEE, saying how standards will be improved.
- New framework of Community, Foundation and Voluntary Schools, with Grant-Maintained Schools becoming Foundation Schools.
- Stronger role for parents, with increased representation on school governing bodies and LEA education committees.
- Maximum delegation of LEA education budgets to schools; routes all government funds through LEAs and abolishes the Funding Agency for Schools (FAS).
- School admissions coordinated by local fora of LEAs, school governing bodies, head teachers, churches and others. Where agreement cannot be reached, new independent adjudicator will decide.
- Each LEA will have to set up School Organisation Committee, with members from the LEA, churches and other bodies, to consider plans for school places.
- Schools cannot introduce selection by ability,but specialist schools can admit up to 10 per cent on the basis of aptitude.
- Local parents can hold ballots on whether grammar schools should keep selective admission.
- All schools to have written home-school agreements.
- LEAs have to publish Early Years Development Plans.
- Secretary of State can intervene where: LEAs are under-performing; Ofsted finds a school to be failing; can close failing schools and reopen them under 'fresh start' schemes.
- Secretary of State can set up Education Action Zones with life-span of 3–5 years; multiagency, innovative approaches to improve standards.
- Other provisions cover minimum class sizes for 5–7 year-olds; safeguard religious ethos of church schools; mimimum standards for school meals; work experience for 14–16 year-olds.

schools are their own admission authorities. For the remainder, the admission authority is the LEA. Selection has, ironically, emerged in a parallel context of parental choice in the arrangements for the future of the 164 grammar schools which had survived the succeeding waves of education reforms. The government proposed that the future of such schools would be dependent on parental ballots, that is, that they would not be phased out on governmental dictat. In November 1998 regulations promulgated under the 1998 School Standards and Framework Act allowed the opportunity for pro-comprehensive campaigners to overturn grammar status if they could secure the signatures of 20 per cent of parents on local petitions to trigger a ballot.

Box 6.5 demonstrates the emphasis now placed on cooperation. Each LEA has to set up a School Organisation Committee (SOC) to supervise the opening, closure or enlargement of schools in their areas. As in other areas of policy, the stress is on collaborative working between councils, local interests and agencies. LEAs continue to have specific responsibilities for children with special educational needs (SEN) and, by late 1998, had to have in place Behaviour Support Plans for the education of children with behavioural difficulties. Otherwise LEAs' spending is limited to a narrow range of core services of special needs, school transport and support for improvements in standards and outcomes.

The changing system of education has also altered the inspection process. Under the Education (Schools) Act 1992 the Office of Standards in Education (Ofsted) is responsible for inspecting all LEA schools in England (in Wales by the Office of Her Majesty's Chief Inspector of Schools in Wales, OHMCI). Unlike the former Her Majesty's Inspectorate, a body of public servants who were responsible for all inspections in the state system, Ofsted lets contracts to Registered Inspectors, who may come from the public or commercial sectors, and members of Her Majesty's Inspectorate to work for Ofsted. The 1997 Education Act gave new powers to Her Majesty's Chief Inspector and his counterpart in Wales to inspect LEAs as well as individual schools. At the same time LEAs fall within the remit of the Audit Commission which is responsible for ensuring that local authorities secure 'best value' for the public money they spend and the Commission has been active in reviewing the role of local authorities in education. In addition, LEAs judged by Ofsted to have failed will have 'improvement teams' drafted in to manage the school system. Schools found by Ofsted to have serious weaknesses are given a six-month period to improve or face a further inspection that could led to closure (with some reopening under a 'fresh start' scheme) or management overhaul, including calling in private consultants. Furthermore, the 1998 School Standards and Framework Act gives the Education Secretary the power to intervene in the LEA itself if he or she is satisfied that the LEA is failing in its performance of any of its functions with regard to schools.

Two further moves are part of the Labour government's social exclusion agenda: measures to combat school truancy and exclusion, and nursery education. The 1998 education legislation requires the governors of each school to set annual targets for the reduction of truancy. Currently, there are at least 1 million children who truant. In addition, there are some 100 000 fixed-term exclusions of pupils from schools, with permanent exclusions rising from 13 000 in 1996 to 16 000 in 1998. The government is committed to reducing this number by one-third over 3 years and is urging schools to work with LEAs, social services, the police and other public and voluntary agencies to meet these targets. In the case of nursery education, local authorities are required to set up public–private Early Years Development Partnerships and a matching development plan, to provide nursery education through private nurseries and voluntary playgroups as well as LEAs. Places will initially be provided for all 4 year-olds and for 3 year-olds in the longer term. In addition, there are improved childcare provisions, 'early excellence centres', after-school clubs and the Sure Start programmes. In 1999 60 Sure Start pilots were set up, with a projected 250 local programmes expected by 2002. The Sure Start projects provide a network of family centres (linked to Early Years Development Plans drawn up by each LEA) in deprived areas for mothers and their children aged from birth to 3, providing a significant infrastructure for the welfare-to-work policy. These developments will help to provide 190 000 extra nursery places and help train more childcare workers.

The 1998 expenditure review increased education funding, including doubling capital investment for school building and repairs and money for additional teachers in reduced class sizes. But the funding increases were targeted and linked to performance outcomes. The government also capped the budget for the central services that local authorities provide (for special needs children, school transport and admissions) to reinforce the trend for more devolution to schools. The Labour victory in the 1997 General Election thus halted the Conservative move towards the autonomy of all schools in which LEAs themselves would have become redundant. But it did not reverse the trend of the past two decades by which many LEAs have moved to a partnership relationship with local schools, meeting the twin objectives of empowered schools and a proactive LEA (Audit Commission, 1998). The government's view is that the role of LEAs is a strategic one of supporting schools, only intervening in their work in inverse proportion to the schools' success, and has instituted a Code of Practice for LEAs to govern the relationship between the authority and schools. In support of this strategic role, LEAs are required to set benchmarks for school performance and advise on best practice. For the best schools, the government is considering exemption from national curriculum and routine Ofsted inspections; this would be a 'third way' between local authority control and reliance on market forces. Improving standards was the prime goal of policy.

Where schools fail, these could be reopened under new management or, in the severest cases, taken over by education associations appointed by the Secretary of State. This has given rise to controversy over the role of the private sector in state education: companies or non-profit organisations can charge consultancy fees, management charges and receive bonus payments. A number of local education authorities are already considering these options in the case of 'failing' schools. This has led to accusations that this amounts to an approach based on 'profits' for shareholders rather than a public service democratically accountable to the local electorate. The government has not ruled out private sector takeovers where management fees are charged and has encouraged private involvement in education provision in Education Action Zones (EAZs).

The emphasis on eliminating 'failing schools' was supported by the establishment of 25 Education Action Zones in poorly performing areas, covering 2–3 secondary schools and their feeder primaries, time-limited to 3–5 years, with additional funding, and with the opportunities to relax the national curriculum and the teachers' national pay and conditions scheme. In EAZs, multiagency partnerships have to be set up between schools, local authorities and business in an Education Action Forum that is responsible for an Action Plan and for the funding that comes from the DfEE. Each Education Action Forum is a statutory body; in effect, a legally constituted surrogate education authority – a major change in education responsibility from a democratically elected body to an unelected one. The zone partnerships have the potential to become deliverers of services outside the framework of municipal control – an ideological Third Way. Indeed, in a speech emphasising that EAZs were an opportunity for partnerships between schools, businesses and parent and community groups, Prime Minister Blair made no mention of local education authorities. In addition, critics fear that EAZs could develop into indirect privatisation on a wide scale, given that managing a single school (which is already occurring in at least one local authority area) is unlikely to be profitable for a business partner. Certain companies are already involved in a wide range of activities including training and employing teachers, running private schools and carrying out Ofsted inspections. This has already occurred in the United States. Overall, local education authorities are now a strategic rather than a controlling element in the local education system characterised by increasingly autonomous schools and detailed central direction.

There are two possible models for the future here. In one, non-profit deliverers (analogous to housing associations) run a local service outside the normal framework of municipal control. The other model is much closer to privatisation. In January 1999 the Education Secretary announced that where a LEA is failing to perform effectively, the task would be handed to contractors, including not-for-profit, the private sector or a neighbouring LEA. But advertisements for potential private sector contracts placed by the DfEE indicate that the private sector could provide the whole education service, with no limitation to one school or mention of handing a school back after the 3–5 year EAZ period. In January 1999, Prime Minister Blair's announcement of a second tranche of EAZs urged more innovation and cash help from business. All but three of the 60 bids for the first 25 EAZs were led by LEAs and the Prime Minister is keen to tip the balance away from local authorities and towards the private sector. This will be reflected in the new bidding criteria for the additional EAZs which demand a much higher level of involvement from business.

If education has become a prime political issue, housing's former high profile has faded.

## Housing

Housing's place on the national political agenda declined in the 1980s. In the twenty-first century there is a new challenge arising from the deficit in social housing; the size of the housing benefits bill and the backlog of repair and maintenance work make it a pressing problem for urban politics. And while council housing was traditionally a desirable tenure for a broad spectrum of the working class, it has become a residual sector for the elderly, the unemployed, female-headed households and those with no other choice. Council housing appears to have become increasingly unpopular, with more than 81 000 empty properties (compared with a figure of 27 000 for housing associations), and council tenants are among the poorest in society. Inequalities between neighbourhoods have increased – a sharpened sociospatial segregation which persists over time (Lee and Murie, 1997). The result is that the goal of social inclusion, of socially mixed communities, remains as elusive as ever. Over the past two decades local authorities have moved from being a major provider of public sector housing to an enabling role of management and maintenance. The Conservative government of 1979 began a programme of sales of council housing to sitting tenants such that by the early 1990s the proportion of owner-occupation had risen to over two-thirds of the stock in England and over 50 per cent in Scotland.

By the mid-1990s housing associations had taken over the task of new build social housing, though local authorities retained certain rights to nominate tenants, generally to a level of around 50 per cent. A variety of schemes have transferred the management of substantial areas of the remaining public sector housing to private landlords or tenant cooperatives. Those estates in exceptional need of refurbishment were passed to government-sponsored Housing Action Trusts in England (in Scotland, Scottish Homes); after renovation of the estates the Trusts could sell them or transfer them to other landlords, including back to the local authority. In addition, there is an increasing trend of estate-size transfers to housing associations and local housing companies, and to non-profit housing trusts with charitable status. In Scotland, Glasgow, Edinburgh, Aberdeen and Dundee are all moving to transfer their council housing to non-profit companies or trusts, driven by the need to overcome the backlog of repairs. These moves are a radical shift which will remove nearly one-third of public housing from local government control in Scotland and the trend is likley to accelerate. In all these cases, one key to success is tenant involvement. The Labour government also continued the previous government's programme whereby local authorities transferred homes to housing associations through Large Scale Voluntary Transfer (LSVT) schemes, and other initiatives allowed the transfer of severely run-down estates to local housing companies. The difference between the local housing company and LSVT is that rather than losing their stock completely, the local council retains a minority stake. The Labour government is also supporting the promotion of the private finance initiative (PFI) in social housing. The aim is to attract private investment; this will largely be used for refurbishment of the existing housing stock, given that it cannot be used to build new dwellings.

The changing structure of housing provision created uncertainty for local authorities. The financial regime also curtailed their scope. Control over capital expenditure in England (in Scotland a simpler regime is operated through the Scottish Office Environment Department) operates through the Housing Investment Programme, HIP. Under HIP, each local authority submits a bid for central government funding and is given a 'credit approval'. Since 1990 these approvals must take account of receipts from the sales of housing. These constraints were eased in 1997 when the Labour government introduced the Local Government (Supplementary Credit Approvals) Act which allowed the phased release of capital receipts to finance housing projects. The Government also provided £900 million for housing and housing-related regeneration between 1997 and 1999. Local authorities could use part of these monies to give grants to housing associations to build new homes. The funding will be extended beyond 2000, with the announcement in July 1998 of the 3-year expenditure plans allocating some £5 billion for housing, including £3.6 billion for repairs. At the same time councils were expected to raise £2.75 billion a year from the sale of assets and land.

While the local authority role in housing diminished, that of housing associations increased. Housing associations are non-profitmaking, non-statutory bodies, overseen by the Housing Corporation (a quango). They are funded by private finance, local authority grants and a competitive system of Social Housing Grants from the Housing Corporation. Housing associations have become a major element in social housing; the effect of their increasing responsibilities has, paradoxically, repeated some of the housing problems that are at the centre of urban policy. Research has shown that where a housing association had taken over council estates and provided renovated and new homes, a greater social mix was not being achieved and many homes were proving hard to let because of their high cost. As a result the majority of those housed were on housing benefit and 8 out of 10 lettings in the mid-1990s were to households where no adult was in paid employment (Crook, Darke and Disson, 1996). In effect, many of the problems of the large council house estates are being replicated in housing association schemes. A number of medium-sized housing associations, however, are involved in Housing Plus initiatives, which are designed to strengthen communities and combat social exclusion by assisting tenants to run their estates, or providing help with specific projects such as youth clubs and training and employment programmes.

A further, and major, problem on the urban agenda is how to reduce homelessness. Since 1977, when the Housing (Homeless Persons) Act was introduced, local authorities have had a duty to house the statutorily homeless. The 1996 Housing Act removed the duty to provide permanent accommodation (replacing it with the duty to provide temporary accommodation for a period of not less than 24 months) and single persons have no clear statutory right to housing. The Labour government has partially remedied this by reinstating homelessness as one of the criteria for permanent housing. The vulnerability of the young single homeless increased as benefit cuts for 16–25 year-olds came into operation in October 1996, though the Labour government removed the planned further cuts for single people aged 25–60 from October 1997. And despite the local authority duty, under the Care in the Community legislation to provide for young people leaving council care, there have been breakdowns in the system. One way forward is the Labour-supported scheme for homeless young people operated by the Foyer Federation. These schemes provide accommodation, employment training and personal support for young people under 25, working with housing associations, training organisations, public agencies and local business. There are currently 78 foyers in the United Kingdom and more are planned.

In London, special measures for relieving homelessness were considered necessary. In July 1998, as part of the anti-exclusion programme, the government announced a new 'rough sleepers' initiative in which a coordinator (a 'streets tsar') with a 3-year £145 million budget was established to cut homelessness by two-thirds by 2002. Similar specialist coordinators, appointed by local authorities, supervised campaigns in other major cities. Councils also have to develop prevention strategies to combat single homelessness, and protect young people leaving care at age 16. The situation for families is somewhat different. In 1997 local authorities accepted 105 260 households as homeless (twice as many as 20 years earlier, but down on the 1991 total of 145 000). These problems have been exacerbated by the dramatic fall in local authority house-building and by the continuing controversies over building on greenfield as opposed to recycled 'brownfield' urban land. An important part of this debate is that, of the projected need of 4.4 million houses between 1991 and 2016 (a projection which is likely to rise to 5 million), some 40–50 per cent of all projected new households will require subsidised housing (Cm 3471, 1996). There is a paradox here, with social housing demand sitting alongside the fall in government funds for the housing associations, and the estimated 250 000 long-standing vacant properties in disrepair waiting to be brought back into use – and the empty refurbished or even new houses that stand empty in unpopular areas. It is estimated that almost a quarter of local authorities are struggling with areas of surplus housing.

Athough local authorities have largely lost their building role, a large number of houses are still owned by councils, giving them an important role as administrators of housing services, including operating the housing benefit system and allocating and managing properties. In housing there have been moves to give tenants a greater say in how their homes are run. Housing management had to be put out to tender under the extended CCT requirements of the 1988 Act. Now, although the universal CCT regime has ended, Labour's best value programme will continue the trend. The government is also requiring councils to give tenants greater management powers. The Tenant Participation Compact will establish common standards throughout the country; this will be backed by £2.2 million of additional funding. Under Labour, council action remains subject to central supervision; this will increase when a new Housing Inspectorate, under the Audit Commission, comes into operation as part of the 'best value' system.

Questions still surround the provision of social housing, homelessness, repair bills and the cost to governments of housing benefits. Some critics also believe that public housing is the problem not the solution, helping to create ghettos of benefit dependency and powerlessness. What is clear is that social housing in Britain has become increasingly marginalised, even though some 12 million people live in council housing, another 3 million in housing association dwellings and with about one-third of the 15 million drawing housing benefit. Social housing is also becoming increasingly polarised. At one end there are established elderly residents who have lived in social housing all their lives and at the other end newer, younger residents, often suffering from multiple problems of unemployment, poverty and poor work skills (Burrows, 1997).

In response to these problems the government is targeting the most deprived housing estates and their multifaceted problems – those 'estates on the edge' of a leading expert in the Social Exclusion Unit (Power, 1997) under the New Deal for Communities programme, as noted above. This concerted effort will, it is hoped, integrate the approaches to housing problems with the wider range of issues facing deprived areas. Among these issues are the multiple factors underlying ill health and the growing pressures to look after vulnerable groups of people in the community.

## Health and community care

One of the major concerns of the Labour government is to deliver improved health services, to tackle the poverty, poor housing and unemployment that are root causes of health inequalities and to end the divisions – Secretary of Health Frank Dobson's 'Berlin walls' – between health and community care at the local level. Local authorities are seen as having the capacity to address these problems through partnerships with health authorities. Local authorities are also an important part of the network of health and social services provision for particular groups of people, including the elderly, people with physical and learning disabilities, work with families and child protection. They also have mental health, drug/alcohol abuse, HIV/AIDS and adoption responsibilities. Local authority social service departments took on fresh responsibilities under the 1990 National Health Service and Community Care Act, which came into force in 1993. The Act laid a statutory duty on local authorities to work with health authorities, housing agencies and users and carers in the production of community care plans. Collaboration has continued to be difficult, however, with different agencies having different professional interests and working practices.

The Labour government is committed to a mixed economy of care. Boundaries between public, private and voluntary sectors are seen as redundant and the trend to private, as opposed to local authority, provision of residential care will accelerate. It is already the case that local authorities are not the major providers of residential care, with only one in seven residential beds provided by social services. This is the result of the transfer of council homes into the independent sector and the requirement that 85 per cent of funds must be spent in the non-council sector. Community care is an area where questions of need and priorities present special problems, particularly over the care of the elderly and the provisions for vulnerable young people. In the case of the elderly, national quality guidelines, a general social services council and a framework for means-tested charges will collectively impose greater central direction on social care. Nine regional inspectorates for England will replace the regulation of nursing homes by health authorities and residential homes by local authorities. To improve the lives of children in care, social services departments will be set targets and brought under a system of central monitoring. In child protection, the Quality Protects scheme launched in September 1998 sets targets for education departments and health authorities and requires all authorities to submit action plans. Additional funding depends on these targets being achieved and intervention if they are not.

In both care for the elderly and young people, the theme of strong central direction and oversight is a clear trend. In December 1998 the government published a White Paper, *Modernising Social Services*, which proposed a network of independent regional inspectorates. These regional commissions for care standards would regulate care homes and agencies, take over the existing regulatory functions of local and health authorities and increase inspection to cover private provision. In addition, there would be national standards and rules for care services. These are significant increases in central control. Local authorities will also have to demonstrate how they contribute to public health goals, working through housing, community development and health agencies to identify needs and how they should be met. As part of the collaboration council chief executives would participate in health authority meetings and there will be a statutory duty placed on local NHS bodies to work in local partnerships to a jointly agreed local health improvement programme (Cm 3807, 1998).

Local authorities will increasingly be drawn into health planning as part of their urban policies. In 1998 the Labour government established Health Action Zones (HAZs) for inner cities to bring together NHS bodies, local authorities, community and voluntary groups and local businesses. As with the other action-zone projects for education and employment and the community safety groups and youth offender teams, HAZs are part of the government's search for cross-cutting, multiagency solutions. The HAZs have a 5–7-year lifespan and are interlinked with social exclusion and SRB regeneration agendas; generally, a HAZ covers at least one health authority. The eleven pilots were launched in April 1998 and in January 1999 provided with a £78 million investment to enable them to develop new ways of improving health services and tackling health inequalities. This investment went into finding new ways of working, new partnerships, new financial arrangements and new structures. Later in 1999, a further 34 HAZs started work. In addition to these specifically targeted projects, further proposals for joint health and social care working are likely from 2000 onwards. These include proposals for local agreements for single agencies to take the lead on health and social care, the pooling of budgets subject to ministerial approval and integrated provision, for example health authorities providing social care services.

The drive for greater collaboration and integration reflects the recognition that housing, education, social and environmental services are essential to improved health. As such, health and community care have become an important element in addressing urban ills. But the well-being of cities extends beyond specialised health programmes: everyone has the right to demand a clean and hazard-free environment in which to live and work.

### The sustainable city

A clean environment and sustainable development have become prominent issues on the urban agenda, influenced by international and EU concern over adverse climate and other environmental problems and by growing public awareness. People are worried about pollution, traffic and transport and related quality of life issues. To match this public concern, local authorities are under pressure to integrate environmental matters with economic development, a concern also reflected in the Labour government's establishment of the Department of Environment, Transport and the Regions to integrate environment, planning and transport. The five key issues are atmospheric pollution, waste, energy, transport, and the built environment.

Sustainable development requires the integration of economic and environmental policies, balancing present demands against the needs of future generations and enhancing democratic involvement in decision-making. This is not an easy task: there is still considerable tension among officials responsible for economic development, planning, environmental issues and within the business community. Sustainable development is also allied to regeneration: in both, the government's commitment is to encourage local communities to contribute and to support them through capacity building – equipping local people to play a key role in developing and running projects. Regional Development Agencies, for their part, have a specific objective of furthering sustainable development as part of their strategic regional brief.

Sustainable development emerged as a major concern for local as well as national politics following the 1992 United Nations Rio de Janeiro Conference on Environment and Development, UNCED (the 'Earth Summit')'s action plan Agenda 21 (Agenda for the 21st Century). Chapter 28 of Agenda 21 focuses on the need for local consultation and the Local Agenda 21 process involves a wide range of interests, local communities and their governments. A second influence has been the European Union's Fifth Environmental Action Programme, 1993–2000, 'Towards Sustainability' (Commission of the European Communities, 1992). In 1997 the European Commission went further, proposing the 'greening' of Structural Funds by developing environmental indicators (Commission of the European Communities, 1997). A third source of pressure came from within the UK, in the White Paper *This Common Inheritance* (Cm 1200, 1990) and the subsequent Environmental Protection Act, 1990. The Act, and the 1994 Sustainable Development Strategy statement, laid new responsibilities on local authorities.

The outcomes of these three sources of action have been mixed, with national and European initiatives supportive but not radical. The Environment Act of 1995 (which set up the Environment Agency for England and Wales) and the establishment of national advisory panels on sustainable development appeared to indicate a new phase. At local level, the 1995 Environment Act set up a new system for improving air quality and systems for local air quality monitoring. Overall, while local authorities are making progress in environmental good practice, much remains to be done, in energy conservation and in recycling (Audit Commission, 1997a). Success in integrating economic and environmental objectives has been mixed (Gibbs, 1997) and while most urban local authorities have published strategies, this is not always reflected in projects or in objectives for improvement.

Local authorities, however, have been encouraged to incorporate Agenda 21 principles into their planning processes (Bateman, 1995) and there are references to Local Agenda 21 in the bidding guidance for the Single Regeneration Budget. More than half the authorities in England, Wales and Scotland are committed to developing Agenda 21 plans, with the Labour government target being for all local authorities to have a Local Agenda 21 strategy in place by the year 2000. Local Agenda 21 projects challenge traditional forms of decision-making. They rely on new forms of urban politics which rest on partnership with groups and interests in a more participatory and flexible approach, including focus groups, citizens' panels, cooption onto committees, working parties and environmental fora. The environmental agenda's emphasis on partnership and participation has been seen as providing important lessons for plans to revitalise local democracy (S. Young, 1996; 1995). Groups of all kinds play a major part in these developments. Young distinguishes between those groups which lobby to change policy and not-for-profit bodies who are concerned with implementation, with getting things done on the ground (S. Young, 1995). Thus not-for-profit groups, for example conservation and wild-life organisations, own and manage sites, organise waste recycling schemes and mount projects for schools and companies. Involving individuals and groups in these new ways are seen as essential to a more collaborative approach drawing in many agencies and services. This is not easy: reconciling major economic and environmental interests is problematic, as is integrating regeneration policies and Agenda 21 concerns.

A contentious area of environmental protection and sustainability lies in energy and transport policies. The privatisation of energy utilities has made it imperative that local authority and other policymakers enter into new coalitions with providers to minimise the environmental costs of infrastructure provision and land-use planning decisions. The second, and high-profile, political issue is transport policy. The Town and Country Planning Act 1990 required local planning authorities to include land-use policies in respect of the management of traffic. Local authorities must produce local transport plans – Transport Policies and Programme (TPP) – which are reviewed annually. In July 1998 the government's integrated transport white paper, *A New Deal for Transport: Better for Everyone*, offered new policies, but implementation would not begin until the year 2000 or later (Cm 3950, 1998). Subsequently, it seemed that there would be further delay, with the timetable for legislation being deferred beyond the 1998–99 parliamentary session.

The key tax measures of the government's proposals were toll and company carpark charges, with the proceeds going to public transport. Other measures include 5-year local transport plans, concessionary bus passes for all pensioners, a national public transport information system, and Quality Partnerships (already operating in some areas) between local authorities and bus companies to improve services. Much of the successful outcomes of the integrated transport policy will depend on the multimodal local transport plans, introduced on a non-statutory basis in 1999. In December 1998 the government's consultation paper *Breaking the Logjam* outlined plans for congestion charges and workplace parking charges (though nationwide charges before 2001 are unlikely) with the money raised to be ploughed back into local transport schemes. It was anticipated that some 150 towns and cities will come forward with local schemes in line with these proposals, with the pilot councils being allowed to charge for road-use and workplace parking and keep all the money raised for public transport improvements. If these pilots are successful then legislation will extend the provisions nationwide.

As the first major transport policy for 20 years, the 1998 Transport White Paper was widely praised, but there was accompanying criticism that the burden of actual responsibility for the hardest choices – for example congestion charges – was laid firmly on local authorities. These strategies, however, have to accommodate the demands of different groups, some of them powerful economic interests and others with considerable public appeal, such as environmental lobbying groups. Considerable political tension continues to surround large-scale development, particularly out-of-town retail and residential projects (Breheny, 1998). The planning guidance issued by government, notably PPG6 *Town Centres and Retailing*, requires that commercial, civic and cultural activity be first located in the town centre and then in descending order of edge-of-town through peripheral locations, but all taking public transport into account. Uncertainty remains, however, over how effective stemming the tide of out-of-town retailing and subsequent residential development really is.

Overall, environmental issues have grown in importance and are an essential part of urban politics. Sustainable development, clean air and water, energy and transport management, must all be integrated into physical and economic planning. It is an area, moreover, where local initiatives, and local involvement – both through 'normal participation' and through protest – are having a sharpening impact.

**Conclusion**

Urban policy at the end of the century means setting priorities to reverse social divisions and deprivation and is especially directed at families with young children, ethnic minorities, the elderly, the long-term unemployed and run-down areas of towns and cities. Urban politics must tackle this agenda, managing conflict over resources and priorities and draw on wide sectors and groups to achieve results. Public services must be embedded in the communities they serve, listening to what local people say and drawing them into both policy and projects; in other words responsiveness to the citizen as consumer who drives modern service delivery. It will be further highlighted by the impact of the 1998 Human Rights Act which incorporates the European Convention on Human Rights into domestic law. These rights include the right to respect for family life, the home and freedom of religion, expression, assembly and association. Local councils, health authorities and schools will all be affected and could face litigation since citizens can take cases of injustice directly to British courts under the 1998 Human Rights Act. Issues could arise, for example, over failure to provide individuals with information, failure to provide appropriate education, failures to repair council houses, or racial discrimination.

Action at the local level reflects pressing urban problems that require collaborative ways of working across the boundaries between services. The problems considered in this chapter illustrate the contemporary pressures of urban politics: how to promote economic growth, ensure safe communities, facilitate improved standards in education, meet the demands for homes, bring together health and social services in community care and protect the environment for present and future generations. Dominating the agenda in recent years have been economic regeneration, education and crime and disorder. Economic regeneration has also highlighted newer preoccupations with social exclusion, where questions of distribution (though not necessarily *re*distribution) are as important as those of economic growth. Nor should the battle for social justice be seen as antipathetic to the search for the sustainable, green city. The two must share the vision for the good city – in housing, health, education and jobs.

This chapter has explored the key themes of the urban political agenda and shown how the role of local authorities has been changing. In all these areas – crime, education, housing, community care, the environment – local authorities must work with and through a wide range of other agencies. This has affected the way services are planned and delivered, how different political interests are accommodated and shows how issues of local input into decisions are as important as political support from voters.

Delivering these services requires a pluralistic system of local politics, with an emphasis on policy networks. This has become both the accepted way of working and the dominant conceptual framework. The pluralist framework, however, cannot be entirely accepted at its face value in urban politics. More apposite are neopluralist and neo-elitist explanations which emphasise policy communities and networks and the dominance of professionals, political leaders and the major groups in each policy arena. The policies and activities considered in this chapter fit this model but the place of the dominant actors within each policy arena varies. In economic regeneration and inner-city policy, the lead actors are the public–private partnerships working to the Single Regeneration Budget process and other projects. In community care, by contrast, the lead role has been given to local authorities, but within frameworks which emphasise multiagency cooperation and planning. In relation to crime and disorder, even though police authorities are autonomous corporate bodies, local authority support for preventive measures remains vital and community partnership working will increase local council inputs. In housing, government legislation has shifted the major responsibility of social housing from the local authority to housing associations and this, together with the contracting out of housing management, has left local authorities with a declining role. In education the centralisation of the curriculum and the imposition of testing and performance indicators, has been matched by decentralisation to governing bodies, parents and head teachers. In the environmental area the input of groups is more eclectic and the emphasis on community participation an essential part of the local policy arena. But it too reflects the fragmented neopluralist arena of urban governance which is characteristic of local policy and politics.

The Labour government has reaffirmed multiagency partnership working to solve urban problems. It has taken this furthest in the highly targeted Action Zone projects for its priority issues of unemployment, education and health. Commentators urge caution in embracing this model; lessons from the urban programmes of the 1960s show that tensions between 'partnerships' is real, with different expectations and ways of working. To succeed, such projects need to work hard to remain focused on their main commitment, rather than becoming mired in organisational battles. By 2000 it is anticipated that there will be some 800 Action Zones and SRB locations which, it is claimed, will be brought together into a national strategy against social exclusion. This is a great challenge: the zones differ enormously in scale and objectives and have been designed to meet individual departmental and ministerial concerns. Other critics argue that the idea is being asked to bear too much weight in the search for realistic improvements and are, moreover, taking on board American initiatives that come from a very different policy and local governmental environment. Nevertheless, the government is firmly committed to radical, integrated solutions. These are emphasised to break down barriers between services, professional prerogatives and public–private sectors. This approach is part of the modernising project, in which local authorities will be major actors in meeting anti-poverty and anti-exclusion objectives but within partnership elite groupings. It is with these developments that the next chapter is concerned.

# 7

# The Modernising Agenda

Urban policy addresses problems of deprivation, quality of life and environmental issues. Urban politics tries to resolve these problems by bringing together resources and people from many parts of city life: public and private, voluntary and not-for-profit. Though different interests may have different agendas and goals, contemporary urban politics is not just about managing conflict between them. The emphasis is on working together for holistic solutions, creating and sustaining partnerships and pursuing consensus. The trends to partnership working to solve urban problems have been growing for the past two decades. Under the present Labour government the modernising project drives the agenda, both promising more powers to local councils while demanding innovative multiagency and democratic reforms. If the traditional model was of decisions being made inside the town hall, now it is urban governance, working across boundaries, that is becoming the dominant form of urban politics.

The outcomes of urban policy in the past 20 years have been judged at best only a partial success. The official and scholarly appraisals, as Chapter 2 showed, point to the lack of a coherent and cohesive strategy, the ad hoc and short-term nature of projects and a concentration on physical renewal which has not produced long-term solutions. Labour after 1997 promised a new approach. The Prime Minister saw social exclusion as the 'big issue', the defining difference between Labour and the previous government. Labour's agenda embraced four key elements: the Social Exclusion Unit in the Cabinet Office reporting directly to the Prime Minister; decentralisation to new Regional Development Agencies; collaboration between centre and localities; new ways of working for local authorities, both within councils and between them and other local bodies.

Collaborative relationships have always existed between local bodies, but pressures from central government and changes in the way services are provided have both opened up the scope of such relationships and entrenched them more formally into urban politics. This has assumed central importance as the issues of reducing poverty, fostering greater social inclusion and improving health and education have come to the top of the political agenda. Local councils have a key role to play in achieving these goals and must do so by delivering services to the best value possible, whether from the town hall, from independent and private providers, or in collaboration with them. But modernisation does not just mean pursuing best value in these ways, it means looking at how councils lead their communities, their internal ways of working and their involving of local people. Modernisation and democracy, the government argues, go hand in hand.

Revitalising urban affairs is an exciting project. Can it fulfil that renewed search for the just society which does, or should, lie at the centre of urban politics? The present chapter examines the changes that are in progress. It begins by looking at the principles that Labour puts forward as the basis of its approach: a Third Way. The chapter then moves to the government's proposals for meeting its objectives, particularly the emphasis on targeting and collaboration. These aims are well demonstrated by the Single Regeneration Budget and New Deal arrangements. Labour aims are also driven by the impact of devolution. The changes in Scotland and Wales have highlighted the debate on a regional dimension in England.

Labour's modernising project is also forcing through changes in the way councils conduct their business, including the introduction of elected mayors and a revamped committee system. There are pressures to improve electoral turnout and involve communities in regeneration projects. More radical are the projects to tackle the worst neighbourhoods through action zones for employment, health and education, that operate through public–private fora and boards. But are these moves enough, or do local councils need wider powers if they are to lead their communities in revitalising urban life? The chapter ends by examining these dilemmas.

## A third way?

Responsible and responsive public bodies, working to high standards and consulting and involving individuals and groups in services, are the key to Labour's aims for a revitalised democracy. But Labour's 'third way' is not identical with the notion of a 'stakeholder' economy with its diffuse ideas of the involvement of interested parties in deci-sion-making, or Hirst's 'associative democracy' of voluntary networks of business, community and other groups (Amin and Graham, 1997; Hirst, 1994). It treads a path, rather, between free market captialism and classical social democracy. In Prime Minister Blair's words, the aim is 'to find a new way, a third way, between unbridled individu-alism and *laissez-faire* on the one hand; and old-style Government intervention, the corporatism of 1960s social democracy, on the other' (quoted in Williams, 1998), that is, between *laissez-faire* and state control, marrying an open and successful economy with a just and humane society.

As Chapter 3 indicated, Blair's definition of a third way is a 'what works' philosophy. The call to the radical centre requires both a new mixed economy and a new democratic state. The institutions of civil society must also be strengthened, supporting the family, investing in skills, reforming welfare and, crucially, redefining equality as inclusion not redistribution. It is evident that this agenda has inmportant implica-tions for urban policy. The central issues can be approached through Le Grand's analysis of the key elements of the third way. These are com-munity, opportunity, responsibility and accountability – CORA (Le Grand, 1998). The Labour government's emphasis is on community, on moves to elected mayors and other suggestions for increasing consulta-tion and participation, and on cooperation between agencies such as health trusts and local councils. These are more than pragmatic responses to low voter turnout or attempts to overcome fragmentation. They reflect a belief in the spirit of cooperation and consultation in opposition to the competitive individualism of the Thatcher years. The fourth CORA theme, accountability, illuminates the thinking of the consultation papers on modernising local government published in the Spring of 1998. The multipurpose local authority of pre-1979 will not be restored, but through partnerships with different local bodies coun-cils will become more open, transparent and responsible to the plural-istic communities they serve. In his pamphlet on local democracy Tony Blair saw local government as crucial to Labour's commitments in education, employment and tackling social exclusion. But it had to improve its legitimacy by overcoming poor local electoral turnout, raising standards of service, having high ethical standards and offering effective community leadership (Blair, 1998a). Le Grand's third 'CORA' element, of personal responsibility, underpins the New Deal, welfare-to-work proposals. Citizens have obligations: those who can work must do so or face loss of benefits, with people taking more responsibility for their own lives. The final theme of the third way is opportunity, particularly opportunity to work and to obtain training and education.

Labour's third way claims to be a different philosophy on which to base policy. Unlike neoliberalism, community is important in promoting the good life. But unlike socialism, the third way is not egalitarian: the social justice it espouses relies on providing minimum standards and equality of opportunity, not on redistribution and equality of outcome. Help is targeted on the most deprived, who would otherwise risk exclusion from society. This help will not depend solely on additional resources but on helping with work and training opportunities and be matched by obligations on those receiving help. The third way is also pragmatic about structures: government sets and guarantees policy objectives but it is not necessarily the agency that delivers them.

**Taking change forward**

In Labour's view, the way forward for democratic renewal lies in more cooperative working. In this cross-cutting approach, civil society is an important check on state power, with an increasingly differentiated range of local bodies having responsibility for decision-making and service delivery (Stoker, 1996b). The changes that the Labour government is introducing reinforces existing trends towards more cooperation between local bodies. Urban governance is used to describe this multiagency working, negotiated agendas and consensus-seeking that increasingly characterises urban politics. Urban governance, that is, is an arena of bargaining and negotiation, with the local council providing leadership of their communities. To legitimise their leadership role, local authorities must move beyond the representative model of periodic elections to an inclusive model of local democracy which incorporates local stakeholders into an active role in decision-making (Cairns, 1996).

The traditional justification for local councils' leadership role in urban politics is democratic as well as functional: a viable system of local democracy, a means whereby people can provide services for themselves (Cmnd 4040, 1969). If it is to do this effectively, it must have the power to vary services according to local need, something that has become a real issue in the wish of successive governments to control finance and impose national standards. Urban politics, that is, is about more than networks and negotiation. It is about responsibility and responsiveness to a local citizenry. Transparent accountability is a major principle. Partnerships and alliances will have to work hard to achieve accountability and transparency within the complexities of contemporary urban governance. It is against these standards that Labour's changes should be judged. The innovative policies include new measures of service delivery, including strengthening the capacity of the core executive in local authorities, changes to the electoral system, and additional powers to act for the community as a whole.

In addition, the Labour government's approach places a greater emphasis on targeting funds on those areas of greatest need (as opposed to the previous government's focus on need plus capacity for improvement). These moves were justified to achieve the overall policy objective of a more just society while making the best use of limited funding. These views are well expressed by the 'three key features' of Labour policy, as set out in Box 7.1.

While partnership working was already a feature of local services, its range and importance increased under Labour. But exclusion was a new theme for urban policy in the form and importance Labour gave to it. Though it had been a part of the European Union social policy discourse since 1988 (and perhaps for that reason ignored by Conservative governments) it was not until Labour was elected to office that it became dominant. It was, claimed Prime Minister Blair, the principle that marked off Labour from previous Conservative governments. The need to make that sharp distinction was put most forcibly by the Social Exclusion Unit's report of September 1998: 'Over the last generation, this has become a more divided country' (Cm 4045, 1998:9). The gap between the worst neighbourhoods and

*Box 7.1*   Labour's 'three key features' of policy

---

- Policies must address social exclusion and need; severely disadvantaged people and areas are unacceptable and uneconomic.
- Develop local partnerships and build the capacity of local authorities to take part in regeneration initiatives – Whitehall does not know best.
- A more collaborative approach between the centre, regional and local levels and across sectors, whilst recognising competition for scarce resources.

the rest of society, said the Prime Minister, 'has left us with a situation that no civilised society should tolerate' (Cm 4045:7). The Social Exclusion Unit report's findings showed the deteriorating state of a 'two nation' Britain. Making Britain a more inclusive society would need efforts on a broad front: innovative ways of getting people into work; creating good neighbourhoods and fighting antisocial behaviour and crime; motivating children at school; providing the poorest people with better access to services (including shops, banks and other services that the middle class take for granted); making government work better, including improved coordination and cooperation at both central and local levels.

### Refocusing regeneration: targeting and partnerships

A new, refocused Single Regeneration Budget exemplified the direction that policy would take to meet the problems of the worst neighbourhoods that Labour had marked out for urgent attention. Table 7.1

*Table 7.1*   Regeneration programmes

| | Additional spending | | | New spending plans | | |
|---|---|---|---|---|---|---|
| *All figures in £m* | *1999–00* | *2000–01* | *2001–02* | *1999–00* | *2000–01* | *2001–02* |
| New Deal for | | | | | | |
|     Communities | 87.5 | 237.5 | 437.5 | 100.0 | 250.0 | 450.0 |
| SRB Challenge Fund | | | | | | |
| (Rounds 1–4) | 69.5 | 2.0 | -138.3 | 636.3 | 568.8 | 428.5 |
| New SRS | 75.0 | 245.0 | 450.0 | 75.0 | 245.0 | 450.0 |
| English Partnerships | -67.7 | -89.7 | -89.7 | 230.7 | 208.7 | 208.7 |
| Housing Action Trusts | 0.9 | 0.9 | 0.9 | 88.4 | 88.4 | 88.4 |
| Estate Action | -32.8 | -35.2 | -59.6 | 66.2 | 63.9 | 39.4 |
| New Towns | -12.9 | -20.9 | -20.9 | -116.0 | -124.0 | -124.0 |
| ERDF | | | | | | |
|     ex-DOE | 35.4 | 0.0 | 0.0 | 221.6 | 186.2 | 186.2 |
|     DfEE transfer for LIPA | 0.0 | 0.0 | 0.0 | 1.4 | 1.4 | 1.4 |
| Other regeneration | -23.2 | -26.9 | -35.2 | 48.5 | 44.7 | 36.5 |
| Regeneration total | 131.6 | 312.6 | 544.6 | 1352.0 | 1533.0 | 1765.0 |

*Source*:   Housing and Regeneration Policy: A Statement by the Deputy Prime Minister and Secretary of State for the Environment, Transport and the Regions (DETR, July 1998).

shows the additional spending proposed for the various regeneration programmes over the 3-year period 1999–2002 and the total spending plans for that period. It shows that following the completion of the SRB Challenge Fund Rounds 1–4, the New SRB and the New Deal for Communities will grow rapidly, while continuing to fund the commitments under the other programmes, including English Partnerships, Estate Action and Housing Action Trusts.

Targeting is the key. As a result of Labour's proposals, the SRB has been reshaped to concentrate 80 per cent of the new resources (some £700 million over the 3-year period from 1998) in the most deprived areas, with at least one new major project in each area by the year 2000. In addition £800 million would go to the New Deal for Communities initiative, offering intensive help to the neediest neighbourhoods, bringing together regeneration and housing programmes and enhancing economic and employment opportunities. Initially the funding would concentrate on 17 'pathfinder' authorities.

Not only targeting, but more cooperation between agencies is essential if regeneration is to work. The aim of the revitalised SRB system is to make bids operate through integrated local partnerships working in cross-cutting ways. Under this system there are longer lead-in times for the projects, more time for consultation and greater resources for capacity building than in the past. In particular, regeneration partnerships have to make clear the linkages between housing, regeneration and other initiatives and demonstrate that local strategies fit well together and complement the regional plans developed by the Regional Development Agencies (DETR, 1998c). They also have to show how they fit with other new area-based strategies such as the Action Zones for employment, health and education.

The emphasis on partnership among local public and private bodies and on attracting private investment were at the centre of Labour's regeneration policy. But not all was new: just as the broad framework of the SRB was a continuation of existing policy, albeit with a different emphasis, so too was the search for a greater input from private investment. To this end Labour relaunched the Private Finance Initiative (PFI) to provide capital assets in health, transport and education services. Originally announced in the (Conservative) Chancellor's 1992 Autumn Statement, the PFI initiative was intended as a means of using private capital to replace government funding for public projects. Under Labour, as part of the PFI, there was a £250 million initial budget (doubling to £500 million in 1998–99) for local authority capital contracts on a design, build, finance and operate (DBFO) basis. The Labour government's 1997 Local Government (Contracts) Act confirmed the powers of local authorities to enter into PFI and other partnership transactions and by the end of 1998 the number of council projects had risen to 87, including schools, children's homes, social housing, fire stations and a light rail system. PFI brings much needed investment and fits the objective of levering in private monies. Not all commentators are happy with this situation, arguing that it gives private companies too much power over terms and conditions and puts large burdens on local taxpayers to pay the interest and charges over the lifetime of the projects.

## Moving decisions from the centre

Labour's commitment to change was not just a matter of prioritising inclusion, reshaping regeneration targets and and attracting private investment. There was a major change to the political climate as Labour fulfilled its pledges to move decisions from the centre, to devolved political assemblies in Scotland and Wales and to new development agencies in the English regions. These were significant departures from the policies of the previous Conservative government which marked a distinctive new era.

In Scotland, a Parliament based on proportional representation and with powers to legislate on local government boundaries and functions challenged local councils to become more open and efficient, moving to elected provosts and reforming their committee structures – a means of attracting high-calibre councillors released from the burden of excessive committee work. The government saw the way forward as councils that carried out the strategic planning of services, not their direct provision, and with a new duty of community planning, following on from the neighbourhood decentralisation plans begun by the previous Conservative administration.

The government also set up an independent commission – the Commission on Local Government and the Scottish Parliament – with a two-task remit: to draw up a framework within which local government and the Scottish Parliament could work together; to examine and develop local councils' democratic accountability to their communities. Its report of November 1998 saw three elements as vital to local government renewal: the separation of the executive role from the scrutiny and representative roles of backbenchers; initiatives to encourage more people to become councillors; the introduction of a more proportional electoral system. There should also be a covenant defining the relationships between local councils, the Scottish Parliament and the new Scottish executive, and a joint fora of MSPs and local representatives to oversee relations between the tiers of government. These proposals, after consultation, went to the Scottish Parliament in June 1999.

In Wales the elected Assembly which, unlike the Scottish Parliament, has no powers to make primary legislation, could be seen as a long-term prototype for English regions. As in Scotland, however, the government was anxious to emphasise that the Assembly would work in partnership with local councils, and there will be a 'partnership council' to effect this. But although the assembly would have no powers to take functions away from councils, there was concern that there might be rivalry between Assembly and councils to expand their respective roles. But the Assembly will be responsible for allocating around half of its total budget to the 22 county councils in revenue and capital funding – small changes in such allocations could have major impacts. The Assembly will also be able to transfer functions from public bodies – for example, some of the functions of the former Tai Cymru (Housing for Wales) – to local government.

Devolution to Scotland and Wales raised the issue of what role, if any, should be given to the English regions. In opposition the Labour party, and John Prescott in particular, had appeared to favour a move to elected regional bodies with important strategic and regeneration powers. The thinking behind these Labour moves had been set out in a number of reports while the party was in opposition. In 1995, proposals for English regional chambers or assemblies, as a parallel to those for a Scottish parliament and a Welsh assembly, were published as a consultation paper. In 1996, the report of the Labour Party's Regional Policy Commission, *New Labour, New Life for Britain* (Labour Party, 1996), rejected any imposition of elected regional assemblies. Because regional cohesion and local support varied, with the North East and North West showing the greatest support, any moves to regional government would be gradual and dependent on popular consent in the areas concerned, expressed through a referendum or other means.

On attaining office in May 1997, John Prescott, Deputy Prime Minister with responsibilities for the merged Department of the Environment, Transport and the Regions, promised to devolve

Whitehall powers to the English regions with a network of multipurpose development agencies (see Chapter 4). The development agencies were set up in the eight standard regions plus Greater London. Legislation was passed in 1998, with the new agencies starting work in April 1999. The argument for development agencies is that effective economic development can only be achieved over wider areas than individual local authorities. In the globalised economy it is argued that the state no longer controls national economic planning as it once did and more emphasis is placed on regional indigenous growth and on attracting investment through the particular qualities of individual regions. Regions have emerged both as units of horizontal integration and as political actors in policymaking (Keating, 1997). As chapter 4 emphasised, the English RDAs are business-led, with 12-member (6 from business, 4 from local councils, 2 from voluntary agencies and universities) boards who have to consult with voluntary regional assemblies made up of councillors, business people, academics and members of the voluntary sectors. Elected assemblies would only follow after local referenda and would be unlikely in the first term of the Labour government. The establishment of RDAs, and nominated chambers to advise them, can be seen in two different ways: as judicious but cautious moves on the road to full regionalism or as business-led 'superquangos' with no guarantees of democratic control.

Research evidence on public support for a future elected regional level of government is mixed. While people have some sense of regional identity, especially in the north, only a quarter of people favoured regional powers of government for England, and 60 per cent were opposed (MORI, 1996). But when people were asked specifically whether they would support the idea for the region where they lived, majorities were in favour, with the exception of East Anglia and the South East outside London (Miller and Dickson, 1996). The result suggests that assemblies could exist in some regions and not others, or for assemblies with varying functions and powers (Constitution Unit, 1996). Though elected regional bodies, if they emerge at all, are some way in the future, urban policy must increasingly be seen within the framework of the new Regional Development Agencies. In Labour's view, Regional Development Agencies are the key element in improving the coordination of land-use, transport and economic development planning at the regional level. The issue of functions, however, remains problematic, given the concern that future regional assemblies would drain responsibilities from local authorities rather than accumulate powers devolved from the central government. From this perspective it is argued this is already an issue for the existing Regional Development Agencies, with RDAs under pressure to intervene in council affairs because central government sees them as forwarding Labour's policy objectives. In the final analysis regional government as such is a political, not a technical question, which depends on where and how democracy is to be expressed and exercised.

## The holistic approach to urban policy

If Labour's third way philosophy meant in practice a 'what works' approach to policy, its stress on collaborative, multiagency working continued trends in local practice that had been evolving over the previous decade. Conservative reforms of the 1980s replaced the traditional all-purpose local authority, providing all services in its area, with the enabling authority that gives strategic direction to services provided from a mix of sources. Though critics have argued that this has led to fragmentation and a lack of coordination, the enabling authority is firmly established. The broad notion is that an enabling authority is one which leads the provision of services – 'steering not rowing' – by working with and through a wide range of public, private and voluntary organisations. The result is a network of partnerships, providing a mixed economy of services, that has been continued and expanded under Labour. The Labour government's belief is that the local authority should use whatever channels of provision are appropriate: the 'best value' approach. 'Networking' and an outward-looking proactive stance are key elements, together with an emphasis on democratic values.

A central theme of the current approach is that of partnership, an approach that now pervades all policy sectors, under the Crime and Disorder Act, the development of primary care groups in the NHS, care in the community, regeneration and anti-deprivation projects. It has become central to urban governance, reflecting the changing relationships between the state, the market and civil society (Geddes, 1997). To push forward urban programmes local councils must now be outward-looking, part of a network of relationships and taking the lead in the wellbeing of the community. Policy success will be judged by this community well-being and councils will need the political acumen to engage with other actors in complex networks of bargaining and

*Box 7.2*   The key to successful partnerships

---

- Genuine joint working; creation of additional benefits – synergy – to those achieved by working alone.
- Commitment of key interests; joint vision of what can be achieved.
- Having a clear agenda, defined objectives, and appropriate level of working between officials/representatives of the various groups.
- Having known systems of accountability; transparent working relationships; interacting with citizen/consumer groups.

---

negotiation. For the Labour government the radical agenda calls for 'joined-up' solutions for joined-up problems.

Partnerships differ in their scope, objectives, and membership. As Box 7.2 shows, the two key elements, however, are the existence of genuine joint working, and the production of some social or non-commercial value-added. The partnership, that is, should be greater than the sum of its parts – synergy – as a result of the collaboration. The result is urban governance working across functional divisions. In the 1980s partnership working was imposed from above, by government requirements that in order to receive funding for urban regeneration projects local councils had to develop bids in conjunction with the private sector and community interests. At that time the Conservative government's guiding principle was in effect the injection of a business culture into urban policy to challenge the bureaucratic workings of the public sector. While continuing the partnership ethos, Labour claims new purposes, both integrating wide expertise into the process and enhancing its democratic nature.

Wanting to work collaboratively has to recognise that success depends on making the links structured and the objectives clear. Partnership working is not easy, given that the different partners have separate systems and procedures, financial regimes and professional cultures and power tends to be unevenly distributed between stakeholders (Bailey, Barker and MacDonald, 1995). Local authorities, in forming partnerships with non-elected bodies, must maintain their democratic responsibility to the community as a whole, with a clear agenda and an ability to mobilise community support. This is a difficult area: partnerships can be seen as threats to formal political accountability as appointed bodies gain influence at the expense of the rest of the councillors not involved in them. Others take the opposite view, that involving a wider range of stakeholders in policy and service delivery increases democracy. A third issue arises from the tendency of these coordinating mechanisms to become institutionalised (Pierre, 1998). The fear then is that they become governing units in their own right – quasi-governments – bypassing democratically elected councils with their party political direction of urban affairs in favour of shadowy boards in which business has a privileged position.

Local authorities have considerable experience of partnership, collaboration and inter-agency working, in economic regeneration, crime and community safety, health and community care and environmental improvements. The scope of collaborative arrangements is wide, including formal and informal mechanisms and different levels of decision-making from the sub-regional to individual projects (Hambleton, Essex and Mills, 1996). Success depends on the exercise of the 'heavenly virtues', including a jointly held vision, a firm plan, jointly owned strategies and parity among partners (Grayson, 1993). In the case of partnership with the voluntary sector, problems can arise where organisations become contracted suppliers, entering into formal contracts and service level agreements with local authorities to deliver specified services. For voluntary bodies, this contract culture alters the nature of partnerships, formalising and legalising them, and raising important issues of accountability to clients and to the community as a whole. Nevertheless, the Labour government is anxious to reaffirm partnership working between local councils and the voluntary sector and proposed a 'compact' to underpin it, which would also deal with funding and contractual relationships.

If partnerships are structured links between organisations, networks are patterns of personal relationships between individuals, albeit in the context of organisations, based on reciprocity and trust. Networks cluster around particular policy or functional areas; policy networks are marked by long-term negotiation strategies to obtain mutual advantages in areas such as economic growth. Active partnerships, however, emerge in much wider activities than urban regeneration. They help to broaden the participatory democracy approach to decision-making. Working with residents' associations, area fora, the users' committees of a variety of facilities such as leisure centres and youth and age groups, are some of the examples of this working with, rather than working for, local people. This then raises issues of equality among partners, given a tendency to a power imbalance in favour of the local authority. It also highlights the criticism that partnerships erode democratic responsibility and accountability, with non-elected bodies and members gaining power at the expense of elected politicians.

## The new local leadership

Labour believes that for democracy to flourish, local leadership must be strengthened and made more responsive and accountable. Historically, the work of local councils has been based on specific functions and implemented through designated committees and departments. Over the past two decades, however, local authorities have sought a more coordinated and strategic approach and this will be accelerated by the Labour government's reform proposals. This acceleration will build on existing changes in how local leadership operates.

The contemporary situation reflects a growing emphasis on a core elite. Most councils have a central coordinating committee, usually a policy and resources committee, with the leader of the majority party group playing a dominant role. In effect most councils have, through this leader and key committee chair system, a political leadership with major executive functions but which falls short of the powers of an elected mayor or local 'cabinet' of the kind proposed by Labour. Although councils have been required, under the provisions of the Local Government and Housing Act 1989, to ensure pro rata representation of all political groups on all committees and sub-committees, including the core policy committee, many authorities have established an informal ruling party group as a policy committee. In practice this acts as an executive, putting decisions to the formal committee for ratification. Deliberations of the informal policy committee will normally also be considered in the wider controlling party group. The chief executive and chief officers may attend the single group committee on an informal basis by invitation, though they continue to maintain their traditional political neutrality. In some authorities where there is no one party in overall control, there are a variety of arrangements, including formal coalitions or some kind of power-sharing.

These arrangements have arisen from the realities of power-holding in local decision-making, which in turn expresses the outcome of democratic processes based on elections. The historic council-committee structure assumed that all councillors were equal. In the present politicised system this is unrealistic. The ruling group and the majority party, where one exists, is the *de facto* executive. This in effect has been recognised in the Labour government's reform proposals. Formally, however, committees have historically been the means of conducting business. The Audit Commission's 1990 report took the view that committee organisation, frequency of meetings and attention to detail could no longer be defended. Instead, members should take on a much more strategic and monitoring role (Audit Commission, 1990). Its follow-up 1997 report showed that councillors continued to spend around half of their time in committees, compared with 30 per cent on their representative work such as ward surgeries or residents' meetings, a position that should be reversed (Audit Commission, 1997b). The main focus of council work should be on policy decisions and on monitoring the performance of officers and contractors.

Labour expressed its determination to address this problem. While its priority for change was evident and its proposals a marked shift from existing practice, there had been previous moves to introduce reforms. Under the impetus of Michael Heseltine's drive to reform local government, the Department of the Environment published a consultation paper on internal council management in 1991. In 1993 a joint DOE/local authority associations working party was set up to examine questions of strategic direction, community leadership and the policy and representative roles of members. The Working Party advocated limited changes to the law to formalise the position of the *de facto* executive. It also considered the possibility of introducing elected mayors and cabinet-style executives and recommended that local authorities should be allowed to experiment with new schemes (Working Party, 1993). These suggestions, however, were never taken further.

Ideas for reform were also put forward by the independent Commission for Local Democracy (1995) and in Lord Hunt's private member's Local Government (Experimental Arrangements) Bill which passed the House of Lords but failed in the House of Commons. The Hunt bill had covered elected mayors, local cabinets and scrutiny committees, and included internal standards committees to maintain ethical standards. But it recommended that changes be left to councils to take up through local experiments. In practice, councils were already experimenting, changing and streamlining their committee systems, scrutinising council work, experimenting with cabinets and producing democracy plans. One example of committee reform is that of the London borough of Hammersmith and Fulham which, in the Spring of 1998, installed an executive mayor chosen by the majority group, a six-member cabinet (the 'Mayor's board') and scrutiny committees. One of the six 'cabinet' members had responsibility for overseeing social exclusion projects and initiatives in run-down areas, reflecting the dominant agenda in urban politics in the late 1990s. Other initiatives, like those in Watford and the London borough of Lewisham, have moved to hold referenda of their voters on whether to opt for an elected mayor. The net effect of these trends is an accelerating downward trend in committee numbers, a slower fall in the number of sub-committees and a fall in the number of committee meetings. At the same time, however, informal member working parties and officer/member working groups have increased significantly. These changes, Young stresses, mark an extension of the decision-making process into small informal groups, and the development of new ways for members and officers to work together (K. Young, 1996a, 1996b).

## Modernising local government

The Labour government took up the debate on how to improve decision-making and made it a central part of its modernising agenda. In 1998 the government published six interrelated consultation papers setting out its vision for revitalised local democracy. These covered democratic renewal, best value in service delivery, a new ethical framework and three papers on aspects of the local government finance system. Following the subsequent White Paper, the Local Government (Organisation and Standards) Bill was published as a consultative draft in March 1999. It was anticipated that the bill would come to parliament late in 1999 and be implemented from the year 2000 onwards. The Local Democracy consultation paper on community leadership, and the White Paper, covered modernising local government, the need for change, modernising electoral arrangements, changing the way councils work, and promoting council leadership of their communities (DETR, 1998d; Cm 4014, 1998). The draft Local Government (Organisation and Standards) Bill was in two parts: Part I covered new political management structures – elected mayors and cabinet style executives – while Part II established a new ethical framework (Cm 4298, 1999).

The incentives for local councils would be that those which embraced change would be rewarded with new freedoms and powers, but this would be dependent on decision-making becoming more transparent, responsive and inclusive. Councils would have to show they accepted change, demonstrate their competence and their willingness to tackle corruption. The government's strong views were based on its determination that change would happen, backed by intervention from the centre if necessary. Included among the suggestions were powers for councils to hold local public fora through which local issues could be aired and local quangos questioned.

Critics believed that the proposals were too centralist, requiring councils to introduce new working practices, instead of allowing them to experiment, as the failed Hunt bill would have done. There were also reservations over the extent of the government's belief in local democracy. In particular, the government's firm rejection of the Local Government Association's (the body that represents local authorities in England and Wales) claim that the return of business rates to local control was fundamental to increasing local autonomy was disappointing. The government's concern was, rather, with improving competence and standards. As the Best Value consultation paper made clear, success would be rewarded and failure punished – with responsibilities transferred to another authority or third party (the threat of 'hit squads' that could take over a council's central administration). The proposals to give the Audit Commission powers to intervene take this process beyond that envisaged by previous Conservative governments. The duty to obtain best value for services permits central government to issue statutory guidance on how councils might comply with that duty. Against these centralising trends, the White Paper of July 1998 gave a degree of financial freedom to the best-performing councils. The best, labelled 'beacon authorities', would be expected to set examples to others, but all councils would have to report to central government on how they would speed-up decision-making.

The prime minister was himself strongly committed to change. In *Leading the Way* Tony Blair, uniquely for a prime minister, set out his ideas through a research think-tank pamphlet (Blair, 1998a). The prime minister both criticised councils and offered solutions. Delivery of the government's key pledges on education, welfare to work, crime reduction, improved health, a sound economy, tackling social exclusion, modernising transport and implementing Local Agenda 21 all required modern local government helping to make change happen. He listed councils' failures as: to explain council tax rises; to encourage participation; to put the needs of service users above those of providers; to be competent housing landlords. A new form of local government action, a third way, was needed with leadership to give vision, partnership and quality of life to their areas.

Blair went on to say that solutions to the weaknesses of the present system lay in collaborative working in matters of health, crime reduction and children's services, matched by revitalised democracy achieved by electoral reforms, referenda and citizens' juries. The executive and representative role of councillors should be separated, with directly elected mayors, overhauled committee structures and strengthened roles for backbenchers. It was crucial to ensure independent investigations into allegations of corruption. Under best value there would be four criteria for ensuring quality services: challenging existing service structures; consultation with users; comparing performance with performance indicators and benchmarking; competing with other providers to maximise cost-effectiveness. These ideas are reflected in the consultation and White Papers.

The *Local Democracy and Community Leadership* Green Paper also emphasised empowerment of people and communities. The government believed in democratic local government because it was vital in ensuring that people have the quality of life they deserve and which, through its democratic mandate, 'can empower citizens locally'. Currently, it fell short of its potential and change was essential to ensure democratic renewal, best value in service delivery and the adoption of a new ethical framework. Like the Blair pamphlet, the green paper advocated cabinet-style executives or directly elected mayors with executive responsibilities. Conducting council business through administrative committees should be abandoned – the reality was that they were not always decision-making bodies since in practice key decisions were taken in group meetings – in favour of a separate political executive of mayor and cabinet and scrutiny committees of backbench councillors. This would make decisions more transparent and accountable. The council would develop a vision for its locality and provide a focus for partnership with others. But as the consultation paper bluntly put it, the days of the all-purpose local authority that planned and delivered everything were gone.

These changes stress the need for a new governing capacity without which the government's economic and social agenda for greater inclusion, tackling health, education and unemployment problems, cannot be delivered. The Labour government was determined that democratic reform would be a major part of these changes. The proposals included annual elections and greater community consultation and participation through, for example, citizens' juries and panels, focus groups, referenda, fora and other mechanisms. These developments will increasingly foster participation that is really responsive between the two sides. Interactive question-and-answer sessions through these various initiatives could also be put on the Web: developing the dialogue through electronic means is now reaching out to a wider audience. What are the implications of these changes for local councils and services? Some of the suggestions raise serious issues of responsibility and accountability: for example, initiatives to put proposals before focus groups of voters instead of council committees, or the use of referenda, blurs the council's answerability for actions. In other words, while citizens' juries are examples of deliberative democracy, where they fit into the representative democracy model remains problematic: how elected councils deal with the verdicts of citizens' juries, in relation to their constituents' views and the wider public interest, is unresolved. For the individuals who take part, citizens' juries can be time-consuming; more preferable might be citizens' priority panels, addressing an agenda set by the local authority – a prioritising and more structured consultation exercise.

A second set of questions on where Labour's changes are taking local action surrounds the potential dramatic reduction in councillors, already lower than in European countries. A parallel issue is increased payment for councillors, reflecting the responsibilities of their new roles and making clear what it is they are being paid for. The future may be for fewer councillors, receiving more pay, with the possibility of executive mayors and cabinet members being paid pensionable salaries. Attendance allowances will be abolished. Councillors will also receive officer support, facilities and training to help them carry out their new roles. The changes will lead to a split between executive and scrutiny functions. A minority of councillors will take executive decisions and the majority will be encouraged into a ward representative and advocacy role which would allow them to be more actively engaged with other organisations and groups. This would be achieved much more effectively once the burden of committee work was removed. Councillors could, for example, become involved in neighbourhood participation fora and locally based regeneration projects. Some councils already have community plans aimed at getting councillors into dialogue with their ward constituents over localised issues. The government believes that greater councillor engagement with their areas will enhance the calibre of candidates. There are major questions here. Given a traditional political culture in which councillors take part in decisions (even acknowledging the existence of leadership groups) there are doubts over whether the backbench role as currently envisaged will be attractive enough. There is a pressing need to emphasise for backbenchers the importance of their role as community representatives who understand their community's priorities, their tasks of monitoring performance and of generating policy ideas.

*Box 7.3*    Modern local government

---

- Annual council elections.
- Councils to produce reform plans to streamline working procedures.
- Elected Mayors or cabinet-style government to be adopted by all councils: where councils delayed reform, government could order a council to hold a referendum asking voters to decide on several options for change.
- Councils to be allowed to experiment with electronic voting, mobile polling stations, postal voting.
- Councils to be allowed to hold referenda on major issues.
- A national independent Standards Board to combat 'sleaze'.
- End to 'universal' capping of council budgets, but government would retain reserve intervention powers.
- Compulsory competitive tendering to be replaced with 'best value' regime overseen by the Audit Commission.
- 'Beacon' status for around 100 best performing councils, with greater financial freedom including powers to set a small additional business rate.

---

The subsequent White Paper, *Modern Local Government: in touch with the people*, of July 1998 reaffirmed Labour's objectives in a comprehensive plan (Cm 4014, 1998) which is summarised in Box 7.3. Councils would have to show that they were changing, and produce plans to put changes into effect. Councils would not be compelled to adopt a particular model, but if they were not modernising, or expanding their consultation of local people, the public would have the right to trigger a referendum ballot on an elected mayor. Under the Local Government (Organisation and Standards) Bill this would be by a petition from at least 5 per cent of local electors. Legislation was needed to put these changes into effect since the existing system is constrained by s 101 of the Local Government Act 1972 under which councillors can only take decisions collectively, preventing delegation of executive powers to individual councillors. Under the proposed mayor or cabinet system this will change. The impact of these proposals are potentially radical. They raise the question of what then becomes the power of the rest of the council. If the council's role is centred on scrutiny, then potential problems of gridlock between executive and council might arise.

The government's plans also raise important questions about the electoral system. The – laudable – aim is to raise electoral turnout from its present average of 40 per cent. To improve turnout and thus democratic accountability, the frequency of elections is to be increased. Unitary Authorities will have 3-member wards and hold elections in 3 out of every 4 years, and 2-tier councils (counties and districts) will hold elections by halves every two years. Voting will be made easier (polling booths in supermarkets, by post or from home by computer or digital television, and by moving polling day to the weekend). These and other measures are welcome, but the rejection of proportional representation for councillors is a weakness. The question of proportional representation, however, will remain on the agenda, given the systems proposed for the Scottish Parliament and for European elections and the likelihood that the use of the Supplementary Vote to elect London's Mayor will be repeated elsewhere. Currently in local government the electoral system has a strong tendency to produce one-party local councils – around one-fifth (Leach, 1998). The result is that people believe that voting changes nothing. There are particular concerns over apathy among young people: more than a third of 18–24 year olds are not registered to vote and 52 per cent say they never vote in local elections. There are two kinds of concern here: one is that one-party rule in some councils is so entrenched that voting will not alter the situation; the other is a reflection on the perceived lack of council powers given the dominance of central control. The government's response, however, has been to reject proportional representation in favour of extending democratic practice beyond the ballot box, particularly in requiring greater consultation before decisions are taken and widening the fora through which they can be done.

## The implications of a mayoral system

The government believes that separating the executive from other council roles brings advantages of efficiency, transparency and accountability. In the Queen's Speech of November 1998 the government announced two local government bills. One dealt with best value (see Chapter 4) while the second, the Local Government (standards and conduct) Bill will allow councils to introduce changes to decision-making structures (including mayoral or cabinet systems) and to impose tough ethics rules. In practice, the Local Government (Organisation and Standards) Bill of March 1999 concentrated on changes to the political executive, the separation of executive and scrutiny functions, and the new ethical framework. The legislation allowed for flexibility in the models chosen: a directly elected mayor who appoints an executive of two or more drawn from councillors; a council leader appointed by the council who appoints an executive drawn from the council or heads an executive appointed by the council (cabinet government); or a directly-elected mayor, with an official, the city manager, appointed by the council. The draft bill lays down that the core executive must not exceed the lower of two levels: either 10, or 15 per cent of the total number of councillors. Councils are required to chose one of the new management forms, and to produce and publish their plans and timetables to do so: the status quo is not an option (Cm 4298).

A mayoral system would be a major change to the way urban politics are conducted, raising a range of important issues, (see Box 7.4). Elected mayors are seen as giving a high profile to a local authority and enhancing accountability – citizens know where responsibility lies and the single executive can take swift action. Strong leaders can use persuasion and political networking to promote new initiatives. Importantly, in a world where communities are increasingly diversified and possibly divided, they can help to bring groups together in cooperative ways of working. More than this, strong leadership is needed if poverty and exclusion is to be tackled and the just city promoted.

*Box 7.4*   Key issues raised by mayoral systems

---

- Nominations, selection and voting systems for an elected mayor.
- Powers of the mayor and of the chief executive, and the relations between them.
- Relations between the mayor and the council and its committees.
- Relations between policy leaders and backbench councillors.
- Powers of committees, particularly their scrutiny role.

The government proposed three alternatives for change. The first one is for a directly elected mayor with a cabinet, as shown in Figure 7.1. The Local Government (Organisation and Standards) Bill requires a local authority to hold a referendum where it proposes to adopt a model including a directly-elected mayor. The mayor is elected by local people on the supplementary vote system (which allows first and second choices) and then appoints a cabinet from among the councillors; s/he can also appoint a deputy mayor. From the consultation papers we can infer that cabinet members could, like their central government counterparts, have portfolios and take executive decisions acting alone. The mayor would lead, propose policy and steer its implementation through officers. The chief executive and chief officers would be appointed by the council, as now. The elected mayor would have significant powers in submitting his budget for council approval. The second model (Figure 7.2) is for a cabinet with a leader: the indirectly elected major model. The leader is elected by the council, with a cabinet of councillors either appointed by the leader or elected by the council. The mayor's powers are narrower than under the directly elected mayor model. The third model is a directly elected mayor with a council manager (Figure 7.3). The mayor gives a lead to a full-time manager appointed by the council. The manager would have delegated power for strategic policy and day-to-day decision-making. The mayor's formal powers are at their weakest in this model, with his powers being those of influence, guidance and leadership.

All three models raise questions of where the powers to act reside and what the degree of control or veto of the mayor on the council, or vice versa, will be. In addition, certain decisions, particularly those for planning, licensing and appeals, will have to remain formally with the whole council rather than with individuals (mayors or cabinet members) or chief executives. Councils will be under a duty to produce a political management plan following these models and a timetable to introduce one of them. This will be in addition to the duty to consult local people about plans and services.

Some advocates of elected mayors point to the experience in the United States to show how mayoral systems could work. In the United States the strong mayor/council model, while still dominant in the largest cities and the north-eastern states, was in the earlier years of this century criticised for corruption and machine-politics. As a result the council-manager form, where the council elects a non-partisan official to run the city administration, became common in smaller cities

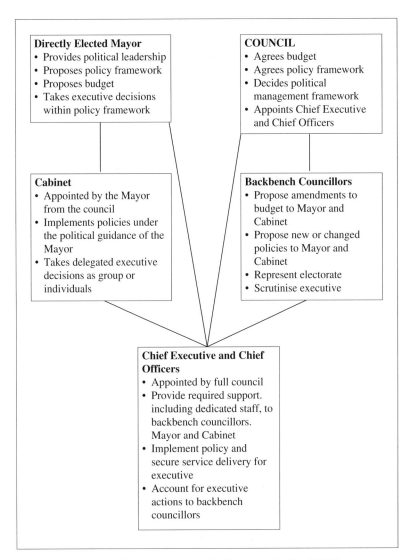

Source: *Modern Local Government: in touch with the people*, Cm 4014 (London: HMSO, 1998).

*Figure 7.1* Directly elected mayor with cabinet

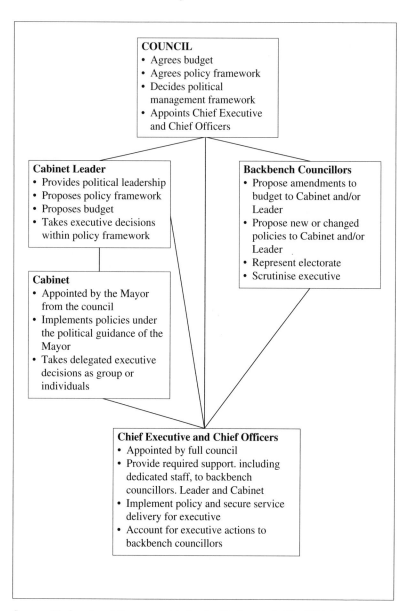

*Source: Modern Local Government: in touch with the people*, Cm 4014 (London: HMSO, 1998).

*Figure 7.2*   Cabinet with a leader

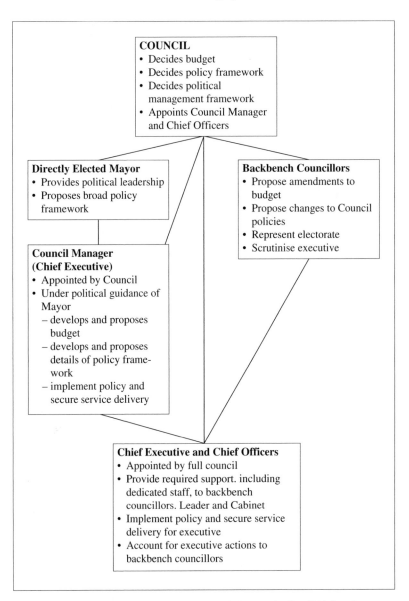

**COUNCIL**
- Decides budget
- Decides policy framework
- Decides political management framework
- Appoints Council Manager and Chief Officers

**Directly Elected Mayor**
- Provides political leadership
- Proposes broad policy framework

**Backbench Councillors**
- Propose amendments to budget
- Propose changes to Council policies
- Represent electorate
- Scrutinise executive

**Council Manager (Chief Executive)**
- Appointed by Council
- Under political guidance of Mayor
  - develops and proposes budget
  - develops and proposes details of policy framework
  - implement policy and secure service delivery

**Chief Executive and Chief Officers**
- Appointed by full council
- Provide required support. including dedicated staff, to backbench councillors. Leader and Cabinet
- Implement policy and secure service delivery for executive
- Account for executive actions to backbench councillors

*Source: Modern Local Government: in touch with the people*, Cm 4014 (London: HMSO, 1998).

*Figure 7.3*   Directly elected mayor and council manager

and the south-west. Structures themselves, however, do not solve problems on their own. City problems are political – disagreements over priorities and resources – and need more transparent accountability and responsibility to local people if they are to be resolved. Even in those American cities with administrative council managers, elected mayors are being established to provide political leadership. Comparison between countries suggests that the lesson is that a strong, visible community political leader – however elected – is the best way to promote coherent policies (Svara, 1990; Elcock, 1995).

Newstyle executives, whether directly elected Mayors or cabinets drawn from among the members of the ruling group on the council, would have important implications for both members and officers. The responsibilities of core executive/committees/full council will change and the powers of a core executive raise questions of openness, accountability and scrutiny. Members will become more clearly divided between policy leaders and backbenchers, a position which is already noticeable in the large urban areas. Members might resist such a split on the grounds that while cherishing their representative role, they would equally defend their power to influence major decisions. Young and Rao's work shows that while councillors criticised the committee burden, they declined to change it, preferring adaptations rather than the abolition of the system (Young and Rao, 1994). The Local Government Management Board survey conducted at the end of 1997 found that 58 per cent of members still sat on five or more committees or sub-committees, and 25 per cent described themselves as full-time councillors (Wright, 1998). It is expected that the reforms will reduce the burden on both councillors and their employers which arose from long hours spent on committee work. This will improve the diversity of candidates and, it is hoped, overcome the under-representation of ethnic minorities, women, the employed and self-employed.

The aim is that under an executive/council system, the full council and committees will need to strengthen their representative and consumer champion roles and develop mechanisms to scrutinise the executive. The scrutiny role of members would become as important as their representative role. These are commendable aims. The potential impact on decision-making has to be seen, however, within the practical realities of politics. Councillors work within party groups; currently these are the place where local problems are considered and decisions taken. This is a particularly important feature of how the ruling party steers policy. To expect backbench councillors to take on new public scrutiny roles of their own front bench will be a major cultural change, challenging group loyalty and cohesion. In theory, far fewer decisions will take place in the secrecy of party group meetings and far more under public scrutiny. If this is to become a reality then local standing orders and whipping systems of party groups will need to undergo fundamental reappraisal. Similarly, inviting communities to share in governance challenges the traditional role of councillors as elected representatives based in party group solidarity. These developments do distinguish Labour's agenda from that of its predecessor and will result in a very different form of urban politics if they are fully implemented.

There will also be significant alterations to the place of officers in decision-making. Officers, now responsible to the council as a whole and employed by it, will also have changed roles. They will continue to be employed by the full council, but in practice leading officers could become responsible to an executive mayor or cabinet. Thought would then need to be given as to how officers would continue to fulfil their responsibility to provide advice to the full council and its committees. It is likely that in future officers will be advising a range of key political figures of mayor and cabinet leaders and will need to develop new skills in organising council work. In modern local government, management teams have become smaller and chief executives increasingly have become powerful general managers. Though there will continue to be a Chief Executive appointed by the whole council, their responsibilities will become even more complex: as a cabinet secretary; as the executant of policy; as chief officer to the council. These complexities would be compounded where a directly elected mayor was of a different party from the council.

Labour's modernising agenda is poised to change urban governance, highlighting the leadership role of individual politicians and their potential for driving through strategies of change and renewal. The most important question of what the impact will be centres on the roles of, and relations between, elected mayors and councillors, that is on policy initiation on the one hand and its scrutiny on the other. As Stoker stresses, in any system with a single-person executive, the council, itself separately elected, plays an important role in checking the performance of the executive and in deciding key budgetary and policy matters (Stoker, 1996c). This will be particularly so given that, under the government's proposals, membership of scrutiny committees would reflect the political balance of the council as a whole. The exact nature of scrutiny will also need determination. Scrutiny could be seen in too negative a light if it only looks at performance outcomes. The potentially positive aspects of scrutiny need to be stressed. Positive scrutiny focuses on the development of policy, considering proposals from the political executive and from members, and reaffirming the councils' overall responsibility both for policy and for expressing the view of local communities. In practical terms this means looking at both policy areas and issues, policy and budgetary proposals put to the council and the actual decisions of the political executive. Such responsibilities do give councillors significant roles. But putting these new roles into practice is going to take time and resolution if members are not to resent what they might see as backbench roles on the – 'lobby fodder' – Westminster model.

A wider issue for the future lies in the potential conflict between cities and regions, should elected regional assemblies come into being. Then the existence of major political actors – city mayors and regional assembly leaders – would inevitably lead to tension over powers, especially economic regeneration and resource management. What these powers will be and the potential conflict between mayors and assembly leaders will become as interesting a political issue in England as they will in Scotland and Wales. This is particularly so if mayors eventually have, as in the London model, powers over economic development and transport planning. The conflict will not be confined to leaders of the respective bodies: there will be rural regional interests meeting urban city concerns head on. Cities versus regions are a real possibility in the future development of urban policy. On the wider political scene, the collective political clout of the elected mayors of major cities will have a significant effect on ministers and Whitehall departments.

Wider political pressures also have important effects on these processes: over party selection of candidates for mayor and cabinet posts and the relation between the mayor and the party groups on the council. In addition, the issue of whether directly elected mayors really help in the empowerment of the people remains important. Critics claim that such a system would be less responsive, giving too much power to the elected mayor (which could raise fears over corruption, given the patronage a mayor would have), politicising senior officials, and weakening rather than strengthening the council's assembly role. Inevitably, the mayor's political role would overlap with the chief executive's managerial task of heading the administration, particularly if this was a strong council manager position. The White Paper's council manager model proposes a directly elected but non-executive mayor alongside the city council, providing political leadership. In this model the council manager is a powerful chief executive: he leads and controls the staff, has delegated strategic policy and day-to-day administrative powers. The manager will be a single focus of responsibility. Though a high-profile role, managers are ultimately dismissible by the council, something that advocates of this model believe offers clear and focused accountability.

## Learning from London

London is leading the way in changes to local democracy. The lessons that can be drawn from it will have a major influence on the rest of the system. Governing London has been a major political issue for more than a hundred years, because of its place as the nation's capital, its size, and its influence over the wider London region and the South East generally. In the 1960s the need for a wider strategic authority was recognised in the London Government Act 1963 (which came into effect in April 1965) which established the Greater London Council (GLC), the London Boroughs and the Inner London Education Authority (ILEA). The system changed again with the abolition of the GLC in 1986 and of ILEA in 1990. Following the abolition of the GLC the Conservative government set up the London Residuary Body to dispose of the assets of the GLC and manage a whole range of services over the transitional period. Its work came to an end in 1992. As well as the London Residuary Body there are a number of other quangos, including the London Docklands Development Corporation (which came to an end in 1996), nine Training and Enterprise Councils, a variety of boards covering the arts, sports and tourism, and the business-led London First and London Forum to promote investment and tourism (Hebbert, 1995; Newman and Thornley, 1997). In essence this amounted to a new system of urban corporatism outside the democratic framework. The coming of a directly elected mayor and assembly system under Labour's reforms will dramatically change the situation in London and is an instructive model for potential changes elsewhere.

The Greater London Authority Act 1999 established a Greater London Authority to consist of the Mayor of London and a London Assembly (see Box 7.5). The new mayor and assembly system has distinctive electoral features, and new roles and responsibilities, that have wider implications. The mayor will be elected by the supplementary

*Box 7.5*    Main provisions of the Greater London Authority Act 1999

- Establishes a Greater London Authority consisting of the Mayor of London and the London Assembly.
- Of the 25 member Assembly 14 are constituency members and 11 are London [ie at-large] members.
- London Authority's purpose is to promote economic and social development and environmental improvement.
- These powers are invested in the Mayor.
- Mayor prepares the transport strategy; London boroughs prepare implementation plans for the transport strategy; Transport for London exercises its powers under the guidance or directions of the Mayor.
- Mayor makes appointments to the London Development Agency (the RDA for London). At least four must be elected councillors of the Assembly, the boroughs or the City of London and at least half must be from business.
- London Development Agency submits draft strategy to Mayor who then publishes the London Development Agency Strategy.
- Act establishes a 23-member Metropolitan Police Authority; the police are under the control of the Commissioner of Police of the Metropolis; the Mayor may make representations to the Secretary of State about applicants for this post.
- Act establishes a London Fire and Emergency Planning Authority.
- Mayor publishes spatial development strategy, after consulting the Assembly and functional bodies (eg Transport, Police, Fire), and receives representations from London boroughs and adjacent local authorities.
- Mayor publishes state of the environment report, following consultation with the Environment Agency, London boroughs and others.
- Other provisions include Mayor's duties to produce a waste management plan and a culture strategy.

vote system, where voters mark their first and second choices. The 25 assembly members will be elected for 4-year terms, using a mix of first past the post (14) and the additional member, party list system (11). The elections for the Mayor will take place in May 2000. The authority itself will start work on 1 April 2000 and will be run in the interim period by ministers and officials.

The new system will be innovative in local government, with a strong leadership at its core that has parallels with the Westminister model. The mayor will be able to appoint 2 political advisors and a small policy and support staff of up to 10 members; the London Authority's remaining staff are appointed by the assembly. The mayor will also appoint the chairs of the new transport and economic development bodies and senior officers' political advisers. The mayor will appoint the deputy mayor, selected from the elected assembly. All will take up and leave office with the mayor. The assembly will elect its own chair and deputy chair from among its members, with the function of chairing assembly meetings. The assembly and mayor will be responsible for transport, economic regeneration, crime, fire and emergency services, environment, land-use planning, arts and sport, but it is the mayor who has the dominant powers. The London Development Agency is appointed by and accountable to the mayor. The mayor also sets London's overall planning system, through what is termed the spatial development strategy, to which individual boroughs will have to conform. Similarly, the mayor will have the duty to produce a 'state of the environment report', a London Biodiversity Action Plan, and a waste management strategy. The mayor will have overall responsibility for transport organised through the Transport for London body, will prepare a transport strategy and will require the London boroughs' implementation plans to be submitted to him/her for approval. The mayor will have responsibility for the police, where the establishment of a 23-member Metropolitan Police Authority who will take over from the metropolitan police commissioner will end the 150 years of the Metropolitan Police reporting to the Home Secretary. The Home Secretary will, however, appoint the members of the Authority and the Commissioner of Police of the Metropolis (after consultation with the mayor). In addition, the London Fire and Emergency Planning Authority will replace the London Fire and Civil Defence Authority. The mayor also has the duty to prepare, each financial year, a capital spending plan for the functional bodies, after consulting both the bodies concerned and the assembly. Collectively, these duties give the mayor an impressive range of powers.

The mayor's powers will be significantly supported by his/her ability to force the budget through the assembly unless there is a two-thirds majority against. There are concerns, however, that the substantial reservation of powers not to the mayor or assembly but to the Secretary of State calls into question the real decentralisation being introduced. Other critics argue, by contrast, that the mayor's powers are so wide compared with the assembly that its role is marginal.

Though it can question and criticise the mayor's monthly report, the assembly has no power to do anything about them. Its financial powers are similarly limited and it is the mayor, not the assembly, who has the duty to promote economic and social development and to seek environmental improvements.

There are also important issues arising over potential conflict between the new Greater London Authority and the London boroughs over responsibilities for the road network, transportation and planning, especially given that the boroughs will be able to collect charges for workplace parking and road-user schemes but the money will go to Transport for London, the transport authority in the mayor's remit. An interesting feature of the London reform is the potentially influential role that black and Asian voters will have in the election of the mayor under the supplementary vote system. In addition, the London model raises questions of the role of the assembly – consisting as it does of full-time salaried politicians – as not only a watchdog over the mayor but a challenger to the mayor's powers and functions. London, however, not only offers a model for revolutionary change in local government, it also suggests a future path for regional assemblies, since in London the London Development Agency (the parallel to the regional RDAs) will become responsible to the London Authority (in effect to the mayor). The LDA will be business-led: the chair and at least half of the members must have business experience. At least four of the LDA members must be members of the London assembly, a London borough or the Common Council of the City of London.

The London Authority or mayor and assembly thus presents an interesting model for other major cities. It points up some important issues: as yet there have not been suggestions for the mixed electoral system to be used elsewhere; the powers of the London mayor are very wide-ranging and it remains to be seen if this will be repeated in other cities; in London, the mayor's leading role in relation to the London Development Agency is unique. In future, elected mayors of major cities could be in conflict over powers and responsibilities with regional political leaders were elected regional assemblies to come into being. Labour's proposals for the modernisation of the wider local government system has received a broadly favourable response, though concern over powers and duties remains and there are differences between councillors and the public over the best way forward. Support from among councillors for elected mayors is mixed, with many (in Scotland as well as in England) favouring cabinet-style executives. The public, for its part, appears extremely supportive of the idea, with 70 per cent in favour (Miller and Dickson, 1996). The mayoral system, in some form, is the model of community leadership for the future. That community leadership is essential to give a new impetus to solving endemic urban problems.

## Conclusion: the new world of urban politics

Governance, enabling, partnership, networking: these terms reflect the ways in which the local world of policy and politics has been transformed by changes to the structure, by the introduction of new agencies and privatisation, by partnership working, and by internal reforms of local councils. To what extent is the local authority now in a position to provide leadership in this new urban world? The assumption of leadership lies in the claim that local authorities are the only bodies that are both local and elected. This is reinforced by two further obligations. The first is the place of local authorities as generalist public bodies with a remit of providing services to the public as a whole. This is likely to remain the case, even though there have been suggestions that other agencies – health trusts, police authorities, or some kind of separate school board – might become directly elected as single-purpose bodies. The second obligation is the legal duty of local authorities as regulators and inspectors of standards, backed by enforcement powers. But a paradox remains, as the House of Lords Select Committee on the relations between central and local authorities revealed. Local authorities, it pointed out, 'hover between being genuine leaders, and being one of several components of local governance' (House of Lords, 1996: para: 4.41).

The qualities that local authorities need to solve the deep-seated problems of deprivation, poor housing, education, health and exclusion are effective leadership in policy networks and partnerships, at the same time heightening the democratic values of openness and accountability. These qualities, and local authorities' abilities to take an overall view of the needs of their area, allow them to act as brokers. The new reforms promoting leadership, consultation and community planning should enable urban politics to overcome the fragmentation and inadequate accountability that has marked them in recent years.

Leading is not dictating. It involves political skills and networking, negotiation, bargaining and consensus-building. But an enhanced leadership role for local councils cannot be achieved, it is argued, unless local authorities are given wider powers beyond those of s 137 of the Local Government Act 1972 to act in the interest of the community as a whole. One suggestion is for a 'local competence' which would be available to authorities who can demonstrate they deliver effective local services and who are prepared to work with other agencies.

The government's White Paper *Modern Local Government* lays a duty on authorities to promote the economic, social and environmental wellbeing of their areas (a duty of community concern). The new statutory duty will include a requirement for councils to produce a community plan. This duty, in the White Paper's words, will enshrine in law the council's role as elected leader of the local community with responsibility for the wellbeing and sustainability of the area and embracing wide-ranging partnerships. The plan will be the backdrop for bids for resources and will be linked to the implementation of other plans. To this end s 111 of the Local Government Act 1972 which allowed authorities to do anything to facilitate their functions, should be replaced with a new and broader power, including entering into joint companies or joint arrangements with other bodies. While the consultation paper supported this, the government then appeared to retreat from a reform of s 111, leaving it unspecified as to the form that giving authorities 'clear discretionary powers to engage in partnerships' will eventually take. Overall, however, the effect of these new powers will be to remove uncertainty as to the extent of councils' powers, rather than extending them significantly. There will also be issues of how community plans at district and county level are linked and how they might be coordinated with the strategies of the new regional bodies.

The 'beacon authorities' proposed in the reform white paper will be rewarded with more independence for offering efficient 'best value' services, including providing effective political systems. In October 1999 the first tranche of 40 beacon councils were phased in, with an emphasis on disseminating best practice. Those chosen must show a proven track record in either community safety, education, housing, modernisation planning, modern service delivery, social services or sustainable development. Councils can also bid to be overall beacons. In the second phase of the scheme, when legislation would confer greater powers, beacons would gain the right to levy the additional business rates, escape reserve capping, be allowed to spend more on capital and be allowed to experiment on new initiatives. They might also take over services from failing councils. While important, these still allow less discretion and variation than many would wish. Those who call for greater freedoms argue that further powers to innovate (through private bills or Orders of Parliament) could be used to extend the scope of local councils, along the lines of the Scandanavian Free Commune experiments. Such moves would be welcome: they also raise again the democratic issue of variation between councils arising from differing local needs and demands. Governments set standards, but local councils can claim a democratic mandate to innovate to meet local needs. Improving democratic politics through new processes will only work if people believe that local councils have power to affect those they represent – including the right to do things of which central government disapproves.

A power of general competence has also been associated with calls for local authorities to be given greater freedoms, including innovations analogous to the Scandanavian 'free commune' idea where national rules are relaxed to allow local experimentation (Clarke and Stewart, 1994; Kitchen, 1995). An interesting example comes from the Republic of Ireland, where the 1990 Local Government Act gives each local authority the power to represent the interests of the community in such a manner as it thinks appropriate (to local non-elected bodies for example), and to undertake surveys and other steps to ascertain local views. In effect, a power of general competence.

The judgement on the effects that Labour's modernising agenda is having on urban politics remains mixed. Labour has accepted much of the changes of functions and structures of the Thatcherite revolution that passed powers and duties to the private sector and to quangos and extended the autonomy of schools. The result was a shift from urban government to urban governance. Enabling, not providing, became an important feature of local decision-making by the mid-1990s. Labour continued this formulation, arguably extending it in the Action Zones for education, health and employment to tackle the problems of the most deprived areas. Nevertheless, as John puts it, a cooperative form of governance both between levels of government and within the urban context is the only practical means of solving modern policy problems (John, 1997a).

Where radical changes are taking place is in the further democratisation of local politics. Leadership, accountability, transparency, openness, consultation, empowerment, are the watchwords of the modernisation project. The political culture that these changes will bring about will be radically different, challenging the traditional roles

of leaders and backbenchers, the relations between mayors and councils, and the ways of conducting party politics. It is this new urban politics that is offering exciting possibilities for the future. Urban policy
depends for its success, governments now argue, on urban politics that
operates collaboratively through networks of interlocking agencies,
and which works for the needs of local communities, leading them and
giving them a real voice in decisions.

# 8

# Conclusion: Cities in Changing Times

Urban policy and politics is not merely a matter of town and country planning or the administration of services through local elected councils. It concerns the basic elements of the good life: how we live together in society, exercise our rights and duties as citizens, resolve our differences and promote justice. On both sides of the Atlantic the emphasis is on participation, involving individuals and groups – as citizens, consumers and clients – in the policy process, both in formulating and implementing programmes. Relatedly there is a search for community – that contested and elusive concept – and an exploration of the relation between this notion and modern urban life. As this book has shown, these ideas have generated an extensive debate. This debate has ranged from the illuminations of Aristotle's concept of civic *virtu*, to the relation between time, space, locality and politics, to questions of exclusion. The debate itself, while grounded in philosophical ideas, has had striking practical outcomes, not only in the physical landscape and economic wellbeing of our cities, but in our provisions for, and attitudes towards, different groups and interests in society. This has become a pressing contemporary political and policy concern in which the establishment of the Social Exclusion Unit in the Cabinet Office, the New Deal welfare-to-work programme, and the emphasis on education, all raise fundamental questions about civic society and urban life.

When we try to define the context within which these issues can be addressed, complexities of space, place and boundaries immediately arise. In contemporary analysis, however, the urban has come to be used to describe areas of population density and their physical and economic characteristics, including their labour markets, residential, business, retail and leisure activities. These forces interact with each other to give rise to urban politics: that complex pattern of power relationships, resource decisions, and networks of negotiating and bargaining skills. If definitions of the urban are problematic, so too is the use of the term urban policy. Since the 1960s urban policy has increasingly come to be defined not in relation to public services largely nationally determined but locally delivered to all citizens, but in terms of problems and defects. In Britain by the 1980s urban policy had become virtually synonymous with the 'inner-city', a notoriously difficult geographical location to define, but which embraced the physical deterioration, concentrated deprivation and complex social problems associated with areas of older housing in urban areas. Such problems were not confined, however, to the older, 'inner' areas of cities, but could also be found on the large post-war estates of public housing, frequently located on the periphery of large towns and cities. These 'problem estates' as they have come to be seen, are now a prime target of the present government's attack on social exclusion.

The current concern of urban policy to target the worst problems of city life should be seen alongside another, equally important, tradition. In this view, the city is a normative order, the natural habitat of civilised humankind, where divergencies of temperament and character are possible. In this tradition the city realm is the site of the good life, of innovation and a rich cultural heritage, of opportunity and fulfilment. 'The urban crisis', the allegations that violence, anxiety and fear permeate social life, with 'fear of crime' heading the list of many people's anxieties in Quality of Life studies, should not be exaggerated. Instead, what must be kept in balance is the contribution of the city to social and political life, the forum within which we experience politics and form those friendship links which are increasingly seen as vital to social cohesion. To this end, what Robert Putnam describes as social capital and civic engagement – that rich mix of voluntary involvement and political participation – must be constantly fostered.

An important element of the good city is that revival of conviviality, of a lively night-life, which is now characteristic of many of our towns and cities. So too is civility – the values of trust and public interaction – which are expressed not just in civil peace and order but also in clean and safe public spaces, in public services as opposed to notions that all needs can be purchased in the private market. It has to be recognised, however, that we are far from the civic pride model of the good city as promoted in Birmingham under Chamberlain before the First World War, or Manchester under the Simons in the 1930s. Most of the development that we now engage in is in the form of shopping malls or supermarkets in the suburbs rather than in city centres. Global market forces erode the public spaces between commercial buildings and society is increasingly polarised into segregated communities. That is the view expounded in Richard Rogers' book, *Cities for a Small Planet*, which calls for changes to the city experience that are close to Prime Minister Blair's agenda: cities where citizenship really flourishes, with a greater emphasis on participation, involving communities in decision-making, with better leadership, and with regard for environmental sustainability (Rogers, 1997). The 'democratisation of democracy' is a key element of the Third Way, paralleling the engagement of government at all levels with the agencies of civil society and the strategy of community renewal (Giddens, 1998a).

## The evolution of policy change

What this book has shown is how policy has evolved and changed between 1945 and 1997 and how, since Labour came to power, it is changing again. The new focus is on modernising local democracy, bringing together resources and agencies to tackle urban decline and work towards a more inclusionary society. How have we arrived at this position? The post-war consensus that set the framework of the welfare state rested on a number of policy assumptions. Prime among these was the need for reconstruction after the trauma of the war years and the depression of the 1930s. Cities would be rebuilt, the urgent need for housing met and the slums demolished. The result would be a pattern of rural and urban development that would both protect the countryside (through the green belt and concentrated development in new towns) and control redevelopment of cities which separated commercial, industrial and residential uses. Such ideas traced their roots to the ideals of harmonious community that go back to the model village and townscapes of philanthrophists and social scientists such as Rowntree, Seebohm, Cadbury and Osbourn. Much of this idealism and pragmatism was realised in the Town and Country Planning Act of 1947. As Chapter 2 showed, the physical planning system it instituted, and its subsequent development though many vicissitudes, has lasted to the end of the twentieth century.

The development of urban policy over the past three decades, however, has seen a questioning of these underlying post-war assumptions which have led to a very different approach to urban problems. The 'rediscovery of poverty' on both sides of the Atlantic in the 1960s, the issues of immigration and race relations, targeting of specific areas and groups instead of the universalism of early welfare state provisions, all brought into question the key assumptions of the welfare state. Since the 1960s, urban policy has gone through two main stages. The first was the concentration on social needs and economic growth, implemented through the public intervention policies of the period between 1968 and 1979. This changed in the 1980s as Conservative governments rejected the precepts of the Keynesian welfare state in favour of deregulation and markets. Entrepreneurship, private investment, business involvement and a reduced role for local councils became the hallmark of the new approach. All highlighted the Conservative government's determination to move from state intervention to market solutions.

By the late 1980s competition among local councils for specific government regeneration funds had become the key policy. After 1979 programmes were time-limited, targeted, heavily business-led and with economic growth their prime objective. The outcomes have been mixed. Physical refurbishment has been significant and real achievements have been made in halting economic decline in some areas. But the worst neighbourhoods remained a seemingly intractable problem. In the early 1990s a series of reports judged the outcomes of these programmes relatively harshly, both as to the extent of the gains that had been made and the piecemeal nature of successive interventions. The review given in Chaper 2 of the evolution of policy enables us to put the Labour government's proposals into context. Though Labour argues from a different set of premises, many of the changes of the 1980s remain in place. The result is that urban policy appears to be coalescing around a consensus of mixed provision by multiagency partnerships.

The government's objectives are to implement policies that are both more targeted and more collaborative, putting resources into the poorest neighbourhoods and estates, setting up experimental action zones and requiring different agencies to work together. These local area-based projects all emphasise multiagency and private and voluntary sector partnerships, seeking to go beyond existing processes. Targeting poor areas is not new: its place in urban policy goes back to the 1969 Urban Programme of the Wilson government and expanded in the 1980s in a multiplicity of economic regeneration programmes. But criticisms of such targeting has consistently argued that area-based policies, as opposed to people-based approaches, particularly where these have a short operating or 'demonstrating' timespan, lack a long-term impact and address only a minority of the people affected. In addition, the lessons of the 1980s remind us that the definition of partnership, and how collaboration can be effectively implemented, are major issues. They not only raise difficult issues of inter-agency cooperation, they also reflect the tensions that exist between governments' desire to implement their national objectives and to decentralise decisions down to locality level. Targeted, area-based efforts will fail, however, unless they are linked effectively to citywide strategies. These in turn must be addressed within their regional context, decentralising policy from Whitehall to Regional Development Agencies to produce solutions that cover areas wider than those of individual cities.

## The importance of ideas

In order to understand where these ideas have come from and where they may take us in the future, Chapter 3 examined the principles underlying action. Within this discourse, three elements dominate. The first are those ideas associated with the New Right; second an increasingly important set of concepts based on political economy; and finally the elite and pluralist frameworks long dominant in political science and sociology. Chapter 3 showed how the term the New Right, including as it does neoliberal and neoconservative strands, came to dominate debate in the 1980s. Its concerns centre on the nature of the post-Keynesian, post welfare-state world: free enterprise, individual choice in the market, and the reduction of state provision in favour of individual, family and voluntary sector responsibility. Conservative governments of the 1980s looked to change the role of all-purpose local authorities, forcing them to divest themselves of certain services to public–private bodies (the quangos) and to the private sector through contracted-out provisions. These changes met the objectives of increased consumer choice and reducing the paternalism and self-interest of bureaucracy.

New right influence on successive Conservative governments has altered the structure and processess of local governance. Political economy discourse, for its part, has been concerned with the relation between modern capitalism and state processes. In the post-Keynesian globalised economy, mass-production and mass-consumption are replaced by niche markets, and by service industries of finance and information technology and, at the other end of the wage scale, retailing and fast-food outlets. In this situation, governments are driven to liberalise and deregulate the economy, promote flexible labour markets and diversify and privatise public services. What is of interest for urban policy is that the mobility of capital, and the demand for 'flexible' labour forces, has given rise to a competition for investment between cities which raises questions about the scope of government management of urban policy. It is also an element of New Labour thinking, where welfare-to-work and education and training promise to enable individuals to survive the ravages of this globalised economy. The political economy approach is also important to contempory urban analysis because of the growing interest in public choice theory, which offers a critique of public bureaucracies. These producer interests and their vote-maximising political leaders maintain public services at high levels to boost their own position rather than that of the public they serve. In the 1980s Conservative governments reflected this perspective when they sought to cut bureaucracies and substitute private for public provision.

The third body of theory looks at urban politics in terms of elites and groups. The elite versus pluralist debate goes back at least to the 1940s. Its contemporary relevance lies in the analysis of urban economic growth through the use of regime theory and urban growth coalitions, and a renewed interest in the neopluralism accounts centred on ethnic, gender and environmental issues. From these perspectives it is important to understand the part that business plays in making and implementing policy. There is as a result renewed theoretical interest in the utility of elite and pluralist theory to describe what has happened to British urban policy. Though traditionally British urban politics has been understood in pluralist terms, more emphasis is now given to elite theory. This is particularly so given the increased role of business in a wide spectrum of local regeneration and other projects, including business leadership in the Regional Development Agencies. As a result the elite accounts of regime theory and urban coalitions have gained in importance. Overall, New Right, political economy and pluralist accounts have added significantly to urban analysis of the changes of the past two decades. More radical analyses have come from postmodernist and feminist theory. Postmodernists criticise both the attempts to explain city life through a body of comprehensive theory, while feminist contributions emphasise new organisational forms, power relations, and specific issues grouped around family and carer relationship responsibilities.

But as this book has shown, the Conservative years have not only profoundly changed the structures and processes of local action, they have permanently altered the political culture within which decisions are taken. The urban arena is now characterised by the neopluralism of traditional approaches but approaches in which coalitions have greater force. That this will change under a Labour government remains open to question. The wide range of theoretical perspectives has had an input into the shaping of urban policy in the 1990s and how we have come to interpret it. But, it is argued, we are now in a new era: the 'third way' of Clinton and Blair which rejects the legacy of both right and left. Instead, the future lies in combining a market and internationally competitive economy with a more inclusive and more truly democratic society. The affirmation of a 'third way' has yet to prove either its uniqueness or its consistency, and no doubt this debate will continue.

## Getting things done

Putting principles into action requires a framework of legislation, a structure of organisations to carry it out, effective management to deliver services and good relations between central and local governments. Chapter 4 showed how this framework operated. Action now depends on alliances between local councils and other local stakeholders, particularly business and voluntary organisations. Although business does not play the prime role in British urban politics that it does in the United States, coalitions in which the private sector is an influential partner are now clearly institutionalised in the system.

While there is considerable debate on whether the involvement of business has become a dominant force in making and implementing policy, there is wide agreement that the 1980s saw increased control by central government over local affairs. '*Rebuilding Trust*', the title of the House of Lords report on central–local relations, indicates the degree of concern over the situation. Under Labour, there is hope for greater partnership and the government is seeking positively to rebuild trust between the centre and the localities. But central direction remains strong: Labour's determination to make radical changes in both policy outcomes and ways of working mean that central control remains firm. Critics are sceptical that structural reforms to change the way councils operate, without giving councils increased powers and financial autonomy, will do enough to rejuvenate the participation and engagement of local people. Such criticism also points to the imposition of government-imposed strategies as expressed in specified local plans: Policing Plans, Early Years Plans, Joint Children's Service Plans, Education Plans, Plans covering Probation Committees and Drug Action Teams – a plethora of plans that reveal how all-encompassing government requirements now are. Chapter 4 goes beyond the national framework to reveal how important relations with the European Union have become. The relations between centre and periphery have broadened to include a European dimension: as a provider of funds the European Union has generated new initiatives and reinforced requirements for collaborative working. The conclusion of Chapter 4's analysis is that urban policy is the result of multi-layered relations: between public and private, central and local and European bodies.

An important argument of this book is that making change happen requires an understanding of how local democracy operates. As Chapter 5 shows, local democracy is grounded in, and reflects, the values and realities of community life. Though community is a contested concept, basing action on communities is an important part of urban politics. Increasing community involvement is part of the new attempts to bring people more actively into decisions that affect them. Making citizenship more responsible and more active is a continuing objective, engaging local people in a variety of new ways in projects, consulting and informing – and hopefully empowering. This is a specific Labour objective. Working towards a more inclusive society, and revitalised cities, depends on establishing new democratic structures and methods. New forms of direct democracy are needed to generate a new politics, more responsive to the public. These reforms are seen by Labour as relevant, indeed crucial, to a revival of democracy at local and regional levels. Referenda, opinion polls, focus groups, lobbies, 'citizens' juries', are all part of the aim of making government more transparent and closer to the people.

## Bringing people together

Economic renewal is a major challenge for the urban agenda. Bringing disadvantaged communities into this process through Single Regeneration Budget projects and through wider anti-poverty strategies depends on forging alliances with many local interests and groups and finding and managing the resources to meet objectives. The parallel concern is with those who are not involved, the excluded and marginalised. This is a major preoccupation of government. Its importance was recognised with the setting up of a special Social Exclusion Unit in Number 10 and the targeting of education, health, employment and other measures on the poorest neighbourhoods. Hard questions have to be asked, however, if enough is being done to tackle the racial discrimination and disadvantage that is suffered by significant minorities of people living in inner cities.

Important questions are raised by these issues: the nature of exclusion; its relation to an 'underclass'; and the substitution of 'exclusion' for 'poverty'. Social exclusion is not synonymous with behavioural notions of the 'underclass' as in some American formulations. At the same time, however, analysts have concluded that working-age households (not individuals) with no integration into the labour market can be seen as a specific category. It has been estimated that this may amount to 10 per cent of all working-age households containing some three million people. Social exclusion is not purely a question of unemployment and income. It refers to the restrictions on taking part in urban politics that arise from these conditions and from the concentration of urban poverty, in ghettos or in peripheral housing estates. The city is not the 'good city' for such people: polarisation between classes, groups and areas increased the problem and threatened ideas of community cohesion and civility, that is severe urban poverty excludes a growing number of individuals from full citizenship, and such poverty is a threat to social cohesion. Exclusion also arises as a result of discrimination on the grounds of gender and ethnicity. In this regard, the issue reflects the wider question of the life experiences of urban minorities. One facet of these experiences is particularly important: that is the problem of urban crime and unrest, particularly in the relation of black youths to the police, and the impact that rioting in inner cities in the 1980s and 1990s had on the evolution of government policy, a response that focused on law and order and economic regeneration rather than on specific anti-racist policies. Discrimination remains, and ethnic and racial problems have not had the prominence in urban policy that might have been expected. But governments have seen problems of deprivation as both cumulative and concentrated in spatial terms: poor housing, poor health, high concentrations of the elderly, young children, crime and joblessness.

Working to tackle exclusion has been prominent in policy at both central and local government levels. The Social Exclusion Unit set up inside Number 10 in 1997 has the remit of tackling school truancy, reducing homelessness in the rough sleepers initiative, and finding new ways to turn around the 2 000 most deprived council estates. Local authorities, for their part, will have an important part to play in New Deal proposals and the health, education and employment action zones. Chapter 5 showed that the key problem is that to be excluded means to be outside the mainstream of social and political life, with little or no voice in how policy is made or in the political structures that implement it. Though attempts are being made to bring communities into the heart of regeneration efforts, it will be some time before this makes any real difference – as the Social Exclusion Unit report *Bringing Britain together* itself acknowledged, the process might take 10–20 years. Government is only now beginning to assess the out-turn of public expenditure locally. Pilot studies reveal the extent to which resources from mainstream programmes go to different areas. Households in the most deprived wards within the pilot cities rely for a majority of their real income on public spending, with actual spending in these areas being about 45 per cent above spending in the least deprived wards. Even so, there is wide variation at similar levels of deprivation, reflecting the complexity of the factors that influence funding decisions. Services which have spending quite strongly skewed towards deprived wards include means-tested social security (income support, housing benefits), social services for children, housing, regeneration and environmental capital spending (Bramley, Evans and Atkins, 1998). The wider problems of improving the quality of city life go beyond economic projects narrowly defined: problems of law and order, improving educational standards, meeting the demand for homes, breaking down the barriers to effective health and community care and achieving a sustainable environment. These form a seamless web of policy objectives. It is these complex, cross-cutting issues and their outcomes in actual services that were analysed in Chapter 6.

Partnership with the private sector, long a feature of economic and physical regeneration schemes of Conservative governments of the 1980s and 1990s, is now charged as a means of harnessing expertise from all sides. A new duty will be laid on local councils to promote the economic, social and environmental wellbeing of their areas, with the possibility of some additional powers. Major changes are imminent in the way councils engage with and lead their communities, through radical democratic renewal, through 'best value' service delivery, and in a new framework of ethical conduct. Local authorities will have to improve their legitimacy and accountability through annual elections, raising voting turnout, and through elected mayors or 'cabinets' facing scrutiny committees of backbench councillors. Councils, for their part, would like greater powers to force local quangos – training and enterprise councils, NHS trusts, and housing associations – to work with them, to participate in this shared way forward. Giving local councils powers to scrutinise local quangos appears, however, not yet to be on the agenda. What the analysis demonstrated is that delivering services requires a system of urban politics that works through networks and partnerships, an approach which Labour has put at the centre of its urban project.

Strengthening urban politics to meet these demands is the rationale behind reforms of local democracy. Chapter 7 showed how the moves to strengthen local leadership are an essential part of Labour's agenda for tackling poverty, unemployment, underachievement and exclusion. The argument is that strengthened leadership through directly elected mayors or cabinet-style executives will enhance accountability and transparency and make backbench councillors more effective representatives of and advocates for their communities. These moves remain the subject of lively debate.

The mixed economy of service provision and the multiagency alliances that deliver it make up a new world of urban governance, radically changed from that of traditional local government and reflecting the fact that problems cannot be neatly parcelled into separate areas. The government, for its part, promises a new framework for redeveloping towns and cities, an 'urban renaissance'. This will be set out in the White Paper expected in 1999 – the first White Paper on urban policy for 20 years. The White Paper will be informed by the work of the government-appointed urban task force led by architect Richard Rogers and charged with establishing a new vision for urban regeneration. The task force is reportedly interested in the French model of the *contrat de ville* (a city agreement) between central and local government, which establishes an agreed strategy on the part of the locality and a commitment to resources for the period of the contract by the central government. The publication in January 1999 of the Urban Task Force's 'Half-Way' report emphasised the need for increased public investment to stem the population drift to the suburbs and reverse the problems of dereliction and vacant land and abandoned properties left behind in the cities. Lord Rogers called for a national strategy of 'compact' urban development in cities to halt this drift, and for a new vision to break down the class and cultural divide between private and public housing. These changes should go alongside a tax on greenfield development, and a tax to penalise owners of land and property which has been left empty for two years or more (Urban Task Force, 1999).

The difficulty with trying to establish a long-term agenda is highlighted by recent research which suggests that we must be wary about assuming that we understand the extent of urban malaise. While we concentrate on the problems of the 'inner-city' and of run-down peripheral council estates, a new and worrying feature of city life is emerging: the traditional suburbs built in the period between the wars are showing signs of stress. A report from the Civic Trust and Ove Arup and Partners for the Rowntree Foundation reveal a level of neglect and under-investment, with suburbs having a much lower priority within the overall urban policy agenda. The better-off residents of the older suburbs ringing the large cities are leaving, potentially concentrating poverty within them and producing the same social problems as the inner-city. Suburban renewal calls for increased mix of uses, revived suburban centres, better transport and improved facilities. In order to adapt, there is a need to establish 'urban parishes' and other forms of community engagement if the hoped-for 'urban renaissance' is to create sustainable city life across the whole area (Gwilliam, Bourne, Swain and Prat, 1999).

Whatever the tensions within objectives – places and people, older suburbs as well as traditional 'inner-city' – urban policy continues to have the lead position on the political agenda. What observers will be looking for is policy that is both coherent and sustainable over the long term, an end to that short-termism and 'initiative-itis' that the Audit Commission and the Social Exclusion Unit have exposed as characteristic of the past 20 years.

Optimism is still appropriate. A people approach is making a steady ascendancy. Crime, dirt and disorder may mark city life after nearly 30 years of specific urban initiatives, but there is room for hope. This hope rests, essentially, on recognising that what is needed is continuous and *sustained* intervention. Time-limited projects, massive resource targeting, localised action teams, all have their place. And some successes are obvious, with enhanced civic pride in the refurbishment – warehouse conversions, heritage and hotel revival, business innovations, a rich mixture of cultures and economic upturn. But the difficulty is that time-limited and targeted interventions will only produce a permanent legacy if they are repeated and reinforced.

## Local communities and local choices

In his first major speech as prime minister Tony Blair stressed the inclusive goal of his government's agenda. How new these new ideas are is a matter of contention, and it is probably premature to judge the coherence or persuasiveness of the Third Way as a theoretical perspective. Considering it as an organising agenda of urban policy – as community, opportunity, responsibility and accountability – does show how the ideas are developing. Labour's modernising project places a major emphasis on community, reflecting a belief in cooperation and consultation as opposed to the competitive individualism of the Thatcher years. A second theme is that of opportunity, particularly opportunity to work and to obtain training and education. Opportunities, particularly focused on the young unemployed, single parents and the disabled, involves penalties: not to take the opportunities offered will result in loss of benefit.

What is the place of local choice and local variation in Labour's perspective? At the moment, such questions have taken second place to making sure central government objectives are met locally. Local government is crucial to Labour commitments in education and tackling social exclusion. But the view of the Labour government is that local government must reform its political management structures, improve legitimacy by overcoming low electoral turnout, improve standards of service, set high standards of conduct and provide effective community leadership that joined with, rather than shut out, business and the voluntary sector. In this way councils would be more effectively accountable to their communities. At the same time councils will also have to be more accountable to the centre. Councils have been warned that while the government wants to give them greater responsibilities, it retains the right to take powers away. And community leadership does not mean the restoration of the multipurpose local authority of pre-1979; those days are gone. It is in partnership with others – with central government and with public agencies, private companies, community groups and voluntary organisations – that will be the core of the modernising project.

Maintaining the quality of city life depends not just on economic growth and improved council services. Community has a special place in the urban renaissance. This is so in spite of the difficulties both with the term and its application in modern, mobile societies marked by commuting for work, shopping and leisure needs. Locality is not synonymous with community in a world marked by mobility, electronic interaction and home-based family lives. Associations of the like-minded ignore physical location. Community is also criticised not merely for the imprecision of definition but also because of its defects: community can be a narrow, excluding mechanism for individuals, intolerant of the outsider, the loner, the non-conformist. Similarly, community can be a labelling and exclusionary device to mark out ethnic, cultural and belief groups.

In spite of these *caveats*, community remains a powerful and evocative precept. In this sense, Labour's agenda meshes with contemporary developments. Grass-roots' citizen action, community involvement in regeneration projects, and area decentralisation of decisions, are all part of the renewed vitality of urban affairs. Clustered around these precepts are ideas – and ideals – of self-help and empowerment. This enhances the practice of citizenship, and fits in with those aims set out in the government's White Paper of creating revitalised cities, with its emphasis on greater participation in decision-making and better leadership. Local authorities have a clear role here. Providing services, acting as leaders of public/private/voluntary partnerships in economic regeneration, in training, meeting needs and striving to integrate economic with social strategies.

## Conclusion

These moves to a new urban politics will mean that power-holders will have to play a different role: less hierarchical, more inclusive, more consultative, more collaborative. This will mean more open policy-making, rather than decision-making in formal committees, in party groups, and largely in secret. In this process elected politicians may not be the sole decision-makers but a part of the 'deliberative democracy' in which genuine forms of bottom-up action can emerge. Local ownership of schemes is a positive way forward, and the unemployment and anti-poverty measures are based on help being channelled not just to individuals but to communities, as in the action zones for employment, health and education show.

This book has taken the hope for the good life in the revitalised city as its rationale. It has shown that British urban policy, as it has evolved over the past 30 years, has been subject to intense scrutiny. The problems themselves are multiple, overlapping and chronic and the search for solutions has embraced a wide range of strategies. A persistent charge has been that projects have been fragmented and limited, biased towards physical development rather than people-led, ameliorative rather than offering fundamental change. This book has examined these issues, setting them in the context of national and local policies, the principles that underpin them, and the variety of programmes that have been established. Judging the outcomes has had two dimensions. One evaluated the tangible results of land redeveloped, economic decline arrested, housing and jobs sustained, and amenities provided. The second judgement is focused on the extent to which local people are part of these efforts, have their social needs met, can make their voices heard effectively. On both counts there have been positive achievements. The vitality of cities has improved, with new jobs, improved shopping, leisure and other facilities. Groups and communities are also finding their voice, pushing for greater information and for a greater say in decisions. It is clear, however, that much needs to be done.

The book has also shown the heart of urban policy: although economic decline and poverty can be found in all areas, their concentration in major towns and cities justifies a special area of analysis. Both central governments and local authorities put these problems high on the political agenda. The task for national leaders is to find policies, and resources, to promote economic growth, jobs and skills, devise new programmes to bring people, especially young people, into work, and ensure safe and harmonious streets and communities. For local leaders the task is to manage conflict between different groups and interests, take decisions on priorities and on how to improve services, and turn around the worst housing estates. Both central and local governments have struggled with these problems for the past 30 years. During that time the economy of Britain, like that of most industrial societies, has changed fundamentally. So too have individuals' lifestyles, families, education and expectations.

The effect of these changes on urban policy has been a mix of both radical interventions and the slow evolution of existing remedies. The land-use planning and slum-clearance approach of the post-war years gave way in the late 1960s to attempts to alleviate social need through

specialised projects in run-down inner-city areas. But the most fundamental changes took place after 1979, replacing planning by markets,
privatising services and fostering entrepreneurship and business
involvement in both devising and running projects. At the end of the
1990s the change from the multipurpose to the enabling local authority
was fully established, but the coming of a Labour government after
nearly two decades of Conservative rule has offered a new approach,
though it is one which mixes a commitment to a more collaborative
partnership between central and local government with strong oversight and potential sanctions if change is not driven through expedi-
tiously. At the same time the highlighting of 'empowerment' in the
governments proposals depend heavily on increasing the capacity of
people to take part and making sure that this participation goes beyond
information or tokenistic measures.

How then might we regenerate the individual's capacity for
engaging in the good life, and foster cohesion and inclusiveness?
Establishing trust, and expanding participation and consultation, will it
is hoped revitalise urban life. Cities are by definition very heterogeneous places, mixing peoples and environments with often unpre-
dictable and sometimes harsh outcomes. At the same time diversity can
be a mark of success, as for example the contribution that ethnic
minority cultures make to city vitality. Communities should not be
seen as melting pots but as variety, retaining different identities and
contributing uniquely to city life. Inclusivity is not about treating
everyone the same but is about recognising equal worth. We can
already see positive outcomes of past programmes, even while recognising their defects. While on the one hand there is evidence of
squalour that has persisted in spite of repeated attempts by governments to revitalise neighbourhoods, on the other there are real
improvements in civic pride as well as in physical refurbishment. As
Anne Power of the Social Exclusion Unit stresses, such sustainable
improvement calls for continuous intervention. Labour hopes that its
New Deal for Communities will be the 'big new idea' to build on past
programmes to make improvements permanent over the next two
decades. Many rounds of renewal are needed to maintain the gains that
are made; time-limited projects with their withdrawal of resources
always leads to decline returning (Power, 1999).

To sustain cities for the future, the great potential that the new roles
and responsibilities for collaborative working bring with them, must be
supported by long-term programmes. They must also be invested with

more transparent and discursive urban politics. The hope now is these developments will result in a more active urban policy, with cities that provide the good life for all their citizens.

# Further Reading

## Chapter 1   Introduction: the Urban Experience

For a broad-ranging account of current debates on the value of a local democratic polity, a more participatory politics, the value of locality, and contemporary theoretical developments including public choice, communitarianism and feminism see King and Stoker (1996). Rogers (1997), reflects on the present state of city life and calls for a more flourishing urban democracy based on participation, the involvement of communities, more dynamic leadership and a sustainable environment.

## Chapter 2   Seeking Solutions: Urban Policy since 1945

Cullingworth and Nadin (1997), is the standard text on land-use planning and development. Deakin and Edwards (1993) examines effects of Conservative governments on urban policy in the 1980s. Edwards and Batley (1978) critically analyses the first of the 'targeted' policy solutions for urban problems. Oatley (1998) looks at urban policy under Conservative governments in the 1990s, including the competitive bidding basis of policy, multi-sector partnerships and an assessment of Labour's proposals. Rydin (1998) considers both the traditional planning system and contemporary concerns with environmental issues.

## Chapter 3   Debating the Issues: the Ideas that Underpin Policy

Giddens (1998) explores New Labour thinking by a scholar close to Prime Minister Blair. Judge, Stoker and Wolman (1995) gives an excellent survey of ideas and arguments that considers both the nature of power and a range of specific theories that underpin urban studies. Tam (1998) reviews the debate on community and communitarianism and challenges the more authoritarian implications of Etzioni's work.

## Chapter 4   Providing the Framework for Action

In Hogwood (1996) the territorial and other issues surrounding the search for a regional dimension to policy solutions are examined in detail. Loughlin (1996) looks at the the relationships between state and localities and how these are moving from a basis in convention to one of greater legal formulations. Judge, Stoker and Wolman (1995) [see Chapter 3] contains accounts of urban alliances and regimes and in Stoker (1999) the results of recent research on 'The New Public Management', including local authorities' involvement in networks in Europe, are presented. Wilson and Game (1998) gives as comprehensive account of local government, with detailed information on powers, duties, structures and processes. Wolman and Goldsmith (1992) examines, among other issues, the issue of local autonomy and the role of the state, as does Gurr and King.

## Chapter 5    Urban Politics: Democracy for All

Burns, Hambleton and Hoggett (1994) looks at arguments, with case studies, for various kinds of decentralisation of decisions and functions to local neighbourhoods. See Coote and Lenaghan (1997) for how local democracy might be revitalised through new forms of consultation and participation. Hill (1994) includes an analysis of citizenship and participation. Jordan (1996) examines power relations in society to work towards a theory of poverty and social exclusion. Pratchett and Wilson (1996) presents the work of the Commission for Local Democracy, providing a detailed survey of the forces that shape local democracy, including political parties, participation in elections, quangos and a power of general competence for local authorities. Stoker (1999) draws on the latest research findings to examine changing power relations, the place of business and other interests, public response to change, and participation and protest.

## Chapter 6    Meeting the Challenge: Reversing Decline and Improving Services

Cm 4045 (1998), *Bringing Britain Together: a national strategy for neighbourhood renewal* is essential reading for understanding the problem of exclusion and the government's long-term strategies for tackling urban problems. Ball (1993) deals with the major reforms of the Conservative governments of the 1980s and early 1990s. Barnes (1997) looks at the issues of care in the community, including how user groups seek to influence policy. Geddes (1997) includes the analysis of policy and examples of local partnerships. Jones (1996) examines the social and economic circumstances of ethnic minority groups. Jones and Newburn (1998) considers the nature of disaffected communities and measures to address the issues. Lee and Murie (1997) shows the connections between housing and deprivation and demonstrates that disadvantaged groups, especially ethnic minorities, are not solely concentrated in council housing. Pole and Chawla-Duggan (1997) is a collection of case studies of aspects of education, including opting-out and the local management and governance of schools. Solomos and Back (1996) looks at how issues and definitions have shaped race relations in Britain. Ward (1996) examines the ways in which local councils are incorporating environmental issues into plans and services. Williams (1997) covers the public and private sectors, housing associations, and housing finance.

## Chapter 7    The Modernising Agenda

Blair (1998a) sets out what he sees as the strengths and weaknesses of local government and how the Labour government will support a revitalised local democracy, provided it delivers reforms. Blair (1998b) is an introduction to the new philosophy. Phillips (1994) examines and restates the classical position, providing a context within which Labour's reforms can be judged. Stoker (1996) discusses the need for a strengthened leadership role in local democracy.

## Chapter 8   Conclusion: Cities in Changing Times

Giddens (1998) puts forward an analysis and definition of the third way and explores the issues of strategies for the renewal of civil society and community. Landry and Bianchini (1995) draws on examples from around the world to urge the need for creative thinking about city problems and solutions, beyond existing preconceptions. Stoker (1999) brings together the latest research findings on partnerships, including the growing prominence of business; new mechanisms of citizen involvement; and innovations in leadership and decision-making.

# References

Agnew, J. (1993), 'Representing Space: Space, scale and culture in social science', in Duncan, J. and Ley, D. (eds), *Place/Culture/Representation* (London: Routledge), pp. 251–271.

Alcock, P., Craig, G., Lawless, P., Pearson, S., and Robinson, D. (1998), *Inclusive Regeneration: Local Authorities' Corporate Strategies for Tackling Disadvantage* (Sheffield: Sheffield Hallam University/University of Humberside and Lincolnshire/DETR).

Allmendinger, P. and Tewdwr-Jones, M. (1997), 'Post-Thatcherite Urban Planning and Politics: a Major Change?', *International Journal of Urban and Regional Research*, vol. 21, 1, pp. 105–16.

Amin, A. and Graham, S. (1997), 'The ordinary city', *Transactions of the Institute of British Geographers*, NS, vol. 22, pp. 411–29.

Armstrong, H. (1998), 'What Future for Regional Policy in the UK?', *Political Quarterly*, vol. 69,3, pp. 200–214.

Arnstein, S.R. (1969), 'A ladder of citizen participation', *Journal of the American Institute of Planners*, vol. XXXV, 4 July, pp. 216–24.

Atkins, D., Champion, T., Coombes, M., Dorling, D. and Woodward, R./Department of the Environment (1996), *Urban Trends in England: Latest Evidence from the 1991 Census*, Urban Research Report (London: HMSO).

Assocation of Metropolitan Authorities (1996), *Local Authorities and Employment: A consultation paper* (London: AMA).

Audit Commission (1989), *Urban Regeneration and Economic Development – the Local Government Dimension* (London: HMSO).

Audit Commission (1990), *We Can't Go On Meeting Like This* (London: HMSO).

Audit Commission (1997a), *It's a Small World: Local government's role as a steward of the environment* (London: HMSO).

Audit Commission (1997b), *Representing the People: the role of councillors* (London: Audit Commission).

Audit Commission (1997c), *Trading Places: The Supply and Allocation of School Places* (London: HMSO).

Audit Commission (1998), *Changing Partners: a discussion paper on the role of the local education authority* (London: Audit Commission).

Aye Maung, N. and Mirrlees-Black, C. (1994), *Racially Motivated Crime: a British Crime Survey analysis*, Home Office Research and Planning Unit Paper 82 (London: HMSO).

Bailey, N. with Barker, A. and MacDonald, K. (1995), *Partnership Agencies in British Urban Policy* (London: UCL Press).

Ball, S.J. (1993), *Education Reform: A Critical and Post-Structural Approach* (Buckingham: Open University Press).

227

Barnes, M. (1997), *Care, Communities and Citizens* (Harlow: Addison-Wesley Longman).

Bateman, D. (1995), 'Local Agenda 21 UK', *Local Government Policy Making*, vol. 22, 2, pp. 16–20.

Bellamy, C., Horrocks, I. and Webb, J. (1995), 'Exchanging Information with the Public: from One-stop Shops to Community Information Systems', *Local Government Studies*, vol. 21, 1, pp. 11–30.

Blair, T. (1998a), *Leading the Way – A new vision for local government* (London: Institute of Public Policy Research).

Blair, T. (1998b), *The Third Way: New Politics for the New Century*, Fabian Pamphlet 588 (London: The Fabian Society).

Bloch, A. (1992), *The Turnover of Local Councillors* (York: Joseph Rowntree Foundation).

Bogdanor, V. (1996), 'Memorandum', House of Lords Select Committee On Relations Between Central And Local Government, *Rebuilding Trust*, Volume II – Oral Evidence And Associated Memoranda, HL Paper-I, pp. 141–50.(London: HMSO).

Boyne, G.A. (1996), *Constraints, Choices And Public Policies* (Greenwich, CT/London: JAI Press).

Bramley, G., Evans, M. and Atkins, J. (1998), *Where Does Public Spending Go? A Pilot Study to Analyse the Flows of Public Expenditure to Local Areas* (London: DETR).

Bramley, G. and LeGrand, J. (1992), *Who Uses Local Services? – Striving For Equity*, Belgrave Paper No. 4 (Luton: Local Government Management Board).

Breheny, M. (1998), *Urban housing capacity: what can be done?* (London: Town and Country Planning Association).

Bryant, C. (1998), 'London's rainbow coalition', *New Statesman*, 8 May, p. 18.

Buchanan, J. and Tullock, G. (1965), *The Calculus of Consent* (Ann Arbor, MI: University of Michigan Press).

Buck, N. (1996), 'Social and Economic Change in Contemporary Britain: The Emergence of an Urban Underclass?', in E. Mingione (ed.), *Urban Poverty and the Underclass* (Oxford: Blackwell), pp. 277–98.

Bulpitt, J. (1983), *Territory and Power in the United Kingdom* (Manchester: Manchester University Press).

Burns, D., Hambleton, R. and Hoggett, P. (eds) (1994), *The Politics of Decentralization: Revitalizing Local Democracy* (London: Macmillan).

Burrows, R. (1997), *Contemporary Patterns of Residential Mobility in Relation to Social Housing in England* (York: Joseph Rowntree Foundation).

Butler, D., Adonis, A., Travers, T. (1994), *Failure in British Government: the Politics of the Poll Tax* (Oxford: Oxford University Press).

Cairns, D. (1996), 'Rediscovering Democratic Purpose in British Local Government', *Policy and Politics*, vol. 24, 1, pp. 17–27.

Castells, M. (1977), *The Urban Question: A Marxist Approach* (translated by A. Sheridan) (London: Edward Arnold).

Castells, M. (1979), *City, Class and Power* (London: Macmillan).

Castells, M. (1983) *The City and the Grassroots* (Berkeley, CA: University of California Press).

Church, J. and Summerfield, C. (eds) (1996), *Social Focus on Ethnic Minorities*, Office for National Statistics (London: HMSO).

Clarke, M. and Stewart, J. (1994), 'The local authority and the new community governance', *Local Government Studies*, vol. 20, pp. 163–76.

Clarke, S.E. (1993), 'The New Localism: Local Politics in a Global Era', in E.G. Goetz and S.E. Clarke (eds), *The New Localism: Comparative Urban Politics in a Global Era* (Newbury Park, CA: Sage), pp. 1–21.

Clarke, S.E., Staeheli, L.A. and Brunell, L. (1995), 'Women Redefining Local Politics', in D. Judge, G. Stoker and H. Wolman (eds), *Theories of Urban Politics* (London: Sage), pp. 205–27.

Cm 1200 (1990), *This Common Inheritance* (London: HMSO).

Cm 2850 (1995), *Standards in Public Life*, Committee on Standards in Public Life, *First Report* (London: HMSO).

Cm 3207 (1996), *Annual Report 1996* (London: Department of the Environment).

Cm 3270–I (1996), *Local Public Spending Bodies*, Committee on Standards in Public Life, Second Report (London: HMSO).

Cm 3471 (1996), *Household Growth: Where shall we live?* (London: HMSO).

Cm 3681 (1997), *Excellence in Schools* (London: HMSO).

Cm 3702–I (1997), Committee on Standards in Public Life, *Third Report* (London: HMSO).

Cm 3807 (1998), *The New NHS – modern, dependable* (London: HMSO).

Cm 3906 (1998), *Annual Report 1998* (London: DETR).

Cm 3950 (1998), *A New Deal for Transport: Better for Everyone* (London: HMSO).

Cm 4014 (1998), *Modern Local Government: In Touch with the People* (London: HMSO).

Cm 4045 (1998), *Bringing Britain Together: a national strategy for neighbourhood renewal*. Social Exclusion Unit, Cabinet Office (London: HMSO).

Cmnd 4040 (1969), *Local Government in England*, Royal Commission on Local Government in England (the Redcliffe-Maud Commission), vol. I Report (London: HMSO).

Cmnd 6453 (1976), *Report* of the Committee of Inquiry into Local Government Finance (the Layfield Committee) (London: HMSO).

Cmnd 6845 (1977), *Policy for the Inner Cities* (London: HMSO).

Cmnd 8427 (1981), *The Brixton Disorders 10–12 April 1981: Report of an Inquiry by the Rt. Hon. the Lord Scarman, OBE* (London: HMSO).

Cmnd 9799 (1986), *Report* of the Committee of Inquiry into the Conduct of Local Authority Business (Chairman, David Widdicombe, QC) (London: HMSO).

Cockburn, C. (1977), *The Local State* (London: Pluto Press).

Cole, A. and John, P. (1995), 'Local Policy Networks in France and Britain: Policy Coordination in Fragmented Political Sub-Systems', *West European Studies*, vol. 18, 4, pp. 89–109.

Coleman, A. (1985), *Utopia on Trial* (London: Hilary Shipman).

Commission of the European Communities (1992), *Towards Sustainability: A European Community Programme of Policy and Action in Relation to the Environment and Sustainable Development* (Brussels: Commission of the European Communities).

Commission of the European Communities (1993), *Green Paper: European Social Policy – Options for the Union*, COM(93)551 (Brussels: Commission of the European Communities).

Commission of the European Communities (1994), *Europe 2000+: Cooperation for European Territorial Development* (Luxemburg: European Commission).

Commission of the European Communities (1997), *Call for Tenders by Open Procedure No. 97.00.57.001 Concerning the Thematic Evaluation on the Impact of Structural Funds on the Environment* (Brussels: Commission of the European Communities).

Commission on the Future of the Voluntary Sector in England (1996), *Report, Meeting the Challenge of Change: voluntary action into the 21st Century* (London: National Council for Voluntary Organisations).

Community Development Project (1977), *Guilding the Ghetto* (London: HMSO).

Constitution Unit (1996), *Regional Government in England*, Local and central government relations research findings no. 50 (York: Joseph Rowntree Foundation).

Cooke, P. (1989), 'Locality, Economic Restructuring and World Development', in P. Cooke (ed.), *Localities: The Changing Face of Urban Britain* (London: Unwin Hyman), pp. 1–44.

Cooke, P. (1990a), *Back to the future* (London: Unwin Hyman).

Cooke, P. (1990b), 'Modern urban theory in question', *Transactions of the Institute of British Geographers*, vol. 15, pp. 331–43.

Coote, A. and Lenaghan, J. (1997), *Citizens' Juries: Theory into Practice* (London: Institute of Public Policy Research).

Council of Europe (1985), *European Charter of Local Self-Government* (Strasbourg: Council of Europe).

Council of Europe (1995), 'The size of municipalities, efficiency and citizen participation', *Local and regional authorities in Europe, No. 56* (Strasbourg: Council of Europe Press).

Crook, A.D.H., Darke, R.A. and Disson, J.S. (1996), *A New Lease of Life? Housing Association Investment on Local Authority Housing Estates* (Bristol: The Policy Press).

Cullingwoth, J.B. and Nadin, V. (1997) *Town and Country Planning in the United Kingdom*, 12th edn (London: Routledge).

Dahl, R. (1961), *Who Governs? Democracy and Power in an American City* (New Haven, CT: Yale University Press).

Dahl, R. (1986), 'Rethinking *Who Governs?* New Haven revisited', in R.J. Wade (ed.), *Community Power: Directions for Future Research* (Newbury Park, CA: Sage).

Dahl, R.A. and Tufte, E.R. (1974), *Size and Democracy* (Stanford, CA/London: Stanford University Press/Oxford University Press).

Davis, M. (1990), *Quartz City: Excavating the Future in Los Angeles* (London: Verso).

Dawson, H. (1995), 'Voting? Why should I bother?', *Local Government Chronicle*, 30 June, pp. 18–19.

Day, G. and Murdoch, J. (1993), 'Locality and community: coming to terms with place', *The Sociological Review*, vol. 41, 1, pp. 82–111.

Deakin, N. and Edwards, J. (1993), *The Enterprise Culture and the Inner City* (London: Routledge).

Dearlove, J. (1973), *The Politics of Policy in Local Government* (Cambridge: Cambridge University Press).

Department for Education and Employment (1997a), *Design of the New Deal for 18–24 year olds* (London: DfEE).

Department for Education and Employment (1997b), *Welfare to Work: Employment Zones* (London: DfEE).

Department of the Environment (1988), *Action for Cities* (London: HMSO).

Department of the Environment (1995a), *Final Evaluation of Enterprise Zones* (London: HMSO).

Department of the Environment (1995b), *Involving Communities in Urban and Rural Regeneration: A Guide for Practitioners* (London: HMSO).

Department of the Environment, Transport and the Regions (1997), *Involving Communities in Urban and Rural Regeneration* (London: DETR).

Department of the Environment, Transport and the Regions (1998a), *Annual Report 1998* (London: DETR).

Department of the Environment, Transport and the Regions (1998b), *Community-Based Regeneration Initiatives: A Working Paper* (London: DETR).

Department of the Environment, Transport and the Regions (1998c), *Housing and Regeneration Policy: A Statement by the Deputy Prime Minister and Secretary of State for the Environment, Transport and the Regions* (London: DETR).

Department of the Environment, Transport and the Regions (1998d), *Modernising local government: Local democracy and community leadership* (London: DETR).

Department of the Environment, Transport and the Regions (1998e), *Modernising Local Government – a new ethical framework* (London: DETR).

Department of Social Security (1997), *Household Below Average Income: A statistical analysis 1979–1994/95* (London: HMSO).

Dowding, K. (1996), 'Public Choice and Local Governance', in D. King and G. Stoker (eds), *Rethinking Local Democracy* (Basingstoke: Macmillan), pp. 50–66.

Dowding, K. and Dunleavy, P. (1996), 'Production, disbursement and consumption: the modes and modalities of goods and services', in S. Edgell, K. Hetherington and A. Warde (eds), *Consumption Matters: The Production and Experience of Consumption* (Oxford: Blackwell), pp. 36–65.

Dowding, K., John, P. and Biggs, S. (1994), 'Tiebout: A Survey of the Empirical Literature', *Urban Studies*, vol. 31, 4/5, pp. 767–97.

Duncan, S. and Goodwin, M. (1988), *The Local State and Uneven Development* (Oxford: Polity Press).

Dunleavy, P. (1980), *Urban Political Analysis* (London: Macmillan).

Dunleavy, P. and Weir, S. (1994), 'Democracy in doubt', *Local Government Chronicle*, 29 April, p. 12.

Edwards, J. and Batley, R. (1978), *The Politics of Positive Discrimination: An Evaluation of the Urban Programme 1967–77* (London: Tavistock).

Elcock, H. (1995), 'Leading people', *Local Government Studies*, vol. 21, 4, pp. 546–67.

Employment Committee (1996), *The Work of TECs*, House of Commons Session 1995–96, First Report, HC 99 (London: HMSO).

Etzioni, A. (1993), *The Spirit of Community: Rights, Responsibilities and the Communitarian Agenda* (New York: Crown).

European Commission (1997), *Agenda 2000: For a Stronger and Wider Union*, DOC 97/6, volume I (Brussels: Commission of the European Communities).

Forrest, R. and Gordon, D. (1993), *People and Places: a 1991 census atlas of England* (Bristol: School for Advanced Urban Studies).

Frazer, E. (1996), 'The Value of Locality', in D. King and G. Stoker (eds), *Rethinking Local Democracy* (Basingstoke: Macmillan), pp. 89–110.

Gamble, A. (1988), *The Free Economy and the Strong State* (London: Macmillan).

Game, C. (1998), 'What's the use of voting?', *Local Government Chronicle*, 26 June, p. 15.

Game, C. and Leach, S. with Williams, G. (1993), *Councillor Recruitment and Turnover: An Approaching Precipice?* (Luton: Local Government Management Board).

Gaster, L. and O'Toole, M. (1995), *Local Government Decentralisation: An idea whose time has come?* (Bristol: The Policy Press).

Geddes, M. (1995), *Poverty, Excluded Communities and Local Democracy*, CLD research report no.9 (London: Commission for Local Democracy).

Geddes, M. (1996), *Extending Democratic Practice in Local Government*, CLD research report No. 17 (London: Commission for Local Democracy).

Geddes, M. (1997), *Partnership against poverty and exclusion? Local regeneration strategies and excluded communities in the UK* (Bristol: The Policy Press).

Geddes, M. and Erskine, A. (1994), 'Poverty, The Local Economy And The Scope For Local Initiative', *Local Economy*, vol. 9, 2, pp. 192–206.

Gibbs, D. (1997), 'Urban sustainability and economic development', *Cities*, vol. 14, 4, pp. 203–208.

Giddens, A. (1985), 'Time, Space and Regionalisation', in D. Gregory and J. Urry (eds), *Social Relations and Spatial Structures* (Basingstoke: Macmillan), pp. 265–95.

Giddens, A. (1998a), 'After the left's paralysis', *New Statesman*, 1 May, pp. 18–21.

Giddens, A. (1998b), *The Third Way: The Renewal of Social Democracy* (Cambridge: Polity Press).

Goldblatt, P. and Lewis, C. (eds) (1998), *Reducing offending: an assessment of research evidence on ways of dealing with offending behaviour*, Home Office Research Study 187 (London: Home Office).

Goldsmith, M. (1995), 'Autonomy and City Limits', in D. Judge, G. Stoker and H. Wolman (eds), *Theories of Urban Politics* (London: Sage), pp. 228–52.

Goodin, R.E. (1996), 'Inclusion and Exclusion', *Archives European Sociology*, vol. 37, 1996, pp. 343–71.

Gordon, D. and Forrest, R. (1995), *People and places 2: Social and economic distinctions in England* (Bristol: The Policy Press).

Gray, C. (1994), *Government Beyond The Centre: Sub-National Politics in Britain* (London: Macmillan).

Grayson, D. (1993), 'Regenerating Britain: Common Purpose, Uncommon Urgency', *Occasional Paper*, Issue 1 (London: Business in the Community).

Greed, C. (1996), 'Promise or Progress: Women and Planning', *Built Environment*, vol. 22, 1, pp. 9–21.

Greenslade, R. (1998), 'Return of the local heroes', *The Guardian*, Media Section, 23 March, pp. 8–9.

Gregory, S. (1998), *Transforming Local Services: Partnership in action* (York: Joseph Rowntree Foundation).

Gurr, T.R. and King, D.S. (1987), *The State and the City* (Basingstoke: Macmillan and Chicago: University of Chicago Press).

Gwilliam, M., Bourne, C., Swain, C. and Prat, A. (1999), *Sustainable renewal of suburban areas* (York: Joseph Rowntree Foundation).

Gyford, J. (1985), *The Politics of Local Socialism* (London: Allen and Unwin).

Hall, D. and Stewart, J. (1996), *Citizens' Juries in Local Government* (London: Local Government Management Board).

Hall, W. and Weir, S. (1996), *The Untouchables* (London: Democratic Audit, University of Essex/Scarman Trust).

Hambleton, R. (1992), 'Decentralisation and democracy in UK local government', *Public Money and Management*, vol. 12, 3, pp. 9–20.

Hambleton, R., Essex, S. and Mills, L. (1996), *Collaborative Councils: a study of inter-agency working in practice* (Tonbridge: LGC Communications).

Harding, A. (1994), 'Urban Regimes And Growth Machines: Toward a Cross-National Research Agenda', *Urban Affairs Quarterly*, vol. 29,3, pp. 356–82.

Harding, A. (1996), 'Is There a "New Community Power" and Why Should We Need One?', *International Journal of Urban and Regional Research*, vol. 70, 4, pp. 637–55.

Harfield, C.G. (1997), 'Consent, Consensus or the Management of Dissent?: Challenges to Community Consultation in a new Policing Environment', *Policing and Society*, vol. 7, pp. 271–89.

Harvey, A. (1998), 'Councils that care', *Local Government Management*, Winter, pp. 18–19.

Harvey, A., Jones, P.A. and Donovan, M. (1998), 'Just do it', *Local Government Management*, Summer, pp. 26–7.

Harvey, D. (1973), *Social Justice and the City* (London: Edward Arnold).

Harvey, D. (1985), *The Urbanization of Capital: Studies in the History and Theory of Capitalism* (Oxford: Basil Blackwell).

Harvey, D. (1989), *The Condition of Postmodernity* (Oxford: Basil Blackwell).

Hayton, K. (1996a), 'A critical examination of the role of community business in urban regeneration', *Town Planning Review*, vol 67, 1, pp. 1–20.

Hayton, K. (1996b), 'Planning policy in Scotland', M. Tewdwr-Jones (ed.), *British Planning Policy in Transition* (London: UCL Press), pp. 78–97.

Healey, P. (1998), 'Collaborative planning in a stakeholder society', *Town Planning Review*, vol. 69,1. pp. 1–21.

Hebbert, M. (1995), 'Unfinished Business: the remaking of London government, 1985–1995', *Policy and Politics*, vol. 23, 4, pp. 347–58.

Higgins, J., Deakin, N., Edwards, J. and Wicks, M. (1983), *Government and Urban Poverty: inside the policy-making process* (Oxford: Basil Blackwell).

Higgins, M. and Davies, L. (1996), 'Planning for Women: How Much has been Achieved?', *Built Environment*, vol. 22, 1, pp. 32–46.

Hill, D.M. (1994), *Citizens and Cities: Urban Policy in the 1990s* (Hemel Hempstead: Harvester Wheatsheaf).

Hills, J. (1998a), 'Does Income Mobility Mean that We Do Not Need to Worry about Poverty?', in A.B. Atkinson and J. Hills (eds), *Exclusion, Employment and Opportunity*, CASE paper 4 (London: Centre for Analysis of Social Exclusion, LSE), pp. 31–54.

Hills, J. (1998b), *Income and Wealth: the latest evidence* (York: Joseph Rowntree Foundation).

Hirst, P. (1994), *Associative Democracy* (Cambrige: Polity Press).

Hirst, P. and Thompson, G. (1996), *Globalisation in Question: The international economy and the possibility of governance* (Cambridge: Polity Press).

Hogwood, B.W. (1996), *Mapping the Regions: boundaries, coordination and government* (Bristol: The Policy Press).

Holman, B. (1997), *FARE Dealing: Neighbourhood Involvement in a Housing Scheme* (London: Community Development Foundation).

Home Affairs Committee (1994), *Racial Attacks and Harassment*, volume I, Report; volume II, Minutes of Evidence and Appendices. House of Commons Session 1993–94 Third Report, 71–I; 71–II (London: HMSO).

Hoover, K. and Plant, R. (1989), *Conservative Capitalism in Britain and the United States* (London/New York: Routledge).

House of Lords (1996), *Rebuilding Trust*, Select Committee On Relations Between Central And Local Government, Volume I – Report, Session 1995–96, HL 97 (London: HMSO).

Howarth, C., Kenway, P., Palmer, G. and Street, C. (1998), *Monitoring poverty and social exclusion: Labour's inheritance* (York: Joseph Rowntree Foundation).

IPPR (1996), *In progress...*, Bulletin of the Institute for Public Policy Research (London: IPPR), Summer.

Janowitz, M. (1967), *The Community Press in an Urban Setting* (Chicago, IL: University of Chicago Press).

Jarvis, R. (1996), 'Structure planning policy and strategic planning guidance in Wales', in M. Tewdwr-Jones (ed.), *British Planning Policy in Transition* (London: UCL Press), pp. 43–60.

Jessop, B. (1995), 'Towards a Schumpeterian workfare regime in Britain? Reflections on regulation, governance, and welfare state', *Environment and Planning A*, vol. 27, pp. 1613–1626.

John, P. (1994a), 'Central-Local Relations in the 1980s and 1990s: Towards a Policy Learning Approach', *Local Government Studies*, vol. 20, 3, pp. 412–36.

John, P. (1994b), *The Europeanisation of British Local Government: New Management Strategies* (Luton: Local Government Management Board).

John, P. (1997a), 'Local Governance', in P. Dunleavy, A. Gamble, I. Holliday and G. Peele (eds), *Development in British Politics 5* (Basingstoke: Macmillan), pp.253–76.

John, P. (1997b), 'The Policy Implications of Tiebout Effects', *Local Government Studies*, vol. 23, 2, pp. 67–79.

John, P. (1998), *Analysing Public Policy* (London: Pinter).

John, P. and Cole, A. (1998), 'Urban Regimes and Local Governance in Britain and France: Policy Adoption and Coordination in Leeds and Lille', *Urban Affairs Review*, vol. 33, 3, pp. 382–404.

Jones, T. (1996), *Britain's Ethnic Minorites* (London: Policy Studies Institute).

Jones, T. and Newburn, T. (1998) *Policing and Disaffected Communities* (London: Policy Studies Institite).

Jones, T. and Newburn, T. (1997), *Policing after the Act* (London: Policy Studies Institute).

Jordan, B. (1996), *A Theory of Poverty and Social Exclusion* (Cambridge: Polity Press).

Jordan, G. (1990), 'The pluralism of pluralism: an anti-theory?', *Political Studies*, vol. 38, 2, pp. 286–301.

Judge, D., Stoker, G. and Wohlman, H. (eds) (1995), *Theories of Urban Politics* (London: Sage).

Katznelson, I. (1992), *Marxism and the City* (Oxford: Clarendon Press).

Kearns, A. (1995), 'Active citizenship and local governance: political and geographical dimensions', *Political Geography*, vol. 14, 2, 1995, pp. 155–76.

Keating, M. (1991), *Comparative Urban Politics: Power and the City in the United States, Canada, Britain and France* (London: Edward Elgar).

Keating, M. (1997), 'The invention of regions: political restructuring and territorial government in Western Europe', *Environment and Planning C: Government and Policy*, vol 15, pp. 383–98.

Keil, R. (1994), 'Editorial: Global sprawl: urban form after Fordism?', *Environment and Planning D: Society and Space*, vol. 12, pp. 131–6.

Kempson, E. (1996), *Life on a low income* (York: Joseph Rowntree Foundation).

Kirby, A. (1995), 'Cities: A research agenda for the close of the century', *Cities*, 12, 1, pp. 5–11.

Kitchen, H. (1995), *A Power of General Competence for Local Authorities in Britain in the Context of European Experiments*, CLD research report No. 16 (London: Commission for Local Democracy).

Labour Party (1996), *New Labour: new life for Britain* (London: Labour Party).

Laudry, C. and Bianchini, F. (1995), *The Creative City* (London: Demos/Comedia).

Lawless, P. (1996), 'The inner cities: towards a new agenda', *Town Planning Review*, vol. 67,1, pp. 21–43.

Laws, G. (1994), 'Oppression, knowledge and the built environment', *Political Georgraphy*, vol. 13, 1, pp. 7–32.

Leach, S. (1998), *It's our Party – democratic problems in local government* (London: Local Government Management Board).

Leach, S. and Stoker, G. (1997), 'Understanding the Local Government Review: a retrospective analysis', *Public Administration*, vol. 75, 1, pp. 1–20.

Leadbetter, C. and Goss, S. (1998), *Civic Entrepreneurship* (London: Demos/Public Mangement Foundation).

Lee, P. and Murie, A. (1997), *Poverty, Housing Tenure and Social Exclusion* (Bristol: The Policy Press).

Lefebvre, H. (1971), *La Revolution Urbaine* (Paris: Gallimard).

Le Grand, J. (1998), 'The Third Way begins with Cora', *New Statesman*, 6 March, pp. 26–7.

Little, J. (1994), *Gender, Planning and the Policy Process* (Oxford: Pergamon/Elsevier Science).

Local Government Chronicle (1998), *Funds Fail Ethnic Minorities* (London: Local Government Chronicle), 1 May, p. 3.

Logan, J.R. and Molotch, H. L. (1987), *Urban Fortunes: the political economy of place* (Berkeley, CA: University of California Press).

Loughlin, M. (1996a), 'Memorandum', House of Lords, *Rebuilding Trust*, Select Committee On Relations Between Central And Local Government, Volume III – Written Evidence, Session 1995–96, HL Paper 97–II, pp. 123–31 (London: HMSO).

Loughlin, M. (1996b), 'Understanding Central-Local Government Relations', *Public Policy and Administration*, vol. 11, 2, pp. 48–65.

Lowndes. V. (1999), 'Management change in local governance', in G. Stoker (ed.), *The New Management of British Local Governance* (Basingstoke: Macmillan).

Lowndes, V. and Stoker, G. (1992), 'An evaluation of neighbourhood decentralisation', *Policy and Politics*, Part I, vol. 20, 1, pp. 47–61; Part II, vol. 20, 2, pp. 143–52.

Lyotard, J.–F. (1984), *The Postmodern Condition: A Report on Knowledge* (Manchester: Manchester University Press).

Mabileau, A., Moyser, G., Parry, G. and Quantin, P. (1989), *Political Participation in Britain and France* (Cambridge: Cambridge University Press).

McLaughlin, E. (1998), 'Taxes, benefits and paid work', in C. Oppenheim, *An Inclusive Society: Strategies for Tackling Poverty* (London: Institute for Public Policy Research), pp. 95–111.

McMarthy, P., Prism Research and Harrison, T., Department of the Environment (1995), *Attitudes to Town and Country Planning* (London: HMSO).

Marr, A. (1996), 'The rise of do-it-yourself democracy', *The Independent*, 18 January, p. 17.

Marshall, T.H. (1950), *Citizenship and Social Class*, The Marshall Lectures, Cambridge (Cambridge: Cambridge University Press).

Massey, D. (1984), *Spatial Divisions of Labour* (London: Macmillan).

Mawson, J. and Spencer, K. (1997), 'The Government Offices for the English Regions: towards regional governance?', *Policy and Politics*, vol. 25, 1, pp. 71–84.

Maynard, W. and Read, T. (1997), *Policing Racially Motivated Incidents*, Crime Detection and Prevention Series Paper 84 (London: Home Office).

Mead, L. (1986), *Beyond Entitlement: the social obligations of citizenship* (New York: Free Press).

Mead, L. (1991), 'The new politics of the new poverty', *The Public Interest*, no. 103, pp. 3–20.

Miller, W.L. (1988), *Irrelevant Elections: The Quality of Local Democracy in Britain* (Oxford: Clarendon Press).

Miller, W.L. and Dickson, M.B. (1996), *Local Governance and Local Citizenship: A Report on Public and Elite Attitudes*, Local Governance Programme Working Paper No. 1 (Glasgow: Local Governance Programme of the ESRC, Strathclyde University).

Mills, C. Wright (1956), *The Power Elite* (New York: Oxford University Press)

Mirrlees-Black, C., Budd, T., Partridge, S. and Mayhew, P. (1998), *The 1998 British Crime Survey*, Home Office Statistical Bulletin (London: Home Office).

Mirrlees-Black, C., Mayhew, P. and Percy, A. (1996), *The 1996 British Crime Survey: England and Wales*, Home Office Statistical Bulletin, Issue 19/96 (London: Home Office).

Modood, T. (1998), 'Racial Equality: Colour, Culture and Justice', in J. Franklin (ed.), *Social Policy and Social Justice* (London: Polity Press/Institute for Public Policy Research).

Modood, T., Berthoud, R., Lakey, J., Nazroo, J., Smith, P., Virdee, S., Beishon, S. (1997), *Ethnic Minorities in Britain* (London: Policy Studies Institute).

Molotch, H.L. (1976), 'The city as a growth machine', *American Journal of Sociology*, vol. 82, pp. 309–30.

MORI (1996), 'Memorandum'; in *Rebuilding Trust*, House of Lords Select Committee on Relations between Central and Local Government, Session 1995–96, vol II, 'Oral Evidence and Associated Memoranda', HL 97–I, pp. 420–25; and 'Examination of witnesses', pp. 425–32; and 'Supplementary memorandum', pp. 433–41 (London: HMSO).

Morris, R. (1994), 'New Magistracies and Commissariats', *Local Government Studies*, vol. 20, 2, pp. 177–185.

Mossberger, K. and Stoker, G. (1997), 'Inner-City Policy In Britain: Why It Will Not Go Away', *Urban Affairs Review*, vol. 32,3, pp. 378–402.

Murray, C. (1984), *Losing Ground* (New York: Basic Books).

Murray, C. (1990), 'The British underclass', *The Public Interest*, no. 99, pp. 4–28.

Murroni, C., Irvine, N. and King, R. (1998), *Future.radio.uk* (London: Institute for Public Policy Research).

Newman, O. (1972), *Defensible Space: Crime Prevention through Urban Design* (New York: Macmillan).

Newman, P. and Thornley, A. (1997), 'Fragmentation and Centralisation in the Governance of London: Influencing the Urban Policy and Planning Agenda', *Urban Studies*, vol. 34,7, pp. 967–88.

Newton, K. (1976), *Second City Politics: Democratic Processes and decision-making in Birmingham* (Oxford: Oxford University Press).

Niskanen, W.A. (1971), *Bureaucracy and Representative Government* (Chicago, IL: Aldine-Atherton).

Oatley, N. (ed.) (1998), *Cities, Economic Competition and Urban Policy* (London: Sage/Paul Chapman Publishing).

Office for National Statistics (1996), *Social Focus on Ethnic Minorities* (London: HMSO).

Osborne, D. and Gaebler, T. (1992), *Reinventing Government* (Reading, MA: Addison-Wesley).

Page, B. (1996), 'Perceptions of local government: what do the public really think about local government?', *Public Policy and Administration*, vol. 11,3, pp. 3–17.

Page, B. (1997), 'Information vehicles stuck in slow lane', *Local Government Chronicle*, 5 December, pp. 12–13.

Page, B. and Elgood, J. (1998), 'The point of view over the parapet', *Local Government Chronicle*, 13 November, pp. 16–17.

Pahl, R. and Spencer, L. (1998), 'The politics of friendship', *Renewal*, vol. 5, nos 3 and 4, pp. 100–107.

Painter, J. (1991), 'Regulation Theory and Local Government', *Local Government Studies*, vol. 17, 6, 1991, pp. 23–44.

Parkinson, M. (1996), 'Twenty-Five Years of Urban Policy in Britain – Partnership, Entrepreneurialism or Competition?', *Public Money and Management*, July–September, pp. 7–14.

Parry, G., Moyser, G. and Day, N. (1992), *Political participation and democracy in Britain* (Cambridge: Cambridge University Press).

Peach, C. (1996), *Ethnicity in the 1991 Census, volume 2: The ethnic minority populations of Great Britain*, Office for National Statistics (London: HMSO).

Peck, J. and Tickell, A. (1994), 'Jungle law breaks out: neoliberalism and global–local disorder', *Area*, vol. 26, 4, pp. 317–26.

Peck, J. and Tickell, A. (1995), 'Business Goes Local: Dissecting the "Business Agenda" in Manchester', *International Journal of Urban and Regional Research*, vol. 19, 1, pp. 55–78.

Percy-Smith, J. (1995), *Digital Democracy: Information and communication technologies in local politics*, CLD research report No. 14 (London: Commission for Local Democracy).

Percy-Smith, J. (1996), 'Downloading Democracy? Information And Communication Technologies In Local Politics', *Policy and Politics*, vol. 24, 1, pp. 43–56.

Phillips, A. (1994), *Local Democracy: The Terms of the Debate* (London: Commission for Local Democracy).

Phillips, A. (1996), 'Feminism and the Attractions of the Local', in D. King and G. Stoker (eds), *Rethinking Local Democracy* (Basingstoke: Macmillan), pp.111–29.

Pickvance, C.G. (1976), 'On the study of urban social movements', in C. G. Pickvance (ed.), *Urban Sociology: Critical Essays* (London: Methuen), pp. 198–218.

Pickvance, C. (1995), 'Marxist Theories of Urban Politics', in D. Judge, G. Stoker and H. Wolman (eds), *Theories of Urban Politics* (London: Sage), pp. 253–75.

Pierre, J. (1998), 'Public–Private Partnerships and Urban Governance: Introduction', in J. Pierre (ed.), *Partnerships in Urban Governance: European and American Experience* (Basingstoke: Macmillan).

Pirie, M. (1992), *Blueprint for a Revolution* (London: Adam Smith Institute).

Plant, R. (1998), 'So you want to be a citizen?', *New Statesman*, 6 February, pp. 30–32.

Pole, C. amd Chawle-Duggan, R. (eds) (1997) *Reshaping Education in the 1990s: Perspectives on Secondary Schooling* (London: Falmer).

Police Complaints Authority (1997), *1996/97 Annual Report* (London: HMSO).

Policy Studies Institute/DOE (1995), *Public Access To Information: an evaluation of the Local Government (Access to Information) Act 1985* (London: HMSO).

Pool, H. (1997), 'Looking to the future', *The Guardian*, Guardian Education, 4 February, p. 9.

Power, A. (1997), *Estates on the Edge: the social consequences of mass housing in northern Europe* (Basingstoke: Macmillan).

Power, A. (1999), 'Pool of Resources', *The Guardian*, 3 February, pp. 2–3.

Power, A. and Tunstall, R. (1997), *Dangerous Disorder: Riots and Violent Disturbances in Thirteen Areas of Britain, 1991–1992* (York: Joseph Rowntree Foundation).

Pratchett, L. and Wilson, D. (eds) (1996), *Local Democracy and Local Government* (Basingstoke: Macmillan).

Preteceille, E. (1990), 'Political paradoxes of urban restructuring: Globalization of the economy and localization of politics?', in J.R. Logan and T. Swanstrom (eds), *Beyond the City Limits: urban policy and restructuring in a comparative perspective* (Philadelphia, PA: Temple University Press), pp. 27–59.

Putnam, D. (1993), *Making Democracy Work: Civic Traditions in Modern Italy* (Princeton, NJ: Princeton University Press).

Putnam, D. (1995), 'Bowling Alone: America's declining social capital' *Journal of Democracy*, vol. 6,1, pp. 65–78.

Pyecroft, C. (1995), 'The Organisation of Local Authorities' European Activities', *Public Policy and Administration*, vol. 10, 4, pp. 20–33.

Rallings, C., Temple, M. and Thrasher, M. (1994), *Community Identity and Participation in Local Democracy*, CLD research report No. 1 (London: Commission for Local Democracy).

Rallings, C. and Thrasher, M. (1995), 'Parties pack a punch', *Local Government Chronicle*, 3 February, p. 16.

Rao, N. (1993), *Managing Change: Councillors and the New Local Government* (York: Joseph Rowntree Foundation).

Rao, N. (1998), 'Representation in Local Politics: A Reconsideration and some New Evidence', *Political Studies*, vol. 46, 1, March, pp. 19–35.

Rao, N. and Young, K. (1993), *Councillors and the New Local Government* (York: Joseph Rowntree Foundation).

Rhodes, R.A.W. (1988), *Beyond Westminster and Whitehall: The Sub-Central Governments of Britain* (London: Unwin Hyman).

Robson, B. (1994), 'Urban Policy At The Crossroads', *Local Economy*, vol. 9,3, pp. 216–23.

Robson, B., Bradford, M., Deas, I., Hall, E., Harrison, E., Parkinson, M., Evans, R., Garside, P., Harding, A. and Robinson, F. (1994), *Assessing the Impact of Urban Policy*, Department of the Environment (London: HMSO).

Rogers, R. (1997), *Cities for a Small Planet* (London: Faber).

Room, G. (1995), *Beyond the Threshold: The measurement and analysis of social exclusion* (Bristol: The Policy Press).

Rydin, Y. (1998), *Urban and Environmental Planning in the UK* (Basinstoke: Macmillan).

Saunders, P. 1983), *Urban Politics: A Sociological Interpretation* (London: Hutchinson).

Saunders, P. (1984), 'Rethinking local politics', in M. Boddy and C. Fudge (eds), *Local Socialism?* (London: Macmillan).

Saunders, P. (1986), 'Reflections on the dual politics thesis: the argument, its origins and its critics', in M. Goldsmith and S. Villadsen (eds), *Urban Political Theory and the Management of Fiscal Stress* (Aldershot: Gower).

Scottish Office (1988), *New Life for Urban Scotland* (Edinburgh: Scottish Office).

Sharpe, L.J. and Newton, K. (1984), *Does Politics Matter? The Determinants of Public Policy* (Oxford: Clarendon Press).

Shaw, K. and Robinson, F. (1998), 'Learning from experience? Reflections on two decades of British urban policy', *Town Planning Review*, vol. 69,1, pp. 49–63.

Skeffington Report (1969), *People and Planning*, Report of the Committee on Public Participation in Planning (Chairman, A. Skeffington) (London: HMSO).

Smith, D.J. (ed.) (1992), *Understanding the Underclass* (London: Policy Studies Institute).

Soja, E.W. (1989), *Postmodern Geographies: The Reassertion of Space in Critical Social Theory* (London: Verso).

Solomos, J. and Back, L. (1996), *Racism and Society* ((Basingstoke: Macmillan).

Stewart, J. (1992), *Accountability to the Public* (London: European Policy Forum).

Stewart, J., Kendall, E. and Coote, A. (1994), *Citizens' Juries* (London: Institute for Public Policy Research).

Stoker, G. (1994), *The Role and Purpose of Local Government*, CLD research report No. 4 (London: Commission for Local Democracy).

Stoker, G. (1995a), 'Intergovernmental Relations', *Public Administration*, vol. 73, pp. 101–22.

Stoker, G. (1995b), 'Regime Theory and Urban Politics', in D. Judge, G. Stoker and H. Wolman (eds), *Theories of Urban Politics* (London: Sage), pp. 54–71.

Stoker, G. (1996a), 'Central control takes stick from polls', *Municipal Review and AMA News*, No. 770, August/September, p. 107.

Stoker, G. (1996b), 'Introduction: Normative Theories of Local Government and Democracy', in D. King and G. Stoker (eds), *Rethinking Local Democracy* (Basingstoke: Macmillan/ESRC), pp. 1–27.

Stoker, G. (1996c), *The Reform of the Institutions of Local Representative Democracy: Is there a role for the mayor-council model?*, CLD research report No. 18 (London: Commission for Local Democracy).

Stoker, G. (1997), 'Local political participation', in H. Davis and C. Skelcher, M. Clarke, M. Taylor, K. Young and N. Rao, G. Stoker, with an Introduction by R. Hambleton, *New Perspectives on Local Governance* (York: Joseph Rowntree Foundation), pp. 157–96).

Stoker, G. (ed.) (1999) *The New Management of British Local Governance* (Basingstoke: Macmillan).

Stoker, G., Hogwood, B. and Bullman, U. (1996), *Regionalism* (Luton: Local Government Management Board).

Stoker, G. and Mossberger, K. (1994), 'Urban regime theory in comparative perspective', *Environment and Planning C: Government and Policy*, vol. 12, pp. 195–212.

Stoker, G. and Mossberger, K. (1995), 'The Post-Fordist Local State: The Dynamics of its Development', in J. Stewart and G. Stoker (eds), *Local Government in the 1990s* (Basingstoke: Macmillan), pp. 210–27.

Stone, C. (1989), *Regime Politics: Governing Atlanta, 1946–1988* (Lawrence, KS: University Press of Kansas).

Svara, J. (1990), *Official Leadership in the City: Patterns of Conflict and Cooperation* (New York: Oxford University Press).

Tam, H. (1998), *Communitarianism: A New Agenda for Politics and Citizenship* (Basingstoke: Macmillan).

Taylor, M. (1995), *Unleashing the Potential: Bringing Residents to the Centre of Regeneration* (York: Joseph Rowntree Foundation).

Thake, S. (1995), *Staying the Course: the role and structures of community regeneration organisations* (York: Joseph Rowntree Foundation).

Thompson, P. (1997), 'Editorial Commentary: A third way?', *Renewal*, vol. 5, No. 3/4, pp. 5–10.

Tiebout, C. (1956), 'A pure theory of local expenditures', *Journal of Public Economy*, vol. 64, 4, pp. 416–24.

Tönnies, F. (1955), *Community and Association* (translated by C.P. Loomis) (London: Routledge and Kegan Paul).

Training and Enterprise Councils (1996), *Disaffection and Non-Participation in Education, Training and Employment by individuals aged 18–20* (London: Department for Education and Employment).

Urban Task Force (1999), *Urban Renaissance – Sharing the Vision*, Urban Task Force Half Way Report (London: DETR).

Urry, J. (1985), 'Social Relations, Space and Time', in D. Gregory and J. Urry (eds), *Social Relations and Spatial Structures* (London: Macmillan) pp. 20–48.

Urry, J. (1990), 'Conclusion: places and policies', in M. Harloe, C.G. Pickvance and J. Urry (eds), *Place, Policy and Politics: Do Localities Matter?* (London: Unwin Hyman) pp.187–204.

Wahlberg, M., Taylor, K. and Geddes, M. (1994), *Enhancing Local Democracy*, Research Report for the Local Government Management Board (Warwick: Warwick Business School, The Local Government Centre).

Walker, D.B. and Richards, M. (1996), 'A Service under Change: Current Issues in Policing in England and Wales', *Police Studies*, vol. 19, 1, pp. 53–73.

Ward, M. (1994), *Rethinking Urban Policy: City strategies for the global economy* (Manchester: Centre for Local Economic Strategies).

Ward, S. (1996), 'Local Authorities and legal agenda 21', *Local Political Economy*, 1, pp. 411–16.

Wilcox, D. (1998), *The Guide to Development Trusts and Partnerships* (London: Development Trusts Association).

Williams, P. (ed.) (1997), *Directions in Housing Policy: Towards Sustainable Housing Policies for the UK* (London: Chapman Publishing).

Williams, S. (1998), 'Don't go blindly down this US welfare road', *The Guardian*, 11 February, p. 17.

Willmott, P. (1996), *Urban Trends 2: A Decade in Britain's Deprived Urban Areas* (London: Policy Studies Institute).

Wilson, D. and Game, C. (1998) *Local Government in the United Kingdom*, 2nd edn (Basingstoke: Macmillan).

Wilson, P.A. (1997), 'Building Social Capital: A Learning Agenda for the Twenty-first Century', *Urban Studies*, vol. 34, 5–6, pp. 745–60.

Wilson, W.J. (1987), *The Truly Disadvantaged: the inner-city, the Underclass, and Public Policy* (Chicago, IL: University of Chicago Press).

Wohlman, H. and Goldsmith, M. (1992), *Urban Politics and Policy* (Oxford: Basil Blackwell).

Working Party on the Internal Management of Local Authorities in England (1993), *Community Leadership and Representation: Unlocking the Potential* (London: HMSO).

Wright, M. (1998), 'Sterling Service', *Local Government Management*, Issue 24, pp. 10–11.

Young, I. (1990), *Justice and the Politics of Difference* (Princeton, NJ: Princeton University Press).

Young, K. (1996a), *Portrait of Change 1995* (Luton: Local Government Management Board).

Young, K. (1996b), 'Reinventing Local Government? Some Evidence Assessed' *Public Administration*, vol. 74,3, pp. 347–67.

Young, K., Gosschalk, B. and Hatter, W. (1996), *In Search of Community Identity* (York: Joseph Rowntree Foundation).

Young, K. and Rao, N. (1994), *Coming to Terms With Change? The Local Government Councillor in 1993* (York: Joseph Rowntree Foundation).

Young, S. (1995), *Participation: Trends and Prospects in the Environmental Sphere*, paper to the ESRC Local Governance Programme Conference, Exeter; cited with permission.

Young, S. (1996), 'Participation Strategies in the Context of Local Agenda 21: Towards a New Watershed?', in I. Hampsher-Monk and J. Stanyer (eds), *Contemporary Political Studies* (Oxford: Political Studies Association of the United Kingdom), pp. 858–70.

# Index